Practice Book 2

**Cornelsen
English
Grammar**

English Edition
Große Ausgabe

Cornelsen

Cornelsen English Grammar: Practice Book 2

Erarbeitet von   Jennifer Seidl, M.A. *sowie* Prof. Hellmut Schwarz

in Zusammenarbeit mit der Englischredaktion   Filiz Bahşi (verantwortliche Redakteurin), Michael Ferguson (Projektleitung), *sowie* Bettina Khalida Abdalla, Dr. Ilka Soennecken, Julie Colthorpe (Assistenz)

Beratende Mitwirkung   Mervyn Whittaker

Illustration   Constanze Schargan (S. 13, 16, 71, 72, 74, 75, 81-83, 128, 137, 145, 155, 164)
Jeong Sook Lee (S. 23, 33, 40, 48)

Umschlaggestaltung   Knut Waisznor

Layout   Katharina Wolff

Technische Umsetzung   Ilona und Ingo Ostermaier *sowie* Eva Baumgart-Catania, Peter Richter, Eva Schmidt

Bild- und Textquellen   s. S. 176

Das *Cornelsen English Grammar: Practice Book 2* bezieht sich auf diese Grammatiktafeln.

◁ ISBN 978-3-464-05334-8

ISBN 978-3-464-06310-1 ▷

www.cornelsen.de

1. Auflage, 12. Druck 2021

Alle Drucke dieser Auflage sind inhaltlich unverändert und können im Unterricht nebeneinander verwendet werden.

© 2003 Cornelsen Verlag, Berlin
© 2018 Cornelsen Verlag GmbH, Berlin

Druck und Bindung: Livonia Print, Riga

ISBN 978-3-464-06312-5

PEFC zertifiziert
Dieses Produkt stammt aus nachhaltig bewirtschafteten Wäldern und kontrollierten Quellen.
www.pefc.de
PEFC/12-31-006

Inhaltsverzeichnis Contents

The article – Der Artikel

The adjective and the adverb – Das Adjektiv und das Adverb

Quantifiers – Mengenbezeichnungen

Pronouns and question words – Pronomen und Fragewörter

Conditional sentences – Bedingungssätze

Relative clauses – Relativsätze

Indirect speech – Die indirekte Rede

Mixed bag – Zusätzliche Übungen

Hinweise zur Benutzung des Practice Book

Liebe Schülerinnen und Schüler,

im Folgenden finden Sie unsere Antworten auf Ihre potentiellen Fragen zum
Cornelsen English Grammar: Practice Book 2 (PB).

1 Wozu dient das PB?

Das *PB* hat zwei Hauptfunktionen. Sie können damit
– überprüfen, wie gut Sie bestimmte Kapitel der englischen Grammatik beherrschen, und diejenigen
– wiederholen und üben, in denen Sie Wissenslücken entdeckt haben. Das *PB* hilft Ihnen also vor allem dann, wenn Sie Ihre Grammatikkenntnisse **selbst testen**, **festigen** und eventuelle **Schwachpunkte beseitigen** wollen. Besonders nützlich ist es in Wiederholungsphasen, z. B. vor und nach Klausuren bzw. vor dem Abitur, insbesondere in Verbindung mit einer Schulgrammatik. Das *PB* bezieht sich eng auf die *Cornelsen English Grammar (CEG)*, kann aber natürlich auch mit jeder anderen Grammatik verwendet werden.

2 Was enthält das PB?

Wie Ihnen das Inhaltsverzeichnis zeigt, besteht das *PB* aus 15 Kapiteln, die in ihrer Reihenfolge – mit Ausnahme von Kapitel 15 (einem „*Mixed bag*") – der *CEG* entsprechen. Allerdings werden im *PB* manchmal zwei Kapitel, die in der *CEG* getrennt behandelt werden (z.B. *Adjektiv/Adverb*), zu einem Kapitel zusammengefasst. Aber auch das Gegenteil kann der Fall sein: So wird das *CEG*-Großkapitel *Satzgefüge* im *PB* in drei Einzelkapitel *(Bedingungssätze, Relativsätze, die indirekte Rede)* aufgeteilt. Die parallele Verwendung von *CEG* und *PB* ist sehr einfach: Im *PB* wird grundsätzlich auf die Paragraphen der *CEG* hingewiesen, auf die sich die Testsätze und Übungen beziehen. Sollten Sie die Bezeichnungen für bestimmte grammatische Phänomene vergessen haben, so können Sie sie in der *CEG* (S. 230-234 bzw. im Register S. 235-247) oder in der Grammatik, die Sie gerade benutzen, nachschlagen.

3 Wie sind die einzelnen Kapitel aufgebaut?

Die Kapitel sind in ihrer äußeren Form alle gleich aufgebaut, sodass man sich leicht zurechtfinden kann. Jedes Kapitel umfasst die beiden Teile *Test* (Ausnahme: *Mixed bag*) und *Exercises*.

a Der Test

Mithilfe der ca. 30-35 Testsätze pro Kapitel können Sie herausfinden, wie gut Sie die Form und den Gebrauch bestimmter grammatischer Erscheinungen beherrschen. Damit Sie das möglichst genau feststellen können, ist der *Test* in unterschiedlich aufgebaute Teilabschnitte gegliedert: Es gibt z.B. *Multiple choice*- und Einsatzübungen sowie Übersetzungen von Satzteilen und ganzen Sätzen und den festen Bestandteil *Spot the mistakes*, bei dem Sie die Fehler in den bereits formulierten Sätzen entdecken und korrigieren sollen. Wenn Sie den *Test* bearbeitet haben und umblättern, finden Sie unter der Überschrift *Correct yourself* die Lösungen. Unterhalb der Lösungen befindet sich der sogenannte *Exercise finder*. In ihm stehen links die Nummern der Testsätze, in der Mitte die Paragraphen der *CEG*, auf die sich die Testsätze beziehen, und rechts die Nummern der *Exercises*, die das in den jeweiligen Testsätzen behandelte grammatische Problem gezielt üben.

▶ Exercise finder		
Sentences	CEG	Exercises
1, 5, 10, 12	▶ 5e	▶ 2, 3

b Die Exercises ▶

Ebenso wie die *Tests* bieten auch die *Exercises* mehrere Varianten von Übungstypen, sodass genügend anregendes Material zum Wiederholen der unterschiedlichen Grammatikbereiche zur Verfügung steht. Die *Exercises* sind in vielen Fällen in a- und b-/c-Teile untergliedert, wobei die b-/c-Teile meistens selbstständige Transferleistungen verlangen. Rechts neben der Überschrift wird bei jeder *Exercise* das behandelte grammatische Phänomen konkret benannt. Die dazugehörigen *CEG*-Paragraphen sind ebenfalls angegeben ▶ **2, 3** . Die Lösungen der *Exercises* sind im separat eingelegten *Key to the exercises* enthalten.

4 *Wie kann man sinnvoll mit dem PB arbeiten?*

Sie können das *PB* sehr flexibel nutzen. Wenn Sie aber seine Vorzüge voll ausschöpfen wollen, ist der folgende Weg am sinnvollsten:

a *Zur Arbeit mit den Tests:*

Die Testaufgaben, die zum ausgewählten Grammatikkapitel gehören, werden in Stillarbeit gelöst. Sie schreiben die Lösungen der Reihe nach auf ein Blatt Papier, blättern anschließend um und überprüfen anhand des *Correct yourself*-Teils, ob Sie Fehler gemacht haben. Es empfiehlt sich, eine fehlerhafte Lösung durch die richtige zu ersetzen. Verstehen Sie eine Lösung nicht, können Sie gleich die *CEG* heranziehen. Den entsprechenden *CEG*-Paragraphen finden Sie im *Exercise finder*. Sie können auch zuerst die als falsch gekennzeichneten Sätze mit der Zuordnung im *Exercise finder* vergleichen. Im Anschluss kann die dort angegebene *Exercise* gelöst und bei Bedarf der entsprechende *CEG*-Paragraph herangezogen werden.

b *Zur Arbeit mit den Exercises:*

Im *Exercise finder* können Sie auf einen Blick sehen, wie viele Fehler Sie pro Grammatikparagraph in den Testsätzen gemacht haben. Bei mehr als einem Fehler sollten Sie in jedem Fall die Übung, auf die verwiesen wird, schriftlich lösen und anschließend deren Richtigkeit – eventuell in Partnerarbeit – mithilfe des *Key to the exercises* überprüfen. Wenn Sie bei der Korrektur viele Fehler entdecken, sollten Sie noch einmal Ihre Grammatik zu Rate ziehen und ein paar Tage später sowohl Testsätze als auch Übung(en) wiederholen.

Andere Arbeitswege:

Neben der hier skizzierten Methode gibt es zahlreiche Varianten, z.B. können Sie
– das betreffende Grammatikkapitel bereits vor dem Lösen der Testsätze durcharbeiten.
– nur die Testsätze ohne die nachfolgenden *Exercises* lösen.
– die *Exercises* unabhängig von den Testsätzen, eventuell aber in Verbindung mit der *CEG* bearbeiten.

Welchen Weg Sie auch immer wählen: Wir wünschen Ihnen viel Erfolg und Spaß bei der Arbeit!

Jennifer Seidl & Hellmut Schwarz

Abkürzungen

aux.	→ *auxiliary/-ies*	pres.	→ *present*
constr.	→ *construction/s*	progr.	→ *progressive*
ex.	→ *exercise/s*	quest.	→ *question/s*
inf.	→ *infinitive*	rel.	→ *relative*
l./ll.	→ *line/s*	sent.	→ *sentence/s*
obj.	→ *object*	subj.	→ *subject*
part.	→ *participle/s*		

The sentence/Word order

A **Put the words and phrases in the correct order to make sentences.**

1 are – which – test results – on – based – your conclusions ?
2 Jason – gets – if – on time – here – can – go – to the cinema – we – all
3 the minister – to all the members of the cabinet – his desicion – announced
4 I didn't know – the machine – how – worked – someone – until – me – showed
5 John – who – did – discuss – with – the new plans ?
6 Tom – didn't pass –although – all his A-levels – a good job with a bank – he – got

B **Make questions from the statements. For questions with a question word ask about the parts underlined.**

7 The Wright brothers made their first flight <u>at Kitty Hawk in North Carolina</u>.
8 <u>The Russian Igor Sikorsky</u> built the first helicopter.
9 Patrick often goes abroad for his company.
10 Joanne has decided against <u>going to Moscow in December</u>.
11 The headmaster pointed out the advantages of the proposed changes.
12 Julie is taking a course in <u>aromatherapy</u>.
13 Noise causes <u>physical and mental stress, as well as lack of concentration</u>.
14 All gases expand when heated.

C **Translate the German sentence parts into English.**

15 If you don't understand the problem, *(kann ich es dir noch einmal erklären.)* …
16 *(Wer holte deine Freundin vom Bahnhof ab?)* … Your sister or her sister?
17 Have you lent those CDs to Cathy? – *(Ja, ich habe sie ihr geliehen.)* …
18 Those people over there are smoking. *(Ich glaube, sie haben das Rauchverbotsschild nicht gesehen.)* …
19 Have you heard the latest? *(Liz ist zur Mannschaftsführerin gemacht worden.)* …
20 *(Ben macht nicht immer)* … what he has been told.
21 *(Was verursachte den Flugzeugabsturz?)* … Was it due to a technical failure?
22 *(Wann erfand Faraday den Dynamo?)* … – I'm afraid I have no idea.

D **Spot the mistakes. There is one mistake in each sentence.**

23 If you could describe me the route, it would save me a lot of time.
24 Never in my life I have felt so miserable as when I spent Christmas on my own a long way from home.
25 The first thing you should do is report the accident the police.
26 I did not the shopping yesterday, so there isn't much in the fridge, I'm afraid. …
27 Only later we realized that we had forgotten to post the visa application forms.
28 I think not you understood fully what I said.
29 We don't know when to use the participle because our teacher didn't explain it us very well.
30 What discovered the British chemist Joseph Priestley in 1774?
31 Max has been voted to captain of the cricket team, hasn't he?
32 Janet mentioned me her plans.
33 Not only the shop assistant was rude to me, she was also slow and unhelpful.
34 I lent to Mandy some of my pocket money because she wanted to buy a friend a present.
35 In what year was Kofi Annan appointed to UN Secretary-General?

The sentence/Word order

A 1: *Which test results are your conclusions based on?*
2: *If Jason gets here on time, we can all go to the cinema.*
3: *The minister announced his decision to all the members of the cabinet.*
4: *I didn't know how the machine worked until someone showed me.*
5: *Who did John discuss the new plans with?*
6: *Although Tom didn't pass all his A-levels, he got a good job with a bank.*

B 7: *Where did the Wright brothers make their first flight?* 8: *Who built the first helicopter?* 9: *Does Patrick often go abroad for his company?* 10: *What has Joanne decided against?* 11: *Did the headmaster point out the advantages of the proposed changes?* 12: *What is Julie taking a course in?* 13: *What does noise cause?* 14: *Do all gases expand when heated?*

C 15: *I can explain it to you again/once more.* 16: *Who picked your girlfriend up from the station?* 17: *Yes, I have lent them to her.* 18: *I don't think they have seen the no-smoking sign. (I think, they haven't seen …)* 19: *Liz has been made team captain.* 20: *Ben doesn't always do …* 21: *What caused the plane crash?* 22: *When did Faraday invent the dynamo?*

D 23: *If you could describe the route to me, …* 24: *Never in my life have I felt so miserable as when …* 25: *The first thing you should do is report the accident to the police.* 26: *I did not do/didn't do the shopping yesterday, …* 27: *Only later did we realize that we had forgotten …* 28: *I don't think you understood fully what I said.* 29: *We don't know when to use the participle because our teacher didn't explain it to us very well.* 30: *What did the British chemist Joseph Priestley discover in 1774?* 31: *Max has been voted captain of the cricket team, hasn't he?* 32: *Janet mentioned her plans to me.* 33: *Not only was the shop assistant rude to me, she was …* 34: *I lent Mandy some of my pocket money …* 35: *In what year was Kofi Annan appointed UN Secretary-General?*

▶ **Exercise finder**

Sentences	CEG	Exercises
1, 5, 10, 12	▶ 5e	▶ 2, 3
2, 4, 6, 15	▶ 16	▶ 8, 11, 12
3, 17, 23, 25, 29, 32, 34	▶ 20a-d	▶ 10
7, 9, 11, 14, 22	▶ 5b	▶ 2-6
8, 13, 16, 21, 30	▶ 6	▶ 4, 5, 6
24, 27, 33	▶ 10c	▶ 7
18, 20, 26, 28	▶ 3	▶ 1
19, 31, 35	▶ 17, 18	▶ 9

1 *An exchange pupil*   **negative statements**   3

A German exchange pupil in Glasgow talks about his impressions of the city, but there is something wrong with the negative forms/constructions/position/etc. Correct the mistakes. Are there 14, 16 or 18?

'The people here are very friendly, I've even got a girlfriend. But they all speak with a strong accent. At first the language sounded not like English to me at all. If my girlfriend not speaks carefully, I understand her not always. I think not she realizes how difficult a strange accent is for a foreigner to understand. I have to ask her to not talk so quickly, but she

5 doesn't remembers most of the time.

I have seen a lot of interesting things in Glasgow, but of course there are some places that I have been not able to visit yet, like Bothwell Castle and the Botanic Gardens.

School? Well, I have learnt a lot of English here, but there's still a lot of grammar that I can use not properly. I'm afraid I do not my homework regularly. In fact, I did not any

10 homework at all yesterday. I doesn't think I take school work here as seriously as I should. The teachers often have to tell me to not waste time in the lessons. They often catch me when I have been not listening. It's hard to concentrate when everything's in English.

I spend a lot of free time playing music and writing songs because I have joined a band here. I would have been not asked to join if I played not the guitar pretty well. I've got some nice

15 friends. They always ask me to their parties. But what I miss most here is being not able to hang around with my friends back home and speak German …'

2 The Airport Express — questions with/without a quest. word; main verbs ▶ 4, 5b/e

a   Margit has just arrived at Newark Airport, on her first visit
to New York. She wants to take the Airport Express bus
to Manhattan, so she asks some questions. Write her
questions using the notes and putting in any missing words.

Margit wants to know:

Examples: when – buses – Manhattan – leave
   Margit: **When do the buses** to Manhattan
   leave?

   if – buses – leave – all terminals
   Margit: **Do buses leave** from all terminals.

Continue.

1 where – buses – leave from
2 buses – what – look like
3 if – driver – sell – tickets – bus
4 how much – one-way ticket – cost
5 if – buses – leave – on time

6 if – have to – queue up
7 which places – bus – stop at
8 if – bus – go – past Central Park
9 how long – journey – take
10 when – next bus – leave

b   Imagine that you are in Manhattan for the first time. What would you want to know?
Write six questions as in part a), with or without a question word.

Example: **What time do** the stores usually **open?**

3 Where do you come from? — questions: mixed exercise ▶ 4, 5a/b/e

a   There's a new girl from Ireland in your class. She doesn't speak much German yet, so the class asked her
some questions. These were her answers. What were the questions?

Examples: A.: Seventeen.   Q.: **How old are** you?
   A.: Just one brother.   Q.: **Have you got/Do you have** any brothers or sisters?

1 A.: His name's Patrick, but everybody calls him Pat.
2 A.: From Dublin.
3 A.: We've been in Germany about four weeks.
4 A.: Yes, I do. It's a nice country.
5 A.: Because my father got a job here.
6 A.: No, I don't know many people here yet.
7 A.: No, not much. Only 'bitte' and 'danke'.
8 A.: Yes, I'm taking an intensive course at a language school.
9 A.: I do karate and I like riding in summer.
10 A.: My hobbies are reading, painting and sending e-mails to my friends back home.
11 A.: All kinds of music, especially punk and hip hop.
12 A.: Go to a party? Tonight? Yes, I'd love to. Thanks.

b   Write five more questions that you would ask someone who has moved to Germany from Dublin.

4 *A film quiz*   **questions with a quest. word; main verbs**   ▶ **5b, 6**

Write a film quiz for your school magazine. You can use the following facts to write your quiz, or you can make up your own questions (8-10) about different films. Make as many suitable questions as possible beginning with different question words.

Examples: Ridley Scott made *Gladiator* in 2000.
Who made 'Gladiator' in 2000?
When did Ridley Scott **make** 'Gladiator'?
Which film **did** Ridley Scott **make** in 2000?

Gladiator won five Oscars in 2001.
How many Oscars **did** 'Gladiator' **win?**
Which film **won** five Oscars in 2001?

1 James Cameron directed *Titanic* in 1997.
2 Julia Roberts starred in *Erin Brockovich* in 2000.
3 *Titanic* won eleven Oscars in1998.
4 Pierce Brosnan and Halle Berry played the main roles in *Die Another Day* in 2002.
5 Denzel Washington won an Oscar for Best Actor in 2002.
6 The first Harry Potter film, *The Philosopher's Stone*, made $961 million worldwide in 2001, second only to *Titanic*.
7 Mel Gibson directed and produced *Braveheart* in 1995.
8 *Die Another Day* cost over $142 million in 2002.
9 Peter Jackson directed *The Fellowship of the Rings* in 2001.
10 Part Two of the *Rings* trilogy, *The Two Towers*, was released worldwide in December 2002.

5 *An interview*   **questions: mixed exercise**   ▶ **4, 5, 6**

Jessica Milani is a shooting star at only 20. The German magazine *Kino* wants to interview her for its readers. The interviewer is going to ask her the following questions in English. Can you translate? Think carefully about the tenses.

Example: Haben Sie eine Schauspielschule besucht (*go – drama school*)?
Q.: **Did you go** to drama school?

1 Wie bekamen Sie Ihre erste Filmrolle?
2 Was machten Sie, bevor Sie zum Film gingen *(start making movies)*?
3 Haben Sie jemals etwas anderes machen wollen?
4 Wer hat Sie entdeckt?
5 Wie fühlten Sie sich, als Sie plötzlich berühmt wurden?
6 Was für Rollen mögen Sie am liebsten?
7 Was macht Sie so beliebt?
8 Würden Sie gern in Komödien mitspielen?
9 Welchen Film drehten *(enjoy making)* Sie am liebsten?
10 Wie viele Filme haben Sie gedreht?
11 Wann kommt Ihr nächster Film in die Kinos *(be released)*?
12 Worum geht es in dem Film?
13 Spielen Sie die Hauptrolle?
14 Wer spielt die männliche Hauptrolle *(male lead)*?
15 Wünschen Sie manchmal, dass Sie nicht berühmt wären?

6 *Sydney Harbour Bridge*   **questions with a quest. word: mixed exercise**   ▶ **4, 5a/b, 6**

a   Thousands of tourists visit the Sydney Harbour Bridge every year. What do they usually want to know about it? Here are the guide's answers, but what are the questions? Ask about the details that are underlined.

Examples: Guide: <u>14,000</u> workers built the bridge.
   Tourist: ***How many** workers **built** the bridge?*
   Guide: It took <u>about eight years</u> to construct.
   Tourist: ***How long did** it **take** to construct?*

Guide:
1 Construction began <u>in December, 1926</u>.
2 <u>A British engineer</u> designed the bridge.
3 It cost <u>13.5 million Australian dollars</u> to build.
4 The bridge is <u>134 metres</u> high.
5 <u>Tens of thousands</u> of tourists visit the bridge every year.
6 The Olympic 2000 Stadium is <u>15</u> kilometres away.
7 The bridge was opened <u>in 1932</u>.
8 <u>16</u> workers died in building accidents.
9 From the top you can see <u>the Blue Mountains in the west and the Pacific in the east</u>.
10 The Opera House is <u>right in front of the bridge</u>.

b   You would like to take the Bridge Climb. The woman at the tourist information office gives you the following information. What exactly did you ask her?

Example: Woman: The tour costs $145 for adults and $100 if you're under 17.
   Your Q: ***How much does** the tour **cost**?*

Woman:
1 It takes about an hour to reach the top. (How long?)
2 You can climb the bridge in the daytime or at night. (When?)
3 The climb takes about three hours. (How long?)
4 You have to wear a special bridge suit and shoes with rubber soles. (What?)
5 You have to wear a special suit because it has no pockets. (Why?)
6 You can't take cameras or coins with you. (What?)
7 It's forbidden to take things with you because you might drop something on people and traffic below. (Why?)
8 Climbs leave every ten minutes. (How often?)

Based on information from *Sydney Online Pty. Ltd.*

A blessing in disguise[1]   inversion

▶ **10a/c**

This is a true story, told by James Porter. He published it in a business magazine years afterwards.
The editor[2] changed some of the sentences to make them more suitable for the literary form of the article.
Change the sentences with numbers as the editor did, using inversion.

'I was lazy in school, I preferred having a good time to learning.

Example: I rarely stayed at home to do school work.
***Rarely did I** stay at home to do school work.*

(1) I had never faced[3] serious problems in my life. Money was certainly no problem. My father had a good job – he had just been promoted[4] – and I had everything. (2) I never thought about what my future might bring. There was no reason to.

Then something happened which made me open my eyes to the realities of life.

understood only later that this day was a turning-point[5] in my life.

Dad was without work for years – mid-forties, not needed, too old to be given a second chance. But me? I changed. After I woke up from the shock I started to learn. (7) I have rarely felt so determined[6] to succeed as on that day. I started to work

(3) My father had hardly got his promotion when his firm went out of business. He lost his job and couldn't get another. Our lifestyle changed dramatically, almost overnight. No more money for big cars, designer clothes and picture phones. No more friends. (4) I have seldom seen my father as sad as on that day …

My mother had no work experience. She was prepared to take a cleaning job – but Dad didn't want that, neither did I. We were too proud. (5) I had never seen my father cry – until the day when mother had to take a cleaning job … (6) I

hard, both at school and in the local supermarket. I passed my exams and studied business management. And today?
(8) One seldom gets a second chance in life – Dad didn't. But I did, and I took it.
(9) I realized only later that Dad's bad luck had been my good luck.'

Editor's note:
Today James Porter is the president of *Porter Enterprises*, an international company which employs thousands of workers – especially if they're in their mid-forties and in need of a second chance.

---

1 a blessing in disguise *Glück im Unglück*   2 editor *Redakteur/in*   3 face *konfrontieren; fertig werden mit*
4 to be promoted *befördert werden*   5 turning-point *Wendepunkt*   6 feel determined *entschlossen sein*

8 *TV advertising* **main clauses, subordinate clauses**

a Do you think you are influenced by TV commercials? Translate the German sentence parts into English.

Example: Dave: Yes, I think so. I sometimes think about buying a product, *(weil ich es im Fernsehen gesehen habe)*.
… *because I have seen it on TV*.

1 Sandra: Not much. I rarely watch commercials. I think *(dass die meisten Werbespots total dumm sind.)* …
2 Leo: Perhaps, subconsciously. But I don't really know *(ob ich von Werbespots beeinflusst werde.)* …
3 Sita: *(Wenn ich in einem Supermarkt einkaufe)* …, I often buy something that I have seen on a TV commercial. Perhaps a new kind of snack or shampoo.
4 Julie: I often buy a new product that I've seen on TV *(weil ich gern neue Sachen ausprobiere.)* … There's nothing wrong with that, is there?
5 Mark: I'm not, but my brother is. *(Er kauft nie etwas, es sei denn* (unless) *er hat es in einem Werbespot im Fernsehen gesehen.)* …
6 Marie: I don't think so. *(Obwohl ich oft Werbespots schaue, höre ich nie wirklich zu.)* …
7 Jeff: Yes, I am influenced by commercials. I bought this new mobile phone *(nachdem ich den Werbespot für Flexifone ungefähr zwanzig mal im Fernsehen gesehen hatte.)* …
8 Lynn: *Wenn ich ein tolles Produkt im Fernsehen sehe, welches mich interessiert, kaufe ich es vielleicht* (might) …

b In your opinion are you influenced by advertising? Write a short paragraph, paying attention to the word order in the main and subordinate clauses.

9 *Famous people* **object complement**  **17, 18**

Write complete sentences from the notes, adding complements from the list in the correct position and prepositions where necessary. Be careful with the verb forms.

Example: _____ B _____ – (ever – make)?
*Was Boris Becker ever **made sportsman of the year**?*

1 T_____ B_____ – (re-elect) – June 2001.
2 S_____ s – (consider).
3 Do you think P_____ C_____ – (will – ever – make)?
4 G_____ – (elect) – December 2000.
5 E_____ II – (crown) – June 1952.
6 When – J_____ R_____ – (make)?

7 P_____ W_____ – (consider).
8 _____ W_____ – (vote) – 2002.

~~sportsman of the year~~

actress of the year
King of England
Queen of England
British Prime Minister
the most popular royal
the world's best woman
  tennis player
actor of the year
President of the USA

▶ **10**   *A big win*   **word order: position of indirect object**   ▶ **20a-d**

a   Mr Tom Wilson won £ 8 million in the National Lottery. Here's his story.
Complete what he says by choosing a suitable position for the objects in brackets, adding *to* or *for* where necessary. Think about style and emphasis. If you think two positions are equally suitable, write both.

Example: I was at home having a beer with my friend Len when the lottery numbers came on TV. I couldn't find my glasses, so I gave *my coupon to Len/Len my coupon*. He checked it and said I'd won. The Big Six.

I thought he was joking, but he showed (1 the numbers – me) and I realized that they were all right. I can't describe (2 anyone – my feelings), half joy, half disbelief. I was in a dream. Then my wife came home. I didn't say (3 her – anything) at first, because I was speechless. Len and I just stared at each other. But then she said she would cook (4 a meal – us). So I just answered, 'Why don't you book (5 a table – us) at the Ritz instead?' It was Len who explained (6 her – the new situation). After two minutes of unbelievable excitement, she phoned our children to tell (7 the incredible news – them). After we had calmed down, we decided to give a big party, so on the next day we sent (8 all our friends, neighbours and colleagues – invitations).

What did we do with the money? Well, we bought (9 our daughter and her family in Scotland – a house), and we bought (10 a nice flat – our 20-year-old son in London). Of course we all owed (11 various banks – money), but now we don't. We gave (12 all our relatives and close friends – generous presents) and of course I wrote (13 the Lottery company – a nice letter of thanks). I sent (14 large cheques – different national charities).

We gave (15 interested radio and TV stations – interviews) and I told (16 a well-known weekly magazine – my story). I donated (17 local charities – all the money I got from the media). I booked (18 a sunshine cruise – us and Len and his wife). It was the first big holiday we had ever had. I didn't really know what to do with so much money, but my family was able to suggest (19 me – plenty of good ideas). Above all, I was able to fulfil my life-long dream – I bought (20 a Harley-Davidson – myself).

b   What would you do with so much money? First, write out the verbs with two objects used in the text, then write a paragraph using as many of them as you can, plus some of the following: *announce, lend, mention, offer, promise*.

11 *Write the story* **word order: mixed exercise** ▶ **6, 10, 16, 20d**

a Write the story by putting the words and phrases in the correct order. Add commas where suitable.

1 home – Sarah – When – got – was – almost midnight – it
2 in the door – the key – Turning – realized – that – she – locked – wasn't – it
3 She – it – couldn't understand – because – with doors and keys – always careful – was – she
4 the door – Had – unlocked – been – while – at the party – had been enjoying – she – herself?
5 nothing – of – afraid – to be – was – there – She – herself – told – that
6 she – had – very quietly – After – opened – went – she – in – the door
7 the door – Before – she – listened – closed – she – carefully
8 that – had – made – What – upstairs – noise?
9 Might – it – who – be – looking for money – was – a burglar
10 Never in her life – she – felt so scared – had
11 she – would – go upstairs – On no account – alone
12 could – do – she – What – if – someone – was – in her bedroom – there?
13 phone – she – Should – the police – and – to them – the situation – explain?
14 Yes. – would – to them – She – report – a break-in – and – give – her name and address – them

Suddenly, …

b Finish the story using complex sentences (combination of main and subordinate clauses) and some of the following: questions with or without a question word, inversion, verbs with two objects.

Read the text carefully, then answer the questions.

Michael Dillon has witnessed an IRA attack. He recognized one of the men, the nephew of a Catholic priest. The priest contacts Michael and warns him not to go to the police and not to testify. Michael does not answer but walks away, having already decided to inform the police. Now Michael has left Belfast and is working in a hotel in London. But he knows that even in London he is in danger because he has contacted the police. He and his girlfriend Andrea are waiting in the hotel for the police to phone back.

'Wait', he said. He took her hand and led her into the lounge. 'I want to talk to you. Let's sit over there, where it's quiet.' [...]
He sat her down. He told her about the priest.
'And you walked away?' she said. 'And now he's going to tell them you'll testify against his
5   nephew?'
'Yes. I suppose so.'
'But why did you do it? You promised me. You're not going to testify, are you?'
'I feel I must. It's the right thing to do.' [...]
'Oh, my God,' she said. 'I knew something terrible was happening. He's off now, phoning
10   them. The priest, I mean. They're not going to let you testify. They're going to kill you.'
He looked at her, at the fear in her eyes. She was trembling and on the edge of tears.
'Andrea, listen. I'll have police protection.'
'And what does that mean? A policeman who sits in your living room and follows you around here in the hotel? Do you know what you're saying? Every time I open the door
15   from now on, I'll be waiting for someone to come in and kill us.'

'Not you,' he said, but remembered that of course she was right. Wives, girlfriends, even bystanders, had been shot dead.

'And why are you doing it? It's for revenge, isn't it? Isn't that what it always is in Ireland? Revenge.'

20 'No.'

'Then what is it?'

'I don't know,' he said. I don't want to be a coward. I don't want to let them frighten me.'

'You're not a coward,' she said. And if you were, is that so terrible? Because that's the choice you're making.'

25 There were tears in her eyes. She was not a coward, nor would ever be. And he, what was he? What did it matter? Why should he risk her life as well as his? Was any country worth the price that Ireland asked, a price demanded again and again and never paid in full?

She did not speak for a moment and then she said, 'I never want to go back there. Never.'

From *Lies of Silence* by Brian Moore

a Look at the language. Find as many examples as you can of the following:

   1 a compound sentence (main clause + main clause)
   2 a complex sentence (combination of main and subordinate clauses)
   3 a question with a question word: + modal aux. + main verb
                                                        + *do* + main verb
                                                        + *do* + *do* as a main verb
   4 a question tag
   5 an imperative

b 1 Andrea says, 'I never want to go back there …' (l. 28). Rewrite the sentence using inversion of the adverbial.

   2 Explain the meaning of *bystander* (l. 17), *revenge* (l. 18) and *coward* (l. 22) using a relative clause for each.

c Answer the questions about the text using complex sentences. You can begin the subordinate clauses with *because*, *when*, *although*, etc. or with *that*.

   1 Why is Michael Dillon going to testify against the priest's nephew?
   2 Why is Andrea so frightened?
   3 How does Dillon try to comfort Andrea?
   4 Andrea questions Dillon's motives for wanting to testify. What does she think his motives are?
   5 Who in your opinion is Andrea most afraid for? For Dillon or for herself? Support your answer by referring to the appropriate lines in the text.
   6 How do you think Andrea feels about the 'troubles' in Ireland . In your answer, consider concepts such as loyalty, patriotism or self-preservation[1]. Find lines in the text to support your answer.

d Write a short summary of the text extract. Pay particular attention to word order in your subordinate clauses.

---

1 self-preservation *Selbsterhaltung*

Modal auxiliaries and be, have, do

A ▶ **Choose the correct or more suitable form from the brackets.**

1. When I was a child, I (was allowed to/might) watch TV for only one hour a day.
2. You (mustn't/needn't) do that now. It can wait until later.
3. If your glasses are broken, you (should have/may have) taken them to be repaired.
4. The roads were icy, but we (managed to/could) get home without an accident.
5. David (ought to/is to) be home by now. It's well past midnight.
6. John will be leaving work soon, but if you phone him now you (might/must) just catch him.
7. We (are to/should) give the maths homework in on Tuesday, and English on Wednesday.
8. Miriam (can/may) be at home now. I'll phone her and see.
9. We (don't have to/mustn't) give back the library books until next week.
10. We (are not supposed to/don't have to) leave our bikes here. Only in the bike-shed.

B ▶ **Complete the sentences with a suitable modal (or substitute form) in the correct tense.**

11. (you) … take photographs inside the cathedral? – Oh, yes. It's quite all right.
12. … we go to visit Mel in hospital? – Good idea. Let's go tomorrow after school.
13. Our flight was delayed, but after about an hour we … take off.
14. From our hotel room we … see the beach. It looked so inviting.
15. In summer school last year we (not) … make any noise after ten.
16. Barbara says we really … go to see the new film at the ABC. It's extremely funny.
17. You … help me with the homework, thanks. I can do it myself.
18. You … tell lies. Don't ever lie to me again.
19. The weather forecast says it will be cold tomorrow. It … even snow in the north.
20. You (not) … put up a tent here. Look, there's a sign.

C ▶ **Translate the German sentence parts in brackets into English using a modal or a substitute.**

21. *(Sie müssen nicht im Bett bleiben)* …, but don't go out until your temperature is normal.
22. The van in front of us suddenly pulled on its brakes. *(Wir konnten gerade noch halten)* … in time.
23. I think the unemployment rate is 3.5 per cent at present. *(Aber ich kann mich irren* [be wrong]*.)* …
24. I didn't go to the youth club meeting last night. *(Ich musste meiner Mutter helfen.)* …
25. If you've got an exam tomorrow, *(du solltest lieber früh zu Bett gehen.)* …
26. Just drop me off at the doctor's. *(Du musst nicht warten.)* … I'll get the bus home.
27. *(Wann musstest du aufstehen)* … when you went to school in England?
28. *(Ich konnte eine Stimme hören)* …, but there was nobody there.
29. *(Sollen wir morgen ins Kino gehen?)* … There's a new Wesley Snipes film on at the Odeon.
30. *(Du darfst mich nicht stören* [disturb] *)* … when I'm working.

D ▶ **Translate the German sentence parts in brackets using a form of *be, have* or *do*.**

31. I'm late this morning. *(Ich habe noch nicht geduscht.)* …
32. Jane won't be long. *(Sie macht gerade den Einkauf.)* …
33. *(Wie viele ausländische Studenten gibt es in* [on] *deinem Kurs?)* … – More than usual this year.
34. *(Hast du schon zu Mittag gegessen?)* … – No, not yet. We can get something in town.
35. *(Macht deine Firma mit Johns Firma Geschäfte?)* … – No, I don't think so.
36. *(Es gab keine leichten Fragen.)* … The whole exam was pretty difficult.

Modal auxiliaries and be, have, do

| ? | **Correct yourself** |

A   1: *was allowed to*   2: *needn't*   3: *should have*   4: *managed to*   5: *ought to*   6: *might*
7: *are to*   8: *may*   9: *don't have to*   10: *are not supposed to*

B   11: *Are you allowed to/Can you*   12: *Shall/Can/Can't/Could/Couldn't*   13: *were able to*
14: *could*   15: *were not allowed to/were not supposed to*   16: *must*   17: *needn't*
18: *mustn't/shouldn't*   19: *may/might/could*   20: *are not allowed to/mustn't*

C   21: *You needn't/don't have to stay in bed, …*   22: *We just managed to/were just able to stop …*
23: *But I may/might/could be wrong.*   24: *I had to help my mother.*
25: *… you had better/should/ought to go to bed early.*   26: *You needn't/don't have to wait.*
27: *When did you have to get up …*   28: *I could hear a voice …*   29: *Shall we go to the cinema
tomorrow?*   30: *You mustn't disturb me …*

D   31: *I haven't had a shower yet.*   32: *She's just doing the shopping.*
33: *How many foreign students are there on your course?*   34: *Have you already had lunch?*
35: *Does your firm do business with John's firm?*   36: *There weren't any easy questions.*

Exercise finder		
Sentences	CEG	Exercises
1, 15	▶ **39d**	▶ **3, 7**
2, 9, 17, 21, 26	▶ **41a**	▶ **2, 3, 7**
3, 5, 7, 10, 16, 25	▶ **42**	▶ **5, 7, 8**
4, 13, 14, 22, 28	▶ **37**	▶ **1, 7**
6, 8, 19, 23	▶ **47**	▶ **6, 7, 8**
11, 20	▶ **39a**	▶ **3, 8**
12, 29	▶ **45**	▶ **4, 5**
18, 30	▶ **39c**	▶ **3, 8**
24, 27	▶ **41c**	▶ **2, 3, 7**
31, 34	▶ **55**	▶ **10**
32, 35	▶ **57**	▶ **11**
33, 36	▶ **52**	▶ **9**

1 *Mini-dialogues*   **ability:** *can, could, be able to, manage to*    **37a-g**

a   Complete the mini-dialogues with *can*, *could* or the correct tense and form of *be able to*. Think about the situation (general or specific) and look out for verbs of perception (*see, hear, feel*, etc.)

Examples: Ed: Luke **won't be able to** play in the team match next Sunday. He twisted his ankle during training. At first he **couldn't** feel anything, but now he **can't** walk at all.

           Jeff: That once happened to me, but I **was able to** play again about a week later.

1 Don: Last night I (1) … hear a strange noise. I (2) … sleep, so I went downstairs to look.

    Tom: And (3) … you see anything?

    Don: Yes, there were two cats fighting in the back garden. I banged on the window and I (4) … frighten them off.

2 Dave: My parents are away, so I'm on my own at home. Unfortunately, I (1) … cook. This morning when I was in the bathroom I thought I (2) … smell something burning.

    Jerry: And what (3) … you smell?

    Dave: My bacon and sausages. Luckily I (4) … get things under control. But what a mess!

3 Jess: I (1) … contact Laura since she moved. (2) … you give me her e-mail address, or her mobile number?

    Lisa: Sorry, I (3) … I haven't got either.

    Jess: Oh, then we (4) … invite her to the party at the weekend.

4 Sarah: Tom's motorbike is making a funny noise these days. He (1) … hear a squeak somewhere. He's looked at it a few times, but so far he (2) … find out what's wrong.

    Janet: Perhaps the mechanic (3) … repair it by tomorrow.

    Sarah: Let's hope so. Tom will hate the idea of (4) … go to the concert on it tomorrow night.

5 Gina: (1) … you swim?

    Tess: Not very well. I don't think I (2) … save my life. My little cousin (3) … swim when he was four. He fell in the lake yesterday, but we (4) … dry his clothes before we took him home.

b   Read the dialogues again. Where could you use *manage to* instead of *be able to*? Look for specific situations in the past and put in *manage to* in the correct form.

c   Think of a time or situation when you (or your friends) had problems or difficulties but managed to overcome them, find a solution, etc. Write a short paragraph. If you can't think of a true incident, use your imagination.

a Have you ever thought about being a contestant[1] on a TV game show? What makes a good contestant? Make sentences with *mustn't* or *needn't* and the words given.

Examples: shy highly intelligent
 *You **mustn't** be shy.* *You **needn't** be highly intelligent.*

1 too serious 2 top fit 3 unfriendly 4 good-looking 5 musical 6 nervous

b Complete the text about game shows with a form of *have to*, *mustn't* or *needn't*.

Contestants in game shows **needn't** look like film stars or be very talented. But they **have to** be fun-loving. Sometimes they also (1) … be adventurous. It isn't easy to be a good contestant. You (2) … be introverted or too quiet. The audience (3) … like you. You (4) … laugh and chat all the time, but you (5) … be outgoing[2] on the show. You (6) … be able to concentrate and react quickly in stress situations. You (7) … be a top athlete, but you (8) … be fit because contestants are often involved in athletic activities.
For some game shows you (9) … have very good nerves – if you haven't, then you (10) … apply. You (11) … be scared of snakes, spiders or worms, for example, because you never know what you may (12) … do. You (13) … refuse to do what the presenter wants, even if you think it is stupid or dangerous. If you lose, you (14) … smile. You (15) … get angry or complain. The show must go on. Game shows are hard work, but then, if you don't like them, you (16) … take part.

✁ c Work with a partner. Write a short dialogue. Imagine that A needs money and has applied to be a contestant in a game show. He/She sent in a full application and was invited to go for interview. B needs money too, and asks questions about the application and the interview. Write the dialogue using the past tense of *have to* in the positive, question or negative form. Use your imagination.

Example: B: **Did you have to** send a photo with the application?
 A: I **had to** send two photos. One full face and one full length.
 B: What kind of questions **did you have to** answer?

———
1 contestant *Kandidat/in* 2 be outgoing *kontaktfreudig sein, aus sich herausgehen*

3 *Signs* permission, prohibition, obligation, lack of obligation: *can/can't,*
be (not) allowed to, must/mustn't, needn't, have to/don't have to ▶ **39, 41a/c/d**

What do the signs mean? Choose the correct answers. More than one may be correct.

Example: a You mustn't pick flowers. ✔
         b You needn't pick flowers.
         c You don't have to pick flowers.
         d You are not allowed to pick flowers. ✔
         e You can't pick flowers. ✔

1    **2**    **3**    **4**    **5**    **6**

1 a You can't camp here.
   b You mustn't camp here.
   c You don't have to camp here.
   d You are not allowed to camp here.

2 a You must be quiet.
   b You needn't be quiet.
   c You are not allowed to play radios.
   d You have to be quiet.
   e You can play radios.

3 a You are allowed to switch on your mobile.
   b You have to switch off your mobile.
   c You needn't switch off your mobile.
   d You must switch off your mobile.
   e You can't switch on your mobile.

4 a You don't have to pay.
   b You have to pay.
   c You needn't pay.
   d You mustn't pay.

5 a You mustn't put in green or brown glass.
   b You needn't put in green or brown glass.
   c You are allowed to put in white glass.
   d You can put in white glass.

6 a You needn't fasten your seat belt.
   b You mustn't fasten your seat belt.
   c You have to fasten your seat belt.

4 *Requests, offers, suggestions* *can, could, will, would, may, shall* ▶ **39b, 43-45**

What would you say in the following situations? There are several possibilities. Choose the modals which are most suitable in the situation. Choose from: *can, could, will, would, may, shall.*

Examples: A friend arrives. It's a hot day. Offer him/her something to drink.
         Can/Shall I *get you something to drink?/* ***Would you*** *like something to drink?*

1 You're at a friend's house. You have forgotten your mobile but you need to make a call.
   Ask your friend's mother if you can use their phone.
2 You see an elderly neighbour struggling with some heavy shopping. You are going his/her way.
3 You are staying with a friend. You would like to check your e-mails on his/her computer.
4 You feel like going to the cinema. Suggest it to a friend.
5 A friend has borrowed some DVDs and you would like to have them back. Ask him/her.
6 You car has broken down at a friend's. It won't start. Ask someone for help.
7 You're shopping with a friend. You haven't got enough money. Ask him/her to lend you £ 20.
8 You need some advice on subjects and universities. Ask your teacher.

5 German 'sollen'

obligation, instructions, advice: *be to, be supposed to, had better, must, shall, ought to, should*

▶ **42, 45**

a Choose the most suitable modal from the brackets. Sometimes more than one may be suitable:

Examples: Mr Fox wants Don to give his paper[1] on Friday, and Anna (***is to***/shall) give hers on Monday. You (***ought to***/***should***) discuss the problem with one of your teachers.

1 (Should/Shall) we go to that art exhibition in town this afternoon?
2 Jan's expecting us at her barbecue at four, so we (had better not/are not supposed to) eat much lunch or we won't be hungry.
3 If you're leaving school in July, you (ought to/should) be studying job ads and writing applications now.
4 When (are we to/shall we) give in our projects? Did Mr Ashley say the twentieth or the twenty-first?
5 It's going to rain this afternoon, so you (ought to/had better) take the bus. You'll get wet if you cycle.
6 Your cough is getting worse. I think you (should/are to) go to the doctor's. He'll give you something for it.
7 I (ought to/had better) be doing maths instead of watching videos. We've got a test tomorrow.
8 You simply (should/must) go to the concert with me. There are some great bands playing.
9 The new Mexican restaurant on Duke Street (is to/is supposed to) be very good. Let's go!
10 I wonder where Susan is. She (had better/was supposed to) be here at four. Now it's almost five.

b Name two things that you are to do for school before Monday next week.
Name two things that you are not supposed to do at home.
Name two things that you think you had better do or had better not do within the next few days.
Name two things that you should do before you go to bed tonight.

Examples: *My brother and I **are supposed to make** our beds and keep our rooms tidy.
I **had better not forget** my best friend's birthday.*

6 Probability and possibility *can, can't, could, will, must, may, might*

▶ **37g/h, 47**

a We use the following modals to express different degrees of probability or possibility: *can, can't, could, will, must, may, might.* Choose a suitable modal and write new sentences without changing the meaning of the underlined words. More than one modal may be possible.

Example: That isn't Rob at the door. It isn't possible. He's in London today.
*That **can't** be Rob at the door.*

1 Dave's brother is a hotel manager in Paris. That's a very interesting job, I'm sure.
2 It's quite possible that John will come this evening.
3 The sun has gone in and it's getting cloudy. It will probably rain.
4 Laura said she would phone at seven. Oh, that's the phone now. That's definitely her.
5 Gemma isn't over 25. It isn't possible.
6 Paul studied physics. It's likely that he will know the answer. Ask him.
7 The weather in Scotland is sometimes sunny and warm.
8 I'm sure that Mrs Hadley isn't a foreigner. She speaks perfect English without an accent.

---

1 give a paper *ein Referat halten*

b   What could have happened? Give a logical reason or explanation. Use a suitable modal + perfect infinitive.
    Choose from: *can't/could/must/may/might* + perfect infinitive. More than one modal is possible.

Examples: John: Tim didn't phone me last night.
            *He **must/could have forgotten**. / He **may/might have been** too busy to phone.*

1 Leo: Peter hasn't given me my DVDs back.
2 Laura: I can't find my physics file anywhere.
3 Ali: Janet doesn't seem to be at home.
4 Dave: Phil was in, but he didn't answer the phone.
5 Jill: Oh no. Look at Brian's car. All the front is smashed in.
6 Sanjay: I saw Mark in a red sportscar this morning.

---

7   *Mixed bag*   modal aux.: mixed exercise   ▶  **37b-d, 39d, 41a-c, 42e, 47**

a   There is one mistake in each sentence or sentence pair. Can you correct it?

1   I must work last weekend, so that's why I wasn't at the football match.
2   I could get up very early this morning, because I went to bed at nine last night.
3   You mustn't sign the contract now. There's no hurry. Tomorrow will do.
4   Terry could repair his bike yesterday, because he bought a few spare parts.
5   Last Saturday my sister may not go to a party because she hadn't done any homework for a week.
6   Don't throw these comics away. Save them for Ben. He could like them.
7   My library books are well overdue. – When must you return them? Last week?
8   Didn't Jan say she was going to Paris this week? – I'm not sure, but you can be right.
9   You mustn't wait for me. There's usually a long queue in the post office. I'll walk home.
10 My little brother could stay up until ten o'clock last night because it was his birthday.
11 The headmaster wants to speak to me. I must go to his room in the second lesson.
12 Mike can have a hammer and some nails. Why don't you ask him?
13 I'm really tired. I simply have to go to bed early tonight.
14 The Robsons have a big house and three cars. They have to be rich.

b   Write new sentences, using modals or their substitutes which express the same as the underlined parts.
    Sometimes there is more than one possibility. If necessary, change the sentence structure.

Example: If you don't want to go to the meeting, it's not necessary for you to go.
            *You **needn't/don't have to go** to the meeting if you don't want to.*

1   It didn't rain yesterday, so it was possible for us to play football.
2   Is it really necessary for us to copy the whole chapter?
3   It is just possible that the story Beth told you is true.
4   I advise you to go to the optician's.
5   I'm quite sure that's the street where John lives. That looks like his car.
6   Scott is always punctual. The only possible explanation is that something has happened.
7   Did you know how to read when you were six?
8   There's no obligation for you to stay for supper if you have a lot to do.
9   They don't let you take photographs here.
10 It isn't possible that you saw Helen. She's in Australia for a month.
11 The car brakes failed, but it was just possible for us to stop in time.
12 I suppose it's possible that Max met Jane on the management course, but it's not very likely.

School rules   modal aux., substitute forms: mixed ex.   ▶ **39a/c, 41a/c, 42a/b/d, 47**

Teen Life Magazine asked teenagers what kind of school rules they have and what they think about them. Here are some extracts from pupils' e-mails. Read the text, then answer the questions.

> In Australia we have a whole book of rules. For example, we have to wear special hats on the way to school, we are only allowed to wear a school uniform. We have to have our hair cut short and we aren't allowed to chew bubble gum. (Marie S., Brisbane)
>
> 5 There must be rules – or school would be chaos. At our school you are allowed to smoke when you turn 16, but you can only smoke outside in the *'Raucherhof'*. You're not allowed to drink alcohol, you shouldn't fight, we mustn't throw snowballs, we mustn't be absent without an absence note[1]. But we can wear what we want, and I think you should be allowed to dress as you want. (Heike, Hamburg)
>
> We're not supposed to leave mobiles on during lessons. We mustn't steal or damage school property. You can't get expelled[2] unless you do something really bad. Two friends of mine sprayed some school walls
> 10 with paint. They only had to repaint the walls. That was OK. I don't think they should have been punished harder. You're not supposed to talk or disturb others in class. If you do, you have to leave the class and stand outside, or you have to write up a protocol of the lesson. I'm glad we don't have to wear a uniform. (Fabian T., Frankfurt)
>
> Our school rules are OK. We mustn't eat in class, we can't listen to walkmans. We can't leave the campus
> 15 until the teacher says so. But we needn't stand up when the teacher comes in. (Liz, Illinois)
>
> We can't have drugs or electronic equipment on campus. If you have drugs at school, you can get expelled. And you'd better not have a knife or a gun, because then you're in big trouble – you *will* get expelled. If you chew gum or if you're late to class twice, you might get a detention[3]. I hate that because you're not allowed to talk. You can't even move! If you wear T-shirts promoting alcohol, tobacco or gang violence, the principal[4] may write to your parents. If you get an F grade for two semesters, you have to
> 20 take the semester over[5] the next year. (Miles K., Georgia)
>
> Adapted from 'School Rules', *The Goldmine*

a Search the text for examples of the following:

   1 a past tense form of *must*   3 three modals that express 'it is possible that …'
   2 a modal + perfect infinitive   4 a modal that expresses 'it is certain that …'

b Express the sentences using different modals without changing the meaning:

   1 'We can't have drugs … ' (l. 16)   2 '… you are allowed to smoke when you turn 16 …'
      (ll. 4-5)   3 'But we needn't stand up when the teacher comes in.' (l. 15)

c Translate the sentences into German:

   1 '… we mustn't throw snowballs …' (l. 6)   4 'You're not supposed to talk or disturb
   2 '… we can wear what we want … (l. 6-7)   others …' (l. 11)
   3 'You can't even move!' (l. 19)   5 '… you'd better not have a knife …' (l. 17)

d Answer the questions in paragraphs using modals and substitute forms:

   1 Write down what you must, mustn't, are allowed to and are not allowed to do at school.
   2 Look at the rules mentioned in the e-mails. Which ones are different from yours?
   3 Write four questions (in all) that you would ask the writers of the e-mails.
   4 Think about punishments at your school and the ones mentioned in the e-mails. Do you think they should be harsher[6] or less harsh? When, in your opinion, ought a pupil to be suspended or expelled?

---

1 absence note *schriftliche Entschuldigung*   2 expel: officially make sb. leave a school   3 detention *Nachsitzen*
4 principal (AE): head teacher   5 take a semester over (AE): repeat a semester   6 harsh *hart*

9 *Hong Kong – past and present*   **be** used as a full verb: *there + be*   ▶ **52**

a   Complete the text about Hong Kong with the correct tense and form of *there + be*.

There are several good reasons for visiting Hong Kong. For a start, **there's** the fascination of the two faces of this dynamic metropolis, a remarkable blend[1] of East and West. (1) … ultra-modern skyscrapers side by side with traditional Chinese markets selling live snakes – and 350 temples. (2) … the new Chek Lap Kok airport on Lantau Island, twice the size of JFK, capable of handling 35 million passengers a year. On Lantau (3) … also the biggest bronze Buddha in the world.

Hong Kong has a population of 6.8 million, 96 % being Chinese. But (4) … thousands of British citizens living there permanently too. Even as early as the 18th century (5) … brisk[2] trade between the British East India Company and the Chinese – in Indian opium, until Peking banned its import. (6) … two Opium Wars because of this. In 1841 the British established a naval base in Hong Kong to protect their economic interests, and since then (7) … increasing prosperity[3]. One could claim that (8 not) … an economic miracle in Hong Kong without the arrival of the British, but more praise is due to the work ethics of the Hong Kong people. (9 not – always) … such wealth in Hong Kong. (10) … a number of contributing factors, one being the millions of refugees – many of them wealthy – who fled from Communist China in 1949.

Although Hong Kong has been under Chinese administration again since 1997, (11) … still a noticeable British presence on the streets. (12) … buildings, street names and MTR[4] stations which are a constant reminder of former colonial times, for example Prince Edward station, the Prince of Wales Building, Queen's Road, Victoria Peak. And (13 may – not) … as many chauffeur-driven Rolls Royces anywhere else in the world as (14) … in Hong Kong Central.

Amidst all the festivities of 1 July 1997, the Handover[5], (15) … a real fear that life would change dramatically for the people of Hong Kong. In the future (16 certainly) … many political, even economic setbacks[6], as the Chinese may try to abolish the democratic reforms introduced by the British. The present law guarantees a high degree of autonomy until 2047. The question that everybody is asking is: And what (17) … after that?

Based on information from *Hong Kong Insight Pocket Guide* by Joseph R. Yogerst

b   Write five questions with *there + be* that you would like to ask someone who lives in Hong Kong.

c   Write a short paragraph telling a penfriend about your home town, using *there + be* in various tenses and forms, both positive and negative. Make sure that you do not leave out *there*.

Example: *In Bad Tölz **there's** a … and **there are** three cinemas. In the town centre **there used to be** a …, and soon **there's going to be** a new …*

---

1 blend *Mischung*   2 brisk *lebhaft*   3 prosperity *Wohlstand*   4 MTR: Mass Transit Railway
5 Handover *die Übergabe*   6 setback *Rückschlag*

10 *Write a story*   **have** used as an activity verb   ▶ **55**

a Max is a medical student in London. He's in his second year, but he doesn't take his studies very seriously. He likes to have a good time. Complete the sentences about him using the words in brackets and *have* as a full verb in the correct tense and form.

Example: Where's Max? He should be at a lecture. – (bath)
          *He's **having a bath**.*

1 Max (never – breakfast) … before nine.
2 What time (lunch) …? – Not before two.
3 Last night he (party) …, but he (not – fun) … because he (a quarrel – girlfriend) …
4 So today he (a day off) …
5 Later he (game of tennis – friend) …

b Use your imagination and write a story about a day in Max's life, using as many of the verbs below as you can in any order. If you are not sure of the correct translation, use a dictionary. Include a conversation between Max and his girlfriend, using question and negative forms.

> frühstücken ▪ duschen ▪ Kaffee trinken ▪ (zu) Mittag essen ▪ schlafen ▪
> etwas trinken ▪ Pause machen ▪ sich vergnügen ▪ eine Party geben ▪
> viel Spaß haben ▪ einen freien Tag nehmen ▪ schwimmen gehen ▪ spazieren gehen ▪
> essen gehen ▪ sich streiten

Examples: *One day Max **was having breakfast**. It was late and he still **hadn't had a shower**. Just then his girlfriend arrived.*

Continue.

11 *Doing things*   **do** used as a full verb   ▶ **57**

Complete the sentences with the correct form and tense of *do* or *make*.

1 How was the maths test? – Not good. I could only … two out of five questions
2 (you) … all the French homework last night? – No, I've still got two exercises to …
3 Somebody has … a mistake. These figures are wrong.
4 The house is a mess at the moment. I (not) … any housework yesterday.
5 Don't worry about the exam. Just concentrate and … your best.
6 (you) … the ironing yet? I need my blue T-shirt.
7 When I called at Mark's house he … a job for his dad, for some extra pocket money.
8 Could you … me a photocopy of these documents, please?
9 My brother's old car still … over 100 mph.
10 Jason … a management training course at the moment.
11 I'll … you an offer for your old computer. How about eighty pounds?
12 The neighbour blamed Ben for breaking her window, but Ben says he … it.
13 How's school? (you) … well at the moment?
14 We (not) … business with Johnsons any more. They don't deliver on time.
15 The storm … a lot of damage last night. It even blew off a few roofs.

A ▶ **Simple or progressive? Choose the correct form from the brackets to complete the sentences.**

1 Pat is in Scotland at the moment. She (stays/is staying) with her cousin for a week.
2 Tim (is cooking/cooks) dinner for his girlfriend right now.
3 I (have worked/have been working) hard on my essay. It's finished now.
4 When I called at Don's, he (assembled/was assembling) his new computer.
5 Emma's eyes were red when I called. She (had chopped/had been chopping) onions for lunch.
6 Liz (always gives/is always giving) parties. I don't think she does much for school.
7 Dave can't hear you at the moment. He (is listening/listens) to his walkman.
8 Last night we (were going/went) to see *Speed 4* at the ABC. It was really exciting.
9 I (cycle/am cycling) to school this week because the weather's so nice.
10 Sam (has kicked/has been kicking) a ball through the neighbours' window, I'm afraid.
11 Judy always (is going/goes) to her ballet class on Thursdays.
12 I couldn't speak to Janice because she (washed/was washing) her hair.

B ▶ **Complete the sentences with the past, present perfect or past perfect in the simple or progressive form. Sometimes a passive verb may be necessary.**

13 What time (your train – arrive) … this morning? – At 8.05 exactly.
14 Phone the police. I think my car (steal) … It's not where I left it.
15 Sarah felt ill because she (eat) … four hamburgers and two ice creams.
16 It's time you made an appointment for a check-up at the dentist's. You (not – be) … there for ages.
17 Do you know where my old boots are? – I (look for) … them in the cellar.
18 How long (you – clean) … your room? – For well over an hour. And I haven't finished yet.
19 I couldn't pay for the cinema tickets because I realized I (forget) … my money.
20 How long (you – know) … your best friend?
21 I was hot and tired when I met Jan. I (run) … down by the river.
22 The police found Laura's stolen moped, but unfortunately it (damage) … by the thief.
23 The unemployment figures (rise) … only slightly this year so far.
24 When Andy and Paul (drive) … up to Glasgow, their car broke down.

C ▶ **Spot the mistakes. There is one mistake in each sentence or sentence group.**

25 We have this house for three years. We got it cheap.
26 Pat is a radiologist. She works at Victoria Hospital for about five years.
27 Last year we have gone on holiday to Corsica.
28 While I was watching TV, the doorbell was ringing. It was Polly.
29 I haven't been to the cinema since about three months.
30 You'll have to drive Paul home, I'm afraid. Don't let him drive. He has drunk.
31 Dad won't be long. He just takes the dog for a walk.
32 I am going to karate classes every Wednesday. Why don't you join too?
33 Tom works at Cole's garage for a few weeks. I don't think he likes it.
34 In the film *Vanilla Sky* Tom Cruise is playing a rich playboy with lots of girlfriends.
35 Can you lend me ten pounds until tomorrow? – No, I can't. You always borrow money.
36 Janet looked very miserable yesterday. I could see that she had cried.
37 We haven't seen Jonathan since ages.
38 In *Bridget Jones's Diary* Helen Fielding is humorously describing the daily life of a single girl over thirty.

? **Correct yourself**

A

1: *is staying*   2: *is cooking*   3: *have worked*   4: *was assembling*   5: *had been chopping*
6: *is always giving*   7: *is listening*   8: *went*   9: *am cycling*   10: *has kicked*
11: *goes*   12: *was washing*

B

13: *did your train arrive*   14: *has been stolen*   15: *had eaten*   16: *haven't been*
17: *have been looking for*   18: *have you been cleaning*   19: *had forgotten*   20: *have you known*
21: *had been running*   22: *had been damaged*   23: *have risen*   24: *were driving*

C

25: *We have had this house for three years …*
26: *… She has worked at Victoria Hospital for about five years.*
27: *Last year we went on holiday to Corsica.*
28: *While I was watching TV, the doorbell rang …*
29: *I haven't been to the cinema for about three months.*
30: *… Don't let him drive. He has been drinking.*
31: *… He is just taking the dog for a walk.*
32: *I go to karate classes every Wednesday …*
33: *Tom is working at Cole's garage for a few weeks …*
34: *… Tom Cruise plays a rich playboy with lots of girlfriends.*
35: *… – No, I can't. You are always borrowing money.*
36: *… I could see that she had been crying.*
37: *We haven't seen Jonathan for ages.*
38: *… Helen Fielding humorously describes the daily life of a single girl over thirty.*

Exercise finder

Sentences	CEG	Exercises
2, 7, 31	▶ 77a	▶ 1, 2, 3, 4, 21
1, 9, 33	▶ 77b	▶ 1, 2, 3, 4
3, 10, 14, 23	▶ 80a	▶ 6, 7, 8, 9, 16, 17, 21
4, 12, 24, 28	▶ 89b	▶ 11, 12, 16, 17
5, 21, 36	▶ 94	▶ 13
6, 35	▶ 77a Anm.	▶ 4
8, 13, 27	▶ 86a	▶ 6, 7, 8, 11, 12, 14, 15, 16, 17, 21
11, 32	▶ 75a	▶ 1, 2, 3, 4, 21
15, 19, 22	▶ 92a	▶ 13, 14, 15, 16, 17, 21
16, 20, 25, 26	▶ 80b	▶ 6, 7, 8, 9, 16, 17, 21
17, 18, 30	▶ 82	▶ 9, 10, 21
29, 37	▶ 84	▶ 10
34, 38	▶ 75c	▶ 5

The tenses of the full verbs   *Ways of expressing future time*

A ▶ **Choose the correct form from the brackets.**

1 Oh, it's starting to rain. Get in. I (drive/will drive) you home.
2 What (will you do/will you be doing) at this time next week? – My English exam.
3 The first bus to Coventry (is leaving/leaves) at 6.15, I think.
4 Look out! The ice (is going to/will) break.
5 I (go/am going) to a barbecue tonight. Do you want to go with me?
6 We (are about to/are to) leave for the airport, so I haven't got much time, I'm afraid.
7 When (will you have finished/have you finished) with my CDs?
8 We (land/are landing) in Chicago at 3.35 and our connecting flight is two hours later.
9 When I get home, my parents (will have/will be having) supper.
10 Mike has just put his boots on. He (will/is going to) post some letters.

B ▶ **Put in the correct tense/form of the verb given. Sometimes two tenses/forms are possible. Choose from: simple present, present progressive, *will*-future, *going to*-future, future progressive, future perfect.**

11 What time (your plane – leave) … tomorrow? Shall I take you to the airport?
12 On Monday next week I (lie) … in the sun on the beach at Rimini.
13 Isn't that the phone ringing? It's OK. I (go) …
14 Dave (not – plan) … to go to university yet. He wants to earn some money first.
15 I expect we (have) … hot weather in Italy. We always do.
16 Mum, by the time you get home, I (clean) … my room. I promise.
17 I think I (walk) … home through the park. I need some fresh air.
18 Sue (study) … pharmacy after school. She's already got a place at Bristol University.
19 Just imagine. At this time tomorrow, we (fly) … over the Atlantic.
20 What time (the last bus – go) …? I mustn't miss it.

C ▶ **Translate the German clauses in brackets into English.**

21 Look at that man standing on the bridge. *(Er wird gleich springen.)* … Call the police!
22 I'm getting the next bus into town. – Oh. Just a minute. *(Ich fahre mit dir.)* …
23   A week today *(werden wir unsere Englischprüfung schreiben* [do]*.)* … I'm nervous already.
24 Sorry I can't come, *(aber morgen Nachmittag spiele ich mit Dave Tennis.)* …
25 Jenny has just put her coat on. *(Sie ist im Begriff, den Hund auszuführen.)* …
26 Don't worry. Pam's a careful driver. I'm sure *(sie kommt bald.)* …
27 Have you seen those dark clouds? It's windy too. *(Es wird einen Sturm geben.)* …

D ▶ **Spot the mistakes (future time). There is one mistake in each sentence or sentence group.**

28 Mick will study microbiology at university.
29 You can't lift that heavy box on your own. Just a moment. I help you.
30 By this time next year we will leave school.
31 Do you do anything tomorrow evening? If not, you could come with me to the concert.
32 Oh, hello. Sorry, but we are just to go out. Can I phone you back later?
33 Why have you put on those old clothes? – I will clean out the garden shed.
34 I suppose Gemma comes late again. She usually does.

The tenses of the full verbs *Ways of expressing future time*

> **? Correct yourself**

A 1: *will drive*   2: *will you be doing*   3: *leaves*   4: *is going to*   5: *am going*   6: *are about to*
7: *will you have finished*   8: *land*   9: *will be having*   10: *is going to*

B 11: *does your plane leave*   12: *will be lying*   13: *I'll go.*   14: *isn't planning*   15: *will have*
16: *will have cleaned*   17: *will walk*   18: *is going to study/is studying*   19: *will be flying*
20: *does the last bus go*

C 21: *He is going to jump. / He is about to jump.*
22: *I'll go with you.*
23: *… we will be doing our English exam.*
24: *… but tomorrow afternoon I am playing/I am going to play tennis with Dave.*
25: *She is about to take the dog for a walk.*
26: *… she'll come soon.*
27: *There's going to be a storm.*

D 28: *Mick is going to study microbiology at university.*
29: *… Just a moment. I'll help you.*
30: *By this time next year we will have left school.*
31: *Are you doing anything tomorrow evening? …*
32: *Oh, hello. Sorry, but we are just about to go out …*
33: *… – I am going to clean out the garden shed.*
34: *I suppose Gemma will come late again …*

> **Exercise finder**

Sentences	CEG	Exercises
1, 13, 22, 29	▶ 96b	▶ 18, 19, 20, 21
2, 9, 12, 19, 23	▶ 102a	▶ 20, 21
3, 8, 11, 20	▶ 100	▶ 19, 20
4, 21, 27	▶ 98b	▶ 18, 19, 20, 21
5, 14, 24, 31	▶ 99	▶ 19, 20
6, 25, 32	▶ 106c	▶ 20
7, 16, 30	▶ 104	▶ 20
10, 18, 28, 33	▶ 98a	▶ 18, 19, 20, 21
15, 17, 26, 34	▶ 96a	▶ 19, 20, 21

1 *Quick and easy*   **aspect: simple form, progressive form**   ▶ **68, 75, 77, 78**

a Match the statements to the pictures. Combine the letters with the right sentence numbers.

Example: *Gemma **is writing** job applications.*

Example: *Gemma **has** already **written** five applications.*

1 Ed is a driving instructor. He gives six to eight lessons a day.
2 Emma plays in the women's team for the local tennis club.
3 Tom has been preparing a presentation for a conference all day.
4 Emma is playing in a tennis tournament.
5 Tom has prepared all his OHTs[1] for the conference.
6 Ed is giving someone a driving lesson.

---

1 OHTs overhead transparencies *Folien für den Overheadprojektor*

b   Would you use the simple or the progressive form to translate these sentences? Write 's' or 'p'.

1   Gina arbeitet für eine Software-Firma in der Stadt.
2   Zurzeit arbeitet sie an einem neuen Projekt.
3   Rob schreibt einen Leserbrief an die *Daily Post*.
4   Er schreibt regelmäßig Leserbriefe.
5   Pam lernt Mathe-Formeln schon den ganzen Tag.
6   Die wichtigsten Formeln hat sie schon gelernt.

2   *Get it right*   **state verbs**   ▶ **70, 75, 77, 78**

a   Which verbs can be used in the progressive form? (✔) Which verbs are not usually used in the progressive form (state verbs)? (✘)

belong to	✘	live	____	mind	____
go	✔	know	____	believe	____
consist of	____	contain	____	collect	____
work	____	own	____	prefer	____
understand	____	visit	____	do	____
cost	____	give	____	seem	____
creep	____	sound	____	doubt	____

b   Choose from the verbs above to complete the sentences. Use a present tense (simple or progressive), and make the verb negative where indicated.

1   A good education (not) … learning facts alone. It also teaches you to think critically.
2   Your essay … a few inaccuracies[1], but on the whole it's a good piece of work.
3   We … hard for A-levels at the moment, so we haven't got much time for parties.
4   Jan says she passed her driving test first time, but I (not) … her. It took her ages to get her licence.
5   John's a good friend of mine, but I (not) … where he lives.
6   Sheila … a course in mulitmedia design in Brighton.
7   It's stuffy in here. … you … if I open the window?
8   I'm not a very sporty person. I … reading a book to climbing a mountain any day.
9   Gina … to be much happier since she left home and started life on her own.
10 Tom (not) … the car he drives around in. It's his brother's car that he just borrows.
11 I … Val's reasons for wanting to change her job. I would do the same in her position.
12 Sarah has all kinds of different collections. At the moment she … glass animals.

---

1 inaccuracy *Ungenauigkeit*

3   *Our website*   **simple present, present progressive**   ▶ **75, 77, 78**

a   The German new metal band *Babylon* has a website in German and English. Here is their English version. Unfortunately, there are ten mistakes in it. The simple present and present progressive sometimes need to be corrected. Look out for 'signal words' and make the necessary corrections.
Make sure that the adverbs are in the right place.

Location: **www.babylon-bavaria.de**

Hi!...........................
Welcome to the *Babylon* website.
Here we are: Marco, Florian, Basti and Tobi.
....

Examples: Well, first a few general things about us and an up-date
about what goes on in the band at the moment. Originally,
we are all coming from Rosenheim in Bavaria.
Correct: … what **is going on** in the band at the moment.
… we **all come from** Rosenheim in Bavaria.

Perhaps you know our home town. Rosenheim is very close to the mountains, so we are all going skiing every winter.

Three of us don't live in Rosenheim permanently any more, but we sometimes are going home at weekends and we often are giving concerts there. Basti is still going to
5   school in Rosenheim. He isn't liking school much usually. Just now he does his Abitur, so he's not too happy at all.

Basti is playing the bass guitar. Marco is our lead guitarist and singer. He usually is writing the lyrics for our songs, but for our new single I am writing them. Florian is on keyboard. I'm on drums.

10   We usually meet twice a week for band practice, but this week we don't meet at all – because of Basti's exams. Just now we work on new songs for our second album.

By the way, *Babylon* is playing at the *Open Air Festival* in Passau on Saturday 1st June, so if you are living close by, or if you are in the area, come and see us.

Bye now, from Tobi and *Babylon*.

b   Write four questions that you could ask the band, with and without question words. Use the simple present and the present progressive.

Examples: **Do you give** concerts in other parts of Germany?
Where are you giving your next concert?

c   Work with a partner or in small groups and design a website in English for your class. Include general information about the school and your class, and say what is happening in your class at present, e.g. if you are planning a class trip, what kind of projects you are doing, what you are reading or discussing in your English lessons, etc. Write mainly in the present, using simple and progressive forms. Think about state verbs and the position of adverbs.

Mini-dialogues   **simple present, present progressive**   ▶ **75a/b, 77, 78**

a Choose the correct verb form from the brackets. If you choose a present progressive form, make sure that the adverb is in the right place. Look out for state verbs.

1 Kim: Emma still (1 looks for/is looking for) a part-time job. She (2 needs/is needing) more money.
   Ann: Emma always (3 needs/is needing) more money. I can't believe it.
   Kim: Well, she (4 spends/ is spending) a lot at the moment. More than usual. She's got a new boyfriend and unfortunately he (5 lives/is living) in Portsmouth, so she (6 goes/is going) down there every weekend. Sometimes she (7 takes/is taking) her sister's car, but petrol (8 goes up/is going up) all the time, and train fares (9 are costing/cost) even more than petrol.
   Ann: Sarah (10 works/is working) at Sainsbury's for six weeks. Perhaps they (11 are needing/need) somebody else as well. I heard that they (12 are paying/pay) quite well.
   Kim: Well, Emma (13 babysits/is babysitting) this week for our neighbours, so I'll see her.

2 Beth: (1 Are you doing/Do you do) a job these holidays?
   Max: I (2 help out/am helping out) at the garden centre on Wentworth Road. First time.
   Beth: Oh. I didn't know you were the gardening type.
   Max: Come on, Beth. It's just a job. Anyway, yes, I (3 like/am liking) being in the fresh air all day, and there's no stress. It's a quiet, relaxing job.
   Beth: And what if it (4 rains/is raining)?
   Max: We (5 work/are working) inside or in the greenhouses. Luke (6 is delivering/delivers) pizzas, I think. Jason (7 empties/is emptying) dustbins, and Jenny and Kathy (8 work/are working) at a kindergarten or day centre – with screaming little kids. So I'm perfectly happy with my geraniums.

▶ b With a partner write a dialogue about holiday jobs, similar to dialogue 2 in a) above. Use the simple present and the present progressive, also in the question and negative forms.

5   *What's it about?*   **simple present to talk about texts (books, articles, films, etc.)**   ▶ **75c**

a Heike is telling an English friend about a film she liked. She makes some mistakes with verb forms/tenses. Correct them.

Heike: *Maid in Manhattan* is starring Jennifer Lopez and Ralph Fiennes. It's a romantic comedy with a happy ending, a kind of modern Cinderella story. Well, Jennifer Lopez is playing Marisa. She was a room maid in a hotel in Manhattan. She made beds and tidied rooms for rich people. She's also a single mum with a son. One day in one of the hotel rooms she is trying on some clothes of one of the rich guests – just for fun. There's a mix-up. She meets a US senator at the hotel. He is thinking she is a rich guest too, and he is falling in love with her. Of course, Marisa is trying to hide the truth at first.
Ann: Well, go on. What happens then?
Heike: Well, get the DVD and watch it yourself.

b What's your favourite film or book? Tell the story in a short paragraph.

A problem   present perfect (simple), simple past   ▶ **80, 86, 87**

Jonathan wants to go to drama school, but his parents are against it. First, read his letter to a problem page, then complete the tasks.

'I have always wanted to become an actor. I have often acted in school drama productions and with the drama group in our town. I have already written my own scripts and in 2002 I won the 'Young Actors' Award'. My parents have tolerated this interest as a hobby, but they have never taken it seriously.

Last year my parents persuaded me to stay on at school to do A-levels. I have already told them that I want to go to drama school, but they say it's a dead-end job with very uncertain prospects. They want me to study law. I'm a creative person – law would be the worst thing I can imagine.

We have spoken a lot about my future recently, but they haven't changed their views. They have had reason to be angry with me. So far I have done reasonably well in school. Up to now my marks have been average or even better. My marks in English have always been very good.

Two months ago I applied for a place at RADA¹. I didn't tell my parents. Last week I received a reply inviting me to go down for interview and first audition². I have considered leaving home if I am offered a place. The trouble is, it would cost a lot of money and my parents wouldn't give it to me. How could I possibly support myself?

I have just had a serious argument with my parents, although I have never really quarrelled with them in my life before. Yesterday my girlfriend said: 'Have you ever done anything that your parents didn't want? Because if you haven't, now is the time.' But I haven't had my 18th birthday yet.

I think I am afraid of the future, but I have not made up my mind yet about leaving home. My parents want what's best for me – but do they really know what that is? What shall I do?'

a Search the text and write down the adverb phrases of time that signal a) the present perfect and b) the simple past.

b In a paragraph, describe Jonathan's problem in your own words. Use the present perfect (simple) as your main tense, and the simple past where necessary. Use suitable adverb phrases of time with both tenses.

c Translate the sentences about Jonathan into English. Use either the present perfect (simple) or the simple past and look out for 'signal words'.

1 Jonathan hat in letzter Zeit viel Streit mit seinen Eltern gehabt *(to quarrel a lot)*.
2 Er hat immer Schauspieler werden wollen.
3 2002 hat er sogar einen Preis gewonnen.
4 Vor zwei Monaten hat er sich um einen Platz bei der RADA beworben.
5 Er hat seinen Eltern noch nichts davon erzählt.
6 Gestern hat er eine Antwort *(reply)* erhalten.
7 Er hat gerade mit *(to)* seiner Freundin gesprochen.
8 Er hat ihr schon von *(about)* seinem Problem erzählt.
9 Bis jetzt haben seine Eltern den Ernst *(seriousness)* der Lage nicht erkannt *(realize)*.
10 Jonathan weiß nicht, was er tun soll. Er hat sich noch nicht entschieden.

---

1 RADA: Royal Academy of Dramatic Art (in London)   2 audition *Termin zum Vorsprechen*

▶ **80, 86, 87**

7 *Have you ever …?* present perfect (simple), simple past

a Complete the mini-dialogues with the correct tense, present perfect or simple past. Look out for 'signal words'.

1 Sean: I (1 never – be) … to Paris.
  Jane: Oh, I (2 go) … there last summer. I (3 do) … a language course there. I (4 make) … a lot of new friends too.
  Sean: And your French is fantastic. (5 you – ever – think) … about studying there?
  Jane: No, thanks. I'm quite happy with our British university system. I (6 apply) … to London, Reading, Bristol and a couple more.
  Sean: (7 you – hear) … anything yet?
  Jane: No, it's too early. I only (8 send off) … the application forms last week.

2 Jill: Rob and I (1 go) … to that new Indian restaurant last night.
  Pete: You mean the one in Hadley Road?
  Jill: That's right. (2 you – ever – be) … there?
  Pete: Not yet. But Trish (3 already – be) … there twice – and it (4 only – be) … open a week. She (5 love) … the meal, especially the sauces. She says she (6 never – eat) … such great Indian food. What (7 you – order) …?
  Jill: Well, I (8 have) … tandoori chicken and Rob (9 order) … a lamb curry.

3 Ann: (1 you – see) … Pat recently? She (2 not – call) … for over a week. I (3 not – see) … her since her birthday.
  Liz: Well, actually I (4 just – speak) … to her. She (5 be) … very busy this week. You know that she (6 start) … her holiday job last Monday. Well, she (7 never – work) … in an office before, so she (8 have to) … learn a lot of new things this week.

➤ b With a partner, write a short dialogue similar to the ones in a) above. Begin with one of the following questions and use both the present perfect (simple) and the simple past (including questions and negative forms):

Have you ever been to …?   Have you ever eaten … food?
Have you ever done a holiday job?   Have you ever seen the film …?

Example: A: **Have you ever been** to the States?
        B: *Yes, I've been a couple of times. The first time I **went** to New York.*
        A: *When **did** you go?*
        B: *I **went** three years ago, in autumn. The year after I **visited** a penfriend in South Carolina.*
        A: ***Have** you **seen** any of the national parks?*

Complete each sentence pair with a verb from the list, using the present perfect or the simple past in the positive or negative form. Think carefully. Sometimes you need the same tense in both sentences.

| be ▪ fail ▪ fall ▪ find ▪ have ▪ hear ▪ lose ▪ see ▪ ~~spend~~ ▪ wear ▪ write |

Examples: When my Dad was younger, he ***spent*** a lot of time travelling around.
I ***have spent*** all morning trying to understand this instruction book.

1 a House prices … sharply since the beginning of the year.

   b I had just invested some money in the stock market when share
      prices … dramatically.

2 a I … these boots every winter for four years, and they still look good.

   b When we were at high school we … a dark blue uniform with stupid hats which
      everybody hated.

3 a The last time I … Gemma was in the shopping mall about a week ago.

   b The accident happened because the van driver … the cyclist coming round
      the corner.

4 a It was a good match yesterday, but unfortunately we … , four goals to two.

   b I … my keys. I just don't know where they are, and neither does anybody else.

5 a We don't know anything about Ben. We … from him.

   b Sorry to keep you standing at the door. I … the doorbell ring.

6 a There … another bad accident on the M1. Apparently, several vehicles were involved.

   b The last big motorway accident … in June last year.

7 a I … these old books in the attic the other day. Are they Dad's?

   b Sue has been looking for her geography file since the last exam, but she … it yet.

8 a Ann's essay is going to be too long. She … six pages so far – and she's only
      half way through.

   b When Emily was on holiday in the States, she … a postcard home every single day.

9 a Janet … her A-levels after all. She's just got the results – two Cs and a B. Not bad.

   b Dave … his driving test again. He's feeling rather depressed at the moment.

10 a We … such an awful summer for years. Nothing but rain for weeks and weeks.

    b The cake was delicious, but I really can't eat any more. I … too much already.

9 Describe the pictures

present perfect (simple), present perfect progr. ▶ 80, 82, 83

Describe the pictures using the present perfect (simple) or the present perfect progressive.

Examples:
swim

Peter enters swimming competitions.
He ***has been swimming*** non-stop for an hour.

Now his training is over.
He ***has swum*** enough for today.

a

1 **read**

b

James is very interested in cars.
He … car magazines all afternoon.

He … at least three magazines.

a

MON	TUE	WED	THU	FRI	SAT	SUN
4	5	6	7	8	9	10
Training			Training			Training

2 **train**

b

Luke wants to compete in a marathon.
He … three times this week.

This is the fourth time.
He … in the woods for at least an hour.

a

3 **drive**

b

Sue is going for a job interview to Manchester.
She … on the motorway for about two hours.

She has arrived at last.
She … over two hundred miles.

a

4 **rain**

b

What terrible weather.
It … every day so far this week.

It … since early this morning.

10 For *or* since? — *for, since*; present perfect progressive ▶ 82, 84

a Where would you use *for*? Where *since*? Put the time phrases into two lists, one with *for* and one with *since*:

Examples: I haven't been to the cinema … **for** *a couple of months.*
… **since** *I saw 'Mission Impossible 3'.*

> last week ▪ ages ▪ about three months ▪ Christmas ▪ my birthday ▪
> a long time ▪ I was on holiday last summer ▪ we moved here ▪ weeks ▪
> 2001 ▪ someone gave me two free tickets ▪ a year or so

b What have the young people been doing since they left school? Use the present perfect progressive with *for* or *since*.

I left school two years ago. After school I started studying medicine.

I left school last summer. I work in my uncle's firm as a management trainee.

Examples: *Kim **has been studying** medicine **for two years**.*

*Rob **has been working** in his uncle's firm as a management trainee **since last summer**.*

1 I started university in October last year. I'm studying economics.

Polly

2 I left school a year ago. I work for a firm of architects in the accounts department.

Doug

3 Chris and I left school eighteen months ago. We're both doing a training course with British Airways.

Scott and Chris

4 I left school last summer. I'm taking a gap year[1].

Val

5 Emma and I are learning fashion design. We started in September last year.

Emma and Lucy

6 After A-levels I joined the RAF[2]. That was two years ago. I'm training as a helicopter pilot.

Owen

c Write a short paragraph to an English-speaking penfriend telling him/her about your favourite hobby, activity, sport, etc. Say when you started it, how you first became interested in it, how long you have been doing it, etc. Use mainly the present perfect progressive and simple past with suitable time phrases.

---

1 gap year: a free year between school and university, to travel or earn money   2 RAF: Royal Air Force

A trip down under   simple past, past progressive   ▶ 86, 89, 90

a   Complete the conversation with the simple past or past progressive. Look out for 'signal words'.

Liz: Hi, Ed. You're back. How was Australia? (1 you – have) … a good trip?

Ed: Yes, great, thanks. I (2 phone) … you last night, but nobody (3 answer) …

Liz: That's strange. We (4 not – go) … out.

Ed: What (5 you – do) … at about 7.30?

Rob: We (6 not – do) … anything special. Oh, now I remember. I (7 hear) … my mobile, but I (8 clean) … my bike when it (9 ring) … I had oil on my hands, so I (10 not – answer) … it. I called Liz, but she (11 listen) … to her walkman. Later I (12 forget) … to look who had called.

Liz: Well, tell us about the trip.

Ed: There's so much to tell. Australia's a great country, and the wildlife's fascinating – if you take care. We (13 drive) … into the outback for a couple of days. I suppose we (14 all – look) … for adventure. Well, Tom (15 just – take) … a few photos when he suddenly (16 look) … down and (17 see) … a snake – not just any snake but an inland taipan, one of the deadliest snakes in Central Australia. It (18 move) … towards him from under a stone, and all the time my heart (19 beat) … so loudly. We were terrified.

Liz: How terrible! So what (20 you – do) …?

Ed: Nothing. We (21 all – wear) … strong shoes and long trousers, but that's not enough if a taipan decides to strike. But I guess it was Tom's lucky day, because then the snake (22 slide) … past him about a foot away and (23 go) … off into some bushes.

Rob: What a lucky escape! So what (24 happen) … after that?

Ed: Well, we all (25 think) … that we had had quite enough 'adventure', so we (26 get) … in our jeep and (27 drive) … non-stop back to civilization and a cool beer.

b   Think of a time when you, your friends or anyone in your family felt really afraid. Where were you? What were you doing? What happened? When did it happen? Tell your story in the simple past with the past progressive when necessary. If you can't remember any real incident, use your imagination. If you wish, you can write your story together with a partner.

Example: *One Sunday night I **was going** for a walk in the park with my girlfriend. It **was getting** dark, so we **decided** to go home. We **were** just **leaving** the park when we **saw** that the main gates were locked. Suddenly someone **grabbed** me by the shoulder from behind.*

a   Read the text about Lincoln's life, then choose the correct verb forms from the brackets, simple past or past progressive. Look out for 'signal words' and state verbs.

Abraham Lincoln was born in Kentucky in 1809, the son of a farmer. He (1 spent/was spending) his childhood doing hard work on the farm and hardly (2 was going/went) to school. He (3 was liking/liked) reading more than farm work, but books were scarce[1] and expensive, so he (4 was always borrowing/always borrowed) books from neighbours.

Being poor, the family often (5 moved/was moving) around. While they (6 looked/were looking) for work in New Orleans, an incident[2] (7 was determining/determined) the future course of Lincoln's life. As he (8 walked/was walking) through the marketplace, he (9 saw/was seeing) slaves for the first time. They (10 were sold/were being sold) to rich, white slave owners who (11 treated/were treating) them like animals on show. From this time on, Lincoln (12 was swearing/swore) that he would work to end slavery.

As a young man Lincoln (13 was trying/tried) various jobs. While he (14 worked/was working) as a postmaster in Springfield, Illinois, he (15 was impressing/impressed) the townspeople with his honest character. Lincoln (16 was working/worked) very hard as an adult. When he (17 was not earning/didn't earn) money, he (18 studied/was studying) law books. He (19 was qualifying/qualified) as a lawyer in 1836.

Lincoln (20 believed/was believing) that the United States (21 was standing/stood) for freedom for all, including slaves. He saw that the issue of slavery (22 divided/was dividing) the country. As a senator he (23 was making/made) many powerful speeches to spread his ideas. Already his name (24 became/was becoming) known across the States.

Lincoln (25 became/was becoming) president in March 1861, at a difficult time. Eleven Southern States who (26 were not agreeing/did not agree) with Lincoln about slavery (27 were leaving/left) the Union and the Civil War (28 began/was beginning) in April 1861. Lincoln (29 wrote/was writing) the Emancipation Proclamation freeing all slaves on 1st January 1863, but the South (30 did not free/were not freeing) their slaves until they had lost the war.

Lincoln had flexible and generous plans for peace, but he (31 was being assassinated/was assassinated) before he could carry them out. While the Lincolns (32 attended/were attending) a play at Ford's theatre in Washington, a fanatic supporter of slavery, John Wilkes Booth, (33 shot/was shooting) Lincoln in the back of the head. The President died the next morning, on 15th April 1865, just 56 years of age.

All Americans and Lincoln's friends and enemies alike (34 were grieving/grieved[3]) at the loss of their president, praising his selflessness, humanity and kind spirit. A statue of Lincoln, 5.8 metres tall, (35 was erected/was being erected) at the Lincoln Memorial in Washington, as a reminder to the American people of one of their greatest leaders.

Based on 'Abraham Lincoln', *Berwick Academy*; 'The life of Abraham Lincoln' by Roger Norton

b   Search the Internet for information on the life of another interesting historical figure. Summarize his/her life using mainly the simple past and the past progressive. Use the Lincoln text as a model.

---

1 scarce: only in small numbers, not many   2 incident: event, happening
3 grieve: show great sadness when someone dies

13 ▶ *Bad luck* past perfect (simple), past perfect progressive   ▶ **92, 94**

Complete the conversation with the correct verb form, past perfect (simple) or past perfect progressive.

Layla: Hi, Pete. How was the rock concert last night?

Pete: Well, when I was getting on the bus to go there,
        I realized that I (1 forget) … my money. So I had
        to get off again. I didn't want to miss the
        concert because I (2 look forward) … to it for a
        few weeks. So I ran, but when I got home, I
        realized that I (3 not – take) … my keys with me
        either, so I couldn't get in. I rang the doorbell
        for ages, but everybody (4 go) … out.
        So there I was – no money, no ticket, no keys. I
        thought about asking Will, but it's a long way
        to his house, and when I got there, I was really
        out of breath.

Layla: Let me guess, Will (5 just – spend) … all his
        money. No, I know. He (6 lend) … it all to
        someone else.

Pete: Wrong. He wasn't even there. He (7 not – come)
        … home yet. His mother could see that I (8 run)
        …, so she asked me in and gave me a drink. She
        put the TV on for me while I was waiting. I (9 watch) … stupid cartoons for twenty
        minutes when I heard somebody come in. But it wasn't Will. When he finally
        arrived, I (10 wait) … for over half an hour. He said he (11 take) … bottles to the
        bottle bank for the neighbour for some extra cash.
        Well, after I (12 explain) … the situation he gave me some money and I rushed for
        the next bus. I (13 waste) … so much time, and when I finally got there, my favourite
        band (14 already – play) …

14 ▶ *Join the sentences* simple past, past perfect (simple)   ▶ **86, 92**

Combine the two sentences in a logical order to make one. Use the word(s) in brackets and make sure that
the time sequence is correct by using the past perfect (simple) for one of the verbs.

Example: I wrote the letter. I went out to post it. (as soon as)
          *As soon as I **had written** the letter, I **went** out to post it.*

1 Ben ate too much at the buffet. He was sick after the party. (because)
2 My pen pal moved to another town. I didn't know. (that)
3 My brother finally passed his exams. He studied for seven years. (after)
4 I started to write the answers. I read the questions through. (as soon as)
5 I didn't eat any breakfast. I felt really hungry in the fourth lesson. (because)
6 I went to the bank. I paid John the money I owed him. (as soon as)
7 I read the novel. I passed it on to a friend. (when)
8 Our maths teacher marked our tests. He gave them back to us straightaway. (after)

The greatest mind ever   simple past, past perfect (simple)   ▶ 86, 92

a   William James Sidis may have been the most intelligent person who ever lived, yet history hardly remembers him. The facts are true. His IQ was assessed at between 250 and 300. Complete the text with the simple past or past perfect (simple). Two verbs require the passive.

William James Sidis **was** born in 1898 to Russian immigrants, Jewish intellectual refugees with brilliant minds. His mother **gave up** her own ambitions to promote the intellectual abilities of their young son. By the time young Sidis **was** 18 months old, he **had learnt** to read – even the *New York Times*. By this time he (1 also – learn) … to count. He (2 teach oneself) … Latin when he was two. As soon as he (3 learn) … Latin, he (4 teach oneself) … Greek. He was now three – and was already typing letters in English and French. After only seven months in grade school he (5 complete) … all seven grades. At the age of seven he (6 take) … an interest in maths. By the time he was eight, he (7 already – write) … four books. At eight he (8 pass) … the Harvard Medical School anatomy examination and the entrance exam for the Massachusetts Institute of Technology. By this time he (9 also – learn) … eight languages.

In high school he (10 take) … six weeks to complete the four year curriculum[1]. From then on, William (11 stay) … at home, because he (12 learn) … everything there was to learn in school. He (13 read) … Einstein and may have corresponded with the great man. By the time he was eleven, he (14 master[2]) … advanced mathematics, so he (15 enrol[3]) … as a 'special student' at Harvard. After he (16 study) … at Harvard for a year, he (17 give) … a lecture[4] on 'four-dimensional bodies' to the Harvard Mathematical Club.
After that, the press (18 follow) … his every move – and his classmates (19 avoid) … him. By the time he was sixteen, he (20 already – graduate) … from Harvard. He then (21 go) … to the Rice Institute, Houston, Texas, as a maths professor, where he increasingly (22 become) … a social misfit[5]. After his students (23 ridicule[6]) … their child professor for eight months, Sidis finally (24 give up) … He (25 go) … back to Harvard to study law. By the time he was eighteen, he (26 already – study) … more than forty languages.

Up to now Sidis (27 drive) … by his parents to become a mental giant, but he now (28 lead) … a totally isolated life. A few years later he (29 disappear) … from society.

In 1983 the physicist Chandra (30 win) … the Nobel Prize for his work on the existence of black holes. Sidis (31 already – predict) … their existence in 1925, in his remarkable book *The Animate and the Inanimate*. But his work (32 ignore) … Sidis (33 die) … of a stroke[7] at age 46. He (34 spend) .. all his adult life running away from the media – and from his parents.

Adapted from 'William James Sidis' by John H. Lienhard; 'William James Sidis' by Jim Morton;
'The greatest mind ever – a lesson from history' by Dave Slater

b   Answer the questions in a few sentences, using the simple past and past perfect.

1   Why do you think Sidis became a social misfit?
2   What had Sidis probably never done in his childhood or as an adult?
3   Why had he probably tried to 'escape' from his parents as an adult?

---

1 curriculum *Lehrplan*   2 master *beherrschen*   3 enrol *sich einschreiben*   4 lecture *Vortrag*   5 misfit: person who does not fit in with society   6 ridicule: make somebody look stupid in public   7 stroke *Schlaganfall*

16   *A plane crash*   **present and past tenses: mixed exercise**   ▶ **75, 80, 86, 87, 89, 90, 92**

Read the report of the plane crash and choose the correct tense forms from the brackets.

Plane crashes in fog

A plane (1 crashed/has crashed) in thick fog near Luxembourg's airport, with 18 dead.
The twin-engine Fokker (2 was carrying/carried) 19 passengers, mostly German businessmen,
and three crew when it (3 came/was coming) down three miles from the airport.
The plane, on a scheduled flight from Berlin-Tempelhof (4 made/was making) its final approach[1]
at around 0915 GMT when it (5 crashed/has crashed). One report said the plane (6 was
circling/circled) the airport after an emergency landing in a field (7 has failed/had failed/failed).
16 people (8 have died/died) at the scene, two critically injured survivors (9 died/have died) later
in hospital. The pilot and one other known survivor (10 remain/are remaining) in critical
condition. Two others (11 have not yet been accounted for[2]/were not yet accounted for).
So far Belgium's defence ministry (12 sent/has sent/has been sending) three helicopters to the
scene. The airport (13 has been closed/was closed) to incoming planes.
A Luxair spokesman (14 has said/said) the plane (15 has been/was/had been) in service since
1991. The crash (16 is believed/has been believed) to be the airline's first fatal accident. The fog
(17 had been said/was said) to be extremely thick and several motorway crashes (18 have also
been reported/are also reported) this morning.

Adapted from 'Plane crashes in fog', *Gaming Magazine Online* 06/11/2002

---

17   *Extract from 'A Pair of Jeans'*   **past tenses: mixed ex.**   ▶ **80, 86, 87, 89, 90, 92**

Miriam lives with her Pakistani family in England. She has just returned from a hill-walking trip with her
college friends – wearing a pair of jeans. She hopes that her future parents-in-law have not arrived yet.

Suddenly she felt odd in her clothing. Yet they were just the type of clothes she needed to
wear today. […] Somehow here, however, in the vicinity[3] of her home she felt different. As
she was crossing the road near her own street, she suddenly became very conscious of her
appearance.

Unfortunately, her future parents-in-law see her arrive home. They are greatly shocked but say nothing.

5   Once in her room, she closed the door behind her and breathed out deeply. That was
another world, one that she had left behind when she waved goodbye to her two friends in
the bus. […] Damn it! Her mind shouted. 'They are only clothes. I am still the same person,
the girl they chose as a bride for their son.' Deny it as much as you like, Miriam, her heart
whispered. It's no use. They have seen another aspect of you. […] When they first saw her at
10 a party, she was dressed in a sari and later on each occasion she had always discreetly
dressed in a shalwar kameze suit. Never at any time had they glimpsed[4] a jean-clad[5] Miriam.
It must have been quite a revelation[6] to them. For now they were seeing her as a young
college woman who was very much under the western influence. One who was dressed like
English girls. […]
15 From her wardrobe she drew out a blue crepe shalwar kameze suit. Only articles of clothing,
but having them on her back she had embraced[7] a new set of values, a new personality in
fact. […] As she went down the stairs she felt a new person. […]

---

1 approach *Anflug*   2 account for sb.: know what happened to sb.   3 vicinity: neighbourhood
4 glimpse: have a short look   5 jean-clad: dressed in jeans   6 revelation *Offenbarung*   7 embrace (here): accept

Once downstairs in the hallway, she hesitated. She felt sick at her hypocrisy[1]. She was now acting out a role, the role that her future in-laws preferred. A role of a demure[2] and elegant
20 bride and daughter-in-law. Yet she was the same person who had earlier traipsed[3] the Pennine countryside in a pair of jeans and wellingtons[4] and who was now dressed in the height of Indian fashion. Or was she the same person? She didn't know. Perhaps there were two sides to her character. […] Now dressed as she was, she was part and parcel of another world; part of the muslim Asian environment. She was now on home ground, and her
25 thoughts, actions and feelings had altered accordingly. Once inside the living room, Miriam felt four pairs of eyes turn in her direction. She stared ahead knowing instinctively that apart from her father they were all comparing her present demure appearance with her earlier one.

From 'A Pair of Jeans' by Qaisra Shahraz, in: Liz Rutherford (Ed.), *Holding Out* (slightly adapted)

a   Understanding the story. Answer the questions in one or two sentences each.

1 Where had Miriam been and who had she been with?
2 How did she feel when she was getting close to her home? Why?
3 What was the 'other world' that she had left behind?
4 Why had her future in-laws never seen her in western clothes?
5 Explain: 'As she went down the stairs she felt a new person.' (l. 17)
6 Why did she feel that she was playing a role? (l. 19)

b   Use the correct past form (past, present perfect, past perfect), in the simple or progressive aspect.

1 When Miriam (come) … home, she (wear) … jeans and wellingtons.
2 Unfortunately, her in-laws (already – arrive) …
3 She (go) … to her room and (change) … into traditional dress immediately.
4 She thought to herself: 'Now they (see) … another aspect of me.'
5 After she (change) … her clothing, she (feel) … like a different person.
6 She (feel) … that she (act) … a role for her in-laws.

c   Look at the language.

1 In which tense are the facts of the story mainly told?
2 Identify and explain the two uses of 'see' in: 'When they first saw her at a party …' (ll. 9-10) and 'For now they were seeing her as a young college woman … ' (ll. 12-13)
3 Explain the use of the present perfect in: 'They have seen another aspect of you.' (l. 9)
4 Explain the use of the past perfect in the sentence: 'Yet she was the same person who had earlier traipsed the Pennine countryside … and who was now dressed … ' (ll. 20-22)

d   Find one example each of the following rules.

1 The past progressive often refers to actions which were in progress when a second action began. The second action is in the simple past.
2 When two or more short actions in the past come directly one after the other, we use the simple past for all the actions.

e   Why did Miriam think that there were perhaps two sides to her character?

Ideas: split identity, two cultures, woman's role in society, freedom, emancipation, education, independence, beliefs, religion, values, tradition, appearance

---

1 hypocrisy *Heuchelei*   2 demure *sittsam*   3 traipse *latschen*   4 wellingtons: high rubber boots

Ways of expressing future time

▶ 96, 98

18 *Make comments*   **will**-future, *going to*-future

a What's going to happen? What are they saying? Make suitable comments on the situations or make a
probable suggestion for the speech bubbles. Use the *will*-future or the *going to*-future.

Examples: *'Hold on! I'll help you.'*

*The books **are going to fall**.*

b Now choose the more suitable verb form from the brackets.

1 How much are these shoes? Seventy pounds? All right I (will take/am going to take) them.
2 How old (are you going to be/will you be) on your next birthday?
3 I (am not going to forget/won't forget) to send you a postcard from New York. I promise.
4 My elder sister (is going to have/will have) a baby.
5 Just imagine. Janet (is going to study/will study) art in Rome.
6 It's starting to rain. Jump on my moped. I (will drive/am going to drive) you home.
7 Ed and Tom (will start/are going to start) their own business. They have already got a few
customers.
8 Terry's a terrible driver. I wouldn't lend him your car – he (is going to crash/will crash) it.
9 I (will stay/am going to stay) with a cousin in Boston in July.
10 I'm sure you (will enjoy/are going to enjoy) the book. It's better than the film.

19 *Future plans* **will**-future, *going to*-future, present progr., simple present ▶ 96, 98-100

a The sixth form pupils at Ashington High School are leaving school in July. They were asked about their future plans. Complete what they said with the correct future form: *will*, *going to*, present progressive or simple present. Sometimes two verb forms are equally suitable.

Examples:

> *I **am doing** a course in fashion design in London. It **starts** in September. If I do well, I **will** probably **get** the chance to work in Paris or Rome. The school has branches all over Europe and they **are going to open/are opening** a branch in New York next year. London's a long way from home. I'**m going to miss** my family*

Ann

1
> I expect I (1 go) … to university if my A-levels are good enough. I'd like to study business administration. I know that it (2 not – be) … easy, but it interests me. I (3 leave) … home. I suppose it (4 be) … strange having to decide things all by myself.

Ali

2
> I (1 do) … a volunteer year in a developing country. I (2 probably – go) … to Africa. The school year (3 finish) … in July, so I (4 sign up) … to start in September. I suppose I (5 miss) … home and family. Africa is a different world. It (6 help) … me to grow up.

Kim

3
> I (1 do) … a gap year straight after school. I think I (2 travel) … around and see a few countries. I (3 definitely – go) … to the States and to Australia. But I (4 do) … a few jobs first to earn some money.

Don

4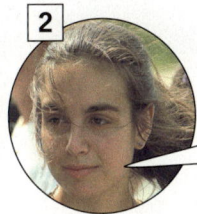
> I hope I (1 be able to) … get a job in a bank or an insurance company. I'm good at maths but I don't want to go to university. I (2 be) … 18 next month, so it's time I earned some money. I've sent off a few applications. I think they (3 send) … me on a training course first. At least I (4 be able to) … live at home.

Owen

5
> I (1 go) … to art school next year in London. I've already got a place. My best friend (2 take) … the same course, so she (3 start) … in October as well. I think it (4 be) … easier having a friend with me. We (5 probably – share) … a bedsit for a start.

Kate

6
> I (1 not – get) … a job straightaway, that's for sure. I need some time to think. I'm very interested in computers, so eventually I suppose I (2 study) … IT. But not just yet. Perhaps I (3 go) … to the States for a year as an au pair, just to gain experience of the country, and to see what kind of IT courses they have to offer. But for a couple of months after A-levels, I (4 relax) … and do nothing.

Mel

b Write a paragraph about your possible plans after school. Are you going to university? What are you going to study? When does the university year start in your country? Will you perhaps take a gap year first? Are you planning to travel?

Read the text about an unusual holiday, then complete the tasks.

Pat and Rob Wilson are about to start out on the holiday of a lifetime. They are going to travel almost 26 thousand kilometres – on their motorbikes. Where are they going? From Alaska to Tierra del Fuego[1].

Pat said, 'We have got the media interested in our trip – a magazine and our local press, of
5 course. We are going to send in a full written report every two weeks. And we'll send lots of photos. They are going to report on our progress to their readers.'

Rob added, 'We're appearing on breakfast TV early tomorrow and when we get back, we are to give a TV special on a local channel and an exclusive interview to the magazine. We hope this will help to cover our costs because I have taken six months' unpaid holiday from
10 work.'

'We know it is not going to be easy,' said Pat, 'but we are about to fulfil a lifelong dream. Our plane leaves from Heathrow at eleven tomorrow morning for Anchorage. If all goes well, next week at this time we will be driving down the west coast of Canada. We will be travelling along the coastal routes as much as possible and sleeping in our tent. We expect
15 to travel up to 250 kilometres a day on average, not more. We need time for sightseeing, meeting people, washing clothes and buying food. The whole trip will probably take us at least five months.'

'I expect we will have some setbacks, probably bad weather in Alaska and extreme heat in South America. We are certain to have a few breakdowns, and the roads are likely to be bad
20 in many parts of Central America. We're taking plenty of spare parts for the bikes,' added Rob. 'I hope we won't have problems at the borders.'

'We will be writing home regularly, and we will be sending our reports from Internet cafés – if we can find them. By the time we get back, we will have seen a lot of fantastic scenery and we will have experienced so many new things,' said Pat. 'I'm going to write a diary.'

25 'We will have driven through quite a few countries too,' continued Rob. 'And in six months from now, I will be sitting at my office desk again …' 'And I will be planning our next unusual holiday,' said Pat, 'but probably not on motorbikes …'

---

1 Tierra del Fuego *Feuerland*

a   Name all the different future forms or tenses used in the text and write down one example of each.

b   Answer the questions in one or two sentences each.

1   What are the Wilsons about to do?
2   The media have shown interest in the trip. What are the Wilsons going to do during and after their trip?
3   Which route will they be taking?
4   What kind of problems will they most likely encounter?
5   What are they probably taking with them? Remember that you can't take much luggage on two motorbikes.
6   What kind of things will they be doing when they are not on the road?
7   When they return to England, how long will they probably have been away?
8   Which countries will they have driven through? Name at least six.
9   About how far will they have driven?
10 What does Pat think she is likely to be doing after they return?

c   With a partner and an atlas, plan an unusual journey to some interesting part of the world, for example, a walking trip through Mexico, a cycle trip around the British coast, New Zealand on horseback. Use as many future forms as possible. Include the following points in your journey description: where and when you are going, what you will probably see, problems you are likely to encounter, what you are going to take with you, what you will probably be doing at which times, what you will have done when you get back.

A question of identity

present, past, future time: mixed ex. ▶ **75, 77, 80, 82, 86, 92, 96, 98, 102**

What makes you British? Read the report on the question of Mary Miller's identity, then complete it with the correct tenses and verb forms, simple or progressive. Sometimes more than one form or tense is suitable. Study the examples first and look out for 'signal words' and passive forms.

Mary Miller **has brought up** four children in the UK and is a grandmother. She **has been living** in the UK for 53 years, yet she **has been told** that she **will be deported** because she **is considered** an American citizen by the British authorities.

Mary Miller, 55, from Trimley St Mary in Suffolk, was born in the United States and (1 move) … to England with her British-born mother in 1949. She (2 live) … in Britain since she was two.

The Home Office (3 order) … her to leave the country by Thursday because she cannot prove that she (4 live) … in the UK for at least 14 years. She (5 be) … not a British citizen.

Mrs Miller (6 say) …: 'I am frightened to open my door. What are the authorities (7 do) …? (8 they – arrest) … me and send me off to the States? (9 I – deport) …? It's all like a bad dream. The last few days (10 be) … a nightmare – I (11 not – sleep) … and I (12 not – eat) …'

Mrs Miller, who was born in Baltimore, Maryland, has ten grandchildren and (13 live) … with her partner Ted Hartley, 61, a builder. She (14 discover) … that there was a problem with her citizenship status when her mother (15 die) … two years ago. Checking through her mother's belongings, she (16 find out) … that she (17 never – register) … as a UK citizen. So she immediately (18 apply) … for UK citizenship, but her application (19 reject) … by the Home Office[1] because officials would not believe that she (20 live) … in the UK uninterrupted for 14 years – although she (21 send) … the Home Office details of National Insurance, income tax and wage slips[2] dating back several years.

Mrs Miller said the only way she could reverse the Home Office decision was to provide a 'right to remain form', which she (22 not – possess) … The authorities should have given her this form when she (23 arrive) … in the UK as a two-year-old.

Her local MP and her neighbours (24 support) … her campaign to stay in the UK by lobbying[3] officials in her favour. 'Everyone (25 try) … to help, but perhaps I (26 sit) … in a plane to the States in a few days' time. I am a Suffolk person, nothing else. My mother (27 be) … British. I (28 live) … in this country with my family for 54 years, and I hope I (29 die) … here. (30 that – not – make) … me British?'

Adapted from 'Grandmother faces deportation', *BBC News World Service, 12/02/2003*

---

1 the Home Office *Innenministerium*   2 wage slip *Lohn-/Gehaltsabrechnung*   3 lobby *beeinflussen*

The passive

A ▶ **Complete the sentences using the correct tense or structure in the passive.**

1 Hatford Hall (build) … in the 18th century, I think.
2 Don't go in there. Applicants (interview) … at the moment.
3 Reference books and magazines (must not – remove) … from the library.
4 It took many years before the warnings of environmentalists (take notice of) …
5 A cure for AIDS (might – find) … within the next few years.
6 Up to the age of 17, John Lennon (bring up) … by his Aunt Mimi and Uncle George.

B ▶ **Put the sentences into the passive using *by* only where necessary.**

7 Somebody must have disturbed the thief.
8 Rowland Hill introduced the first postage stamps in 1840.
9 They have awarded Tony the first prize in the essay competition.
10 A hundred years ago, they had never heard of air pollution.
11 A company in Canada has offered Gina a two-year contract.
12 The police have arrested three teenagers on suspicion of car theft.
13 I think Elton John wrote this song.
14 If Mike fails his driving test the third time, people will laugh at him.
15 When I got to the buffet, people had already eaten most of the food.

C ▶ **Translate the German parts into English.**

16 *(Man erwartet)* … that unemployment figures will rise sharply in winter.
17 *(Man hat meinem Bruder eine Stelle in Berlin angeboten.)* …
18 *(Das neue Hotel wird im Mai eröffnet werden.)* …
19 *(Uns wurde gesagt)* … that the exam date is going to be put forward.
20 *(Man erwartet von Polizisten, dass sie ehrlich und hilfsbereit sind.)*
21 *(Meiner Schwester ist geraten worden)* … not to study medicine.
22 *(Handys sollten nicht in den Prüfungsraum mitgenommen werden.)* …
23 *(Man hat uns gezeigt)* … how to write a correct job application.

D ▶ **Rewrite the sentences using an alternative passive structure, beginning with the words in brackets.**

24 Two thirds of the world's Grey seals are thought to live in British waters. (It …)
25 It was said that the minister of transport had resigned. (The minister …)
26 The new computers have been shown to the class. (The class …)
27 The injured man is reported to be in a critical condition. (It …)

E ▶ **Spot the mistakes. There is one mistake in each sentence or sentence pair.**

28 330 million tonnes of toxic waste are produced from industry every year.
29 At Heathrow Airport, at least 20 mobile phones are lost every day by people.
30 To Jason was promised a better salary and a company car, so he took the offer.
31 Her was thanked for her hard work and support during the whole of the project.
32 My car was damaged through hailstones. They were as big as ping-pong balls.

The passive

A ▷ 1: *was built*   2: *are being interviewed*   3: *must not be removed*   4: *were taken notice of*
5: *might be found*   6: *was brought up*

B ▷ 7: *The thief must have been disturbed.*   8: *The first postage stamps were introduced by Rowland
Hill in 1840.*   9: *Tony has been awarded the first prize in the essay competition. / The first prize in
the essay competition has been awarded to Tony.*   10: *A hundred years ago, air pollution had never
been heard of.*   11: *Gina has been offered a two-year contract by a company in Canada. / A two-
year contract has been offered to Gina by a company in Canada.*   12: *Three teenagers have been
arrested on suspicion of car theft.*   13: *I think this song was written by Elton John.*   14: *If Mike
fails his driving test the third time, he will be laughed at.*   15: *When I got to the buffet, most of the
food had already been eaten.*

C ▷ 16: *It is expected …*   17: *My brother has been offered a job in Berlin.*   18: *The new hotel will be
opened/is going to be opened in May.*   19: *We were told/have been told …*   20: *Policemen are
expected to be honest and helpful.*   21: *My sister has been advised …*   22: *Mobile phones/Mobiles
should not be taken into the exam(ination) room.*   23: *We were shown/We have been shown …*

D ▷ 24: *It is thought that two thirds of the world's Grey seals live in British waters.*   25: *The minister
of transport was said to have resigned.*   26: *The class has/have been shown the new computers.*
27: *It is reported that the injured man is in a critical condition.*

E ▷ 28: *330 million tonnes of toxic waste are produced by industry every year.*   29: *At Heathrow
Airport, at least 20 mobile phones are lost every day.*   30: *Jason was promised a better salary and a
company car, so he took the offer.*   31: *She was thanked for her hard work and support during the
whole of the project.*   32: *My car was damaged by hailstones. They were as big as ping-pong balls.*

▶ **Exercise finder**

Sentences	CEG	Exercises
1, 2, 18	▶ 108	▶ 1, 3, 8, 9, 10
3, 5, 22	▶ 115	▶ 1, 3, 9, 10
4, 6, 10, 14	▶ 113	▶ 6
7, 12, 15, 29	▶ 109a	▶ 5, 7, 9, 10
8, 13, 28, 32	▶ 110	▶ 2, 7, 8, 10
9, 11, 17, 23, 26, 30	▶ 112	▶ 5
16, 20, 24, 25, 27	▶ 114	▶ 7, 8, 10
19, 21, 31	▶ 111	▶ 4, 5

1 Quiet, please! forms of the passive ▶ 108, 115

How many passive forms can you find in the text? Write a list, as in the examples.

We <u>are exposed</u> to all kinds of noise every day, to everything from car radios to aeroplanes. We have become so accustomed to noise that we sometimes do not notice it. But just how much noise <u>can be tolerated</u>?
The human ear is exposed to noise levels between 30 and 90 decibels daily. In discos young people 'enjoy' levels of up to 130 decibels, louder even than an aircraft at take-off.
A study carried out in Japan revealed[1] that housewives living in cities were exposed to just three decibels less than factory workers. The people exposed to the most noise were reported to be not only factory workers but, believe it or not, kindergarten teachers.
Unfortunately, the effects of noise cannot be measured as accurately as the levels of noise – until the damage has been done. In recent years young people especially have been found to be suffering from tinnitus. In most cases the damage had not been noticed. The condition had slowly worsened before the patients realized that their hearing had been irreversibly damaged.
Noise affects us in many areas of everyday life. Concentration at school or work can be disrupted[2], our sleep may be disturbed. Stress levels are increased. In some countries laws are being introduced to reduce noise levels, for example, in Holland. At Schiphol Airport in Amsterdam levies[3] have to be paid to provide insulation[4] for buildings affected by aircraft noise in the whole region.
In medical circles across Europe it is hoped that new EU laws on maximum noise tolerance will be enforced in discotheques within the next few years. Most doctors agree that laws against excessive noise in discos should have been introduced years ago.

The passive forms are:

simple present: ***are exposed***
present progressive:
simple past:
present perfect:

past perfect:
will-future:
modal aux. + present infinitive: ***can be tolerated***
modal aux. + perfect infinitive:

Based on 'Noise', in: Nick Middleton, *Atlas of environmental issues*

2 Famous 'firsts' simple past passive + *by* ▶ 110

a Test your knowledge of famous people and events. Answer the quiz questions with sentences in the simple past passive + *by*. Choose answers from the box.

~~Volta in 1800~~	Christiaan Barnard in 1967	the Montgolfier brothers in 1783
Louis Daguerre in 1837	Galvani in 1780	Emil Jannings in 1927
Plato in 387 BC	the Russians in 1961	Benz in 1885

Example: Who invented the first battery?
(I think) *The first battery **was invented by** Volta in 1800.*

1 Who made the first balloon flight?
2 Who took the first sharp photograph?
3 Who put the first man into space?
4 Who first produced an electric current?

5 Who set up the first school?
6 Who developed the first petrol-powered car?
7 Who performed the first heart transplants?
8 Who won the first Oscar for Best Actor?

b Write three more questions as in a), then ask a partner or the class to give the answers in the passive.

---

1 reveal: show   2 disrupt: interrupt, disturb   3 levies: taxes   4 insulation: the act of protecting sth. with a material

3 *School rules* **modal auxiliary + passive infinitive** ▶ 108c, 115

a   The passive is typically used in official notices and in rules. Write rules for the following dos and don'ts, using a modal auxiliary + passive infinitive.

Example: Pupils must park bicycles in the bicycle sheds only.
           *Bicycles **must be parked** in the bicycle sheds only.*

1 Pupils should not remove school property[1] from the premises[2].
2 You must lock the computer room after use.
3 Pupils may use electronic equipment during the breaks only.
4 You should not hang wet clothing on radiators[3].
5 Pupils must switch off mobile phones during lessons.
6 Pupils should not leave food and drinks in classrooms overnight.
7 You must return sports equipment to the gymnasium after use.
8 Pupils may not remove equipment from the music room without permission.

b   What rules do you have at your school? Are there any rules about smoking, absence, sick notes, clothes and jewellery, eating and drinking? Write down four, using a modal auxiliary + passive infinitive, as in a).

4 *A trip to Ireland* **verbs with one object, *'persönliches Passiv'*** ▶ 111

Translate the missing sentence parts using a passive form with the person as subject.

Example: *(Mir wurde mal geraten)* to spend a holiday in Ireland.
           ***I was once advised** …*

1 *(Den Schülern der Oberstufe* [sixth form] *wurde es erlaubt),* … to organize a class trip to Ireland.
2 *(Man hat uns empfohlen)* … to book the trip through a travel agency.
3 *(Uns wurde … geholfen.)* … a lot with the planning.
4 *(Man sagte uns)* … to visit the beautiful, old castles.
5 *(Es wurde allen Schülern geraten)* … to take warm clothing – even in summer.
6 The trip was great. *(Man wird sich … an sie erinnern.)* … for a long time.

---

1 property: possessions   2 premises (here): school building(s) and grounds   3 radiator *Heizkörper*

a Some teenagers are talking about their NT (National Traineeship) experiences. Rewrite the parts which are underlined without changing the meaning. Use the structure *'persönliches Passiv'*, i.e. beginning with the person as subject.

Example: Marion: On the first day <u>they gave me a long list of jobs to do</u>.
On the first day ***I was given a long list of jobs to do***.

1 Lauren: I'm working in Customer Service in a department store. On the first day <u>they taught me how to deal with complaints</u>.
2 Benny: I think my employer must be satisfied with me. <u>He has already given me a 20% discount card</u>. That's great because I work at the HMV mega-store.
3 Tom: My firm's OK too. I'm in a bakery. I had only been working for two weeks when I broke my leg. <u>They sent me a really nice get-well letter and a big cake</u>.
4 Karen: A friend of mine works for a chain of sports shops. She's almost finished her apprenticeship[1] and <u>they have promised her a job in one of their London branches</u>.
5 Mike: I haven't been quite as lucky. I'm doing my NT in engineering. <u>The people in the workshop haven't even shown me how to work the machines yet</u>. It's hopeless.
6 Lucy: I'm doing my NT with the City Council. There are two of us in the computer centre. <u>They have offered both of us the chance to stay on</u> after our training.
7 Sarah: I'm one of three trainees in a large computer store. <u>They pay us £50 a week</u>. Not much, but I can get computer parts cheap.
8 Simon: I'm with a firm of architects. I'd like to stay on, but there are two other applicants as well. <u>They'll tell me their decision</u> at the end of the month.

b Translate the sentences using the same passive structure as in a) above, i.e. begin with the person as the subject. Note that German *'man'* is usually translated with the passive.

1 Mir wurden von der Firma Bewerbungsformulare *(application forms)* zugeschickt.
2 Beim Interview gab man mir einen Fragebogen *(questionnaire)* zum Ausfüllen.
3 Ich musste auch einen Eignungstest *(aptitude test)* machen. Leider wurden uns diese Dinge in der Schule nicht beigebracht *(teach)*.
4 Man gab uns weitere Informationen über die Firma.
5 Eine Woche später schickte man mir einen Brief.
6 Mir wurde eine Stelle als Azubi *(trainee)* in der Personalabteilung *(personnel department)* angeboten.

---

1 apprenticeship *Lehre*

6   *Street chat*   **prepositional verbs and fixed phrases**   ▶ **113**

Complete the dialogues with the verbs given in the correct passive form. Pay attention to the position of the prepositions and look for 'signal words' which indicate tense (e.g. *last night*, *since*, *next week*).

Example: Kim: I heard the story of what happened to you at Jerry's party last night.
             Phil: You too? I expect it (talk about) … for weeks to come.
                                         … ***will be talked about*** …

1   Kim: I'm going to the Internet café later. Do you want to come with me?
     Ann: Haven't you heard? It's closed today. It (break into) … last night.
2   Ben: What will happen to your dog while you're on holiday? Who'll look after him?
     Kim: He (look after) … by some friends across the road.
3   Ann: I like your new moped. It must be great to ride. How much did it cost?
     Phil: More than enough. I would enjoy riding it more if it (pay for) …
4   Ben: Would you like to go with me to see *Matrix 3* tonight?
     Ann: Yes, sure. Thanks. I (not – ask out) … since my birthday.
5   Kim: There goes Sam on her new motorbike. What a noise it makes!
     Ann: Well, you know Sam. She likes to (take notice of) …
6   Kim: Why was your dad so angry with you yesterday?
     Ben: I took his car without asking and backed it into a sportscar. He went wild.
            I (not – shout at) … like that since I was a kid.
7   Ann: Why aren't you wearing your stars-and-stripes pants today?
     Phil: Well, I wore them yesterday, but I (laugh at) … by some kids in our street.
8   Kim: Did you complain to the store about your computer?
     Ann: Yes, I did. The manager said the problem (deal with) … next week.

7   *The threat to the environment*   **passive sent. with/without *by*;**   ▶ **109a, 110, 114**
                                                       verbs of speaking/thinking

a   Remember that *by* is not always used in passive sentences, e.g. when the 'doer' of the action is unknown, unimportant, or obvious. Write the following sentences in the passive, using *by* only where necessary.

Example: About ten years ago acid rain had already damaged 67% of trees in Britain.
          *About ten years ago 67% of trees in Britain **had** already **been damaged by** acid rain.*

1   In the past CFC's, for example in aerosols and fridges, destroyed ozone.
2   If people damage the ozone layer, the sun's ultra-violet rays can cause skin cancer.
3   New technologies have eliminated or reduced the use of CFC's.
4   Too much ozone caused by traffic smog attacks the lungs.
5   People still dump domestic and industrial waste in landfills[1].
6   Fertilizers[2] and pesticides still pollute the soil.
7   They still use rivers, lakes and seas as dumping grounds for toxic waste.
8   The greenhouse effect causes global warming.
9   Every year we destroy an area of rainforest as big as Denmark.
10   We destroy rainforest plants which might give us a cure for diseases.

---

1 landfill: area of land where waste is buried   2 fertilizer *Düngemittel*

b The passive is often used with verbs of thinking and speaking (in German 'man glaubt, man sagt, man vermutet', especially in newspaper reports. Rewrite the sentences in the passive beginning with It … + passive verb + that ('unpersönliches Passiv').

Example: People believe that the death of our forests is mainly due to acid rain.
It is believed that the death …

1 We know that some nations hunt whales and dolphins in spite of international agreements.
2 People have often claimed that the 'ozone hole' is the earth's greatest problem.
3 We think that half the world's species of birds, insects, flowers and trees live in tropical rainforests.
4 They believe that the Amazon rainforest alone produces 25% of the world's oxygen.
5 We expect that the world population will have doubled by 2050.
6 They estimate that an average American uses twice as much energy as an average European.
7 People have often said that unlimited population growth is the most important issue facing the world.

c Now change the structure of the sentences in b) beginning with subject + passive + to-infinitive. This structure is also common in reports and newspapers.

Example: People believe that the death of our forests is mainly due to acid rain.
The death of our forests is believed to be mainly due to acid rain.

Based on *Saving the Planet* by Geoff Sammon

8 *An accident report*   **passive: mixed exercise**   ▶ **108, 110, 114**

a A local reporter has to report on a motorway accident for his newspaper. Change the sentences into the passive to make them more suitable for written style. Be careful, one sentence cannot be changed into the passive. Remember to use passive structures ('persönliches Passiv', 'unpersönliches Passiv') with verbs of speaking and thinking.

Man dies in M4 crash

A man has died and two people are in critical condition after a crash on the M4 in Wiltshire. The accident happened on Tuesday at 2100 on the westbound carriageway between Swindon and Chippenham.

Continue:

An air ambulance took one crash victim, a 25-year-old man, to hospital. They say he is in critical condition. Passing motorists pulled an injured woman from a burning car.

Unfortunately, they could not rescue the driver. People think that the car was a silver Toyota.
They airlifted the woman to hospital. The passenger in the Ford was unhurt but in shock. They also took him to hospital in Swindon, where they are keeping him under observation.
They believe that the driver of the Ford had lost control on the wet road before he crashed into the Toyota. The police are interviewing motorists who witnessed the accident.

---

b Look for an accident report in your local paper. It need not be a traffic accident. Summarize it in English using the passive and read it to the class.

USA

Green Card Lottery 2003 (DV-2005)

50,000 Immigrant Visas available to work and live in the USA. **Free Info**. Send your Name, Postal Address and Country of Birth to:

Green Card Service Inc, 4001 Santa Barbara Blvd. PMB 333, Naples, Florida 34104, USA

Fax: +1-239-352-4293
E-mail: greencardservice@msn.com
www.GreenCardService.com

Every year there are millions of qualified applicants for US 'Green Cards', or permanent work and residence visas. Alan is telling Brian about it. Complete the dialogue using the correct passive forms of the verbs given. Sometimes, more than one tense is possible.

Alan: The Green Card Lottery, which is actually a controlled immigration scheme[1], ***is carried out*** annually by the US Department of State. Only citizens of certain 'low-rate US immigration countries' (1 invite) … to apply and the countries (2 change) … every year. Applications (3 must – send) … to a specified US National Visa Center, and the forms (4 have to – fill in) … correctly. If only a slight mistake (5 make) …, it will cause an applicant (6 disqualify) … Last year hundreds of thousands of applications (7 reject) … before the envelopes (8 even – open) … The application mail-in period[2] is just four weeks. Some applications had arrived at the wrong time because they (9 post) … too early or too late. Others (10 fill in) … wrongly. If more than one application (11 receive) … from an applicant within one year, he or she (12 automatically – disqualify)… But usually ten to eleven million qualified applicants remain. After (13 select) … at random by computer, the 90,000 'winners' (14 notify) … by post, so if you have not heard anything by a certain date, then you (15 not – select) …

Brian: That's all very interesting. I have a couple of questions.
(16 I – inform) … if I (17 reject) …?

Alan: No, you won't. There's no correspondence, only to the 'winners'. They don't automatically get a Green Card, but selection gives them the right to apply for one. Winners (18 inform) … that they (19 soon – invite) … for interview.

Brian: And where (20 applicants – interview)…?

Alan: At their nearest US consular department, where they must give proof of their eligibility[3], high school education or qualified work experience. From the 90,000 applicants 50,000 (21 usually – issue[4]) … with a Green Card. So if you are interested in living and working in the States, look up the website to find out when the registration period for next year (22 announce) … If you're lucky enough (23 select) … , you must be prepared to act quickly. In September, it's all over and the next year's lottery begins.

---

1 scheme: plan, system   2 application mail-in period: period in which applications must arrive
3 eligibility: suitability, right qualifications, age, etc.   4 issue: give officially

When Adrian was on holiday in California, he visited Death Valley National Park. A park ranger told him some interesting facts. Read the conversation, then carry out the tasks.

R.: Death Valley is even bigger than Yellowstone, 3.3 million acres of desert, mountains, sand dunes and salt flats[1]. Much of the valley is below sea level. In fact, Badwater is recognized as the lowest point in the Western Hemisphere, 280 feet or 85 meters below sea level.

5 A.: Can you tell me something about the history of Death Valley?

R.: Well, it dates back to the end of the last ice age. When the glaciers retreated[2] from the Sierra Nevada Mountains, the valley became an area of fresh water lakes. But the lakes

10 dried up. Climatic changes, wind and water have shaped the landscape over millions of years. Below the valley floor there are at least a thousand feet of different layers of salt and sediments deposited from dried up lakes. The hottest temperature measured here was in July 1913, 134°F – that's

15 57°C. On average it rains only 1.9 inches a year.

A.: Has anyone ever lived here?

R.: Sure. 10,000 years ago the ancestors of the Shoshone people made their homes here. You can find evidence of the presence of man through hundreds of years in almost

20 every part of the valley, for example, in rock drawings. The extreme conditions here have attracted tough, adaptable, and sometimes eccentric people. The first white settlers came in the 1870's. They started to mine borax[3]. Prospectors[4] followed, looking for silver and precious metals. Then in the 1930's they discovered a new industry – tourism. President Hoover proclaimed Death Valley a

25 national monument in 1933, but it wasn't established as a national park until 1994.

A.: I read that Death Valley got its name from gold-seekers in 1849. They were looking for a short cut to California. It's believed that they all died here. Is that right?

R.: That's a myth. People often forget that the Forty-Niners crossed other Nevada and California deserts, not only Death Valley. People wrongly believe that the pioneers died

30 here and that's why it's called 'Death Valley'. The truth is, only one of the pioneers died in the valley, an old man named Culverwell, who was half dead from the ordeals[5] of the Nevada desert before the pioneers even arrived in Death Valley. Secondly, people think that it was very hot when the pioneers crossed the valley. The truth is, they arrived here in December when it is extremely cold in the higher regions of the Nevada desert, and

35 some pioneers were saved from dying of thirst by a snow storm and by the ice on puddles of water. The best temperatures the pioneers encountered[6] on the whole journey were here. The third myth is, people say that there was no water in Death Valley. The truth is, the pioneers found the Travertine Springs near Furnace Creek, which have an output of 2,000 gallons of water a minute. They also found water at Salt Creek and snow on Pinto

40 Peak.

A.: So how did Death Valley get its name?

R.: Some of the pioneers had to slaughter their oxen for food in order to survive. Then they burned their wagons to cook the meat. You can visit 'Burned Wagons Camp' located near the sand dunes. They continued their journey on foot, seeking a trail westward out of the

45 valley. As they left the valley, one of the women looked back happily and cried

---

1 flats: area of low, flat land   2 retreat: move back   3 borax *Borax, Natriumsalz der Borsäure*   4 prospector: person searching land for gold, minerals, etc.   5 ordeal: very unpleasant experience   6 encounter: meet, confront

'Goodbye, Death Valley', and that's how it got its name. Eventually the pioneers were discovered and rescued by Spanish cowboys from a ranch in California.

A.: Well, they have certainly improved the roads through the valley since then. Do you close the valley in winter?

50 R.: Oh no. You can enjoy the scenery best in winter. We close many of the side roads in summer to stop people from getting lost. A German tourist died here in 2001. But his death could have been prevented. He took a three-mile hike in the midday sun in June, and had only one liter of water with him. He died of heatstroke[1] just five hours after he had set out. Death Valley gets over 1.2 million tourists a year. We are improving

55 campgrounds and facilities continually. Most visitors come from February through mid April. Not many visit in December and January, although that's the best time. We have some park rules, of course, that visitors must obey for their own safety at all times. For example, you must park vehicles on roads and parking lots only, not off-road. You must avoid contact with animals, even if they appear friendly. You may not pick flowers or

60 collect rocks. You must not enter mineshafts[2] or tunnels. Visitors should wear strong shoes and hats. And if you have a breakdown, don't leave your vehicle. Someone will come by, some time.

Based on information from 'The Lost 49ers' by Ranger Roger Brandt

a Write down the passive forms used in the text and identify the tense or structure.

b Write these sentences in the passive, as would be preferred in written style. Use *by* where necessary:

1 Climatic changes, wind and water have shaped the landscape … years. (ll. 10-11)
2 You can find evidence of the presence of man … (ll. 18-20)
3 Then in the 1930's they discovered a new industry – tourism. (ll. 23-24)
4 President Hoover proclaimed Death Valley … in 1933 … (ll. 24-25)
5 Well, they have certainly improved the roads through the valley since then. (l. 48)
6 Do you close the valley in winter? (ll. 48-49)
7 We close many of the side roads in summer … (ll. 50-51)
8 We are improving campgrounds and facilities continually. (ll. 54-55)

c Define the following using the passive: 1 a national park   2 a myth

d What does the ranger tell Adrian about the myths that surround the pioneers of 1849? Use your own words and the passive beginning with *It* … ('*unpersönliches Passiv*').

e Translate the following sentence, then rewrite it, beginning with the person as subject ('*persönliches Passiv*'):
It is believed that several pioneers died in Death Valley.

Now translate your new sentence. There is more than one possibility.

f Write out the park rules for visitors using the passive.

g Adrian is asked to write a short article about Death Valley for the school magazine. How would you write it? Use the information that Adrian got from the ranger, and write about the aspects you find most interesting e.g. the formation of Death Valley, its history and inhabitants, myths, visitor rules, best times to visit, tourist numbers, etc. using the passive wherever suitable.

---

1 heatstroke *Hitzschlag*   2 mineshaft: long, narrow, vertical passage

The infinitive and the gerund

A ▶ **Complete the sentences with *to* where necessary.**

1 The authorities will not allow you … enter the country without a valid visa.
2 I think I'd better … get some books from the library for my history essay.
3 My Dad used to let me … borrow his old car, but I'm not allowed to have his new one.
4 'Who was the last … leave the house this morning?' the detective asked.
5 I'd rather … spend my money on an interesting book than on a CD.
6 EU countries should work together … reduce the high level of unemployment.

B ▶ **Infinitive or gerund? Choose the correct form.**

7 How can the government justify (spend) … so much money on new weapon systems?
8 It's no use (try) … to persuade Leo to join the drama group. He won't.
9 When she was introduced, Jenna wasn't sure whether (stand up) … or remain seated.
10 Cutting down on staff costs will probably mean (make) … some workers redundant.
11 Patrick and Marie were the only ones (give in) … their essays on time.
12 There's no point (stay up) … half the night. I'm too tired to finish the project anyway.

C ▶ **Translate the German sentence parts using an infinitive or a gerund construction.**

13 The teacher warned the pupils (*während des Diktats nicht miteinander zu reden.*) …
14 Sarah was really angry about John's remarks. She left the room (*ohne zu sprechen.*) …
15 I don't like to be kept waiting, so I really hate (*wenn meine Freunde zu spät kommen.*) …
16 Environmentalists are opposed to the idea (*dass weitere Kernkraftwerke gebaut werden.*) …
17 I am totally against the plan, but I would like (*dass Sie meine Gründe verstehen.*) …
18 Diana doesn't seem to mind (*dass ihr Freund keinen Job hat.*) …
19 Gina's essay was so bad (*dass der Lehrer sie ihn noch einmal schreiben ließ.*) …
20 Conservationists work hard (*um die Umgebung und die Natur zu schützen.*) …
21 May I remind you (*das Geld für die Klassenfahrt morgen mitzubringen?*) …
22 (*Ich erinnere mich daran, wie ich die Garage zusperrte*) … after I had put my bike in.
23 What was the reason for (*dass Sally nach Glasgow umgezogen ist?*) …
24 Tim didn't know (*wo er die Informationen für sein Projekt finden konnte.*) …
25 Ann is always (*die Erste, die sich beschwert*) … if the maths homework is too difficult.
26 Adrian is not proud (*dass er beim Mogeln* [cheat] *erwischt* [caught] *wurde.*) …

D ▶ **Rewrite the sentences using the word(s) in brackets.**

27 Eventually, we managed to find enough people to support our scheme. (succeed in)
28 My penfriend in Chicago says I should visit her this summer. (want)
29 Most people don't follow complicated diet plans. They just eat less. (Instead of …)
30 Why did Max decide to leave school? (What made …)
31 I don't want to get a job. I'd prefer to go to university. (would rather … than)
32 Mike surprised his friends. He showed them his brand-new driver's licence. (… by…)

E ▶ **Spot the mistakes. There is one mistake in each sentence.**

33 It takes me an hour to get to school, so I am used to get up early on weekdays.
34 Mr Williams doesn't want that his daughter goes to a secretarial college.
35 Do you mind me to open the window?
36 The government is considering to introduce new immigration laws.
37 Try being here about an hour before the concert starts.
38 I'm sure we are all looking forward to finish our exams.

The infinitive and the gerund

? **Correct yourself**

A 1: *to*   2: –   3: –   4: *to*   5: –   6: *to*

B 7: *spending*   8: *trying*   9: *to stand up*   10: *making*   11: *to give in*   12: *staying up*

C 13: *… not to talk to each other during the dictation.*   14: *… without speaking.*   15: *… my friends coming late.*   16: *… of further nuclear power plants/stations being built.*   17: *… you to understand my reasons.*   18: *… her boyfriend not having a job.*   19: *… that the teacher made her write it again.*   20: *… to protect the environment and nature.*   21: *… to bring the money for the school trip tomorrow?*   22: *I remember locking the garage …*   23: *… Sally moving/to move to Glasgow?*   24: *… where to find the information for his project.*   25: *… the first to complain …*   26: *… of being caught cheating.*

D
27: *Eventually, we succeeded in finding enough people to support our scheme.*
28: *My penfriend in Chicago wants me to visit her this summer.*
29: *Instead of following complicated diet plans, most people just eat less.*
30: *What made Max leave school?*
31: *I would rather go to university than get a job.*
32: *Mike surprised his friends by showing them his brand-new driver's licence.*

E
33: *It takes me an hour to get to school, so I am used to getting up early on weekdays.*
34: *Mr Williams doesn't want his daughter to go to a secretarial college.*
35: *Do you mind me opening the window?*
36: *The government is considering introducing new immigration laws.*
37: *Try to be here about an hour before the concert starts.*
38: *I'm sure we are all looking forward to finishing our exams.*

Exercise finder

Sentences	CEG	Exercises
1, 13, 21	▶ 123a	▶ 1, 5, 16, 17
2, 5, 31	▶ 132	▶ 5, 14
3, 19, 30	▶ 133	▶ 5, 14, 16, 17
4, 11, 25	▶ 125	▶ 16
6, 20	▶ 129	▶ 2, 5, 16, 17
7, 36	▶ 139a	▶ 6, 13, 14, 15, 17
8, 12	▶ 147	▶ 14, 17
9, 24	▶ 128	▶ 4, 15, 17
10, 22, 37	▶ 139c	▶ 7, 13, 15, 16, 17
14, 29, 32	▶ 144	▶ 10, 12, 13, 16, 17
15, 18, 35	▶ 149	▶ 11, 12
16, 23	▶ 142	▶ 9, 13, 16
17, 28, 34	▶ 123b, 127a	▶ 1, 2, 16, 17
26, 33	▶ 141	▶ 8, 12, 13, 15
27, 38	▶ 143	▶ 13, 14, 15, 16, 17

1 *At an activity camp*   verb + object + *to*-infinitive   ▶ **123a/b**

A youth group is spending a week at an activity camp. The camp leader tells them about camp rules. What does he tell/ask/advise/warn/etc. them to do or not to do?

Examples: 'Take part in two or three activities every day.' (advise)
*He **advises them to take part in** two or three activities every day.*
'Don't go swimming in the lake after dark.' (warn)
*He **warns them not to go** swimming in the lake after dark.*

1 'Activities are tiring, so get enough sleep.' (advise)
2 'Non-swimmers, don't go canoeing alone.' (warn)
3 'Stay in your groups during outdoor activities.' (tell)
4 'Please do what your instructors say.' (ask)
5 'Don't forget to register for activities the evening before.' (remind)
6 'I hope everybody will keep the washrooms clean.' (expect)
7 'Please don't be late for meals.' (ask)
8 'Please look after camp equipment.' (would like)
9 'You shouldn't play loud music in your tents after ten p.m.' (tell)
10 'And campers under 18, don't leave the camp without permission.' (warn)
11 'And everybody should read the information on the noticeboard regularly.' (remind)
12 'Campers under 14, don't make camp fires without supervision. OK?' (advise)

2 *Jeff's future*   verb + obj. + *to*-inf.; subj. in inf. constr.; *to*-inf. of purpose   ▶ **123b, 127a, 129**

a Translate the text into English. Remember that German constructions such as *wollen/möchten, dass ...* are translated with a verb + object + *to*-infinitive construction.

Jeffs Vater ist Arzt und er möchte, dass Jeff auch Medizin studiert. Jeffs Mutter will auch, dass er auf die Universität geht, um etwas Nützliches zu studieren. Sie sagen ihm oft, er sollte in der Schule mehr tun, um bessere Noten zu bekommen, denn *(because)* sie erwarten von ihm, dass er sein Abitur ohne Schwierigkeiten *(difficulty)* besteht. Sie möchten natürlich, dass er einen guten Start ins Leben haben wird und erwarten, dass er sich bald um einen Studienplatz *(university place)* bewirbt.

Jeffs Freundin will, dass er zu Hause bleibt. Sie möchte nicht, dass er in einer anderen Stadt weit weg studiert. Aber Jeff erwartete, dass sie mehr Verständnis zeigen würde *(be more understanding)*.

Sie erwarten alle, dass er das tut, was sie wollen. Aber Jeff hat andere Vorstellungen *(ideas)*. Er will nicht, dass andere sein Leben für ihn planen. Er sagt ihnen, dass sie sich keine Sorgen um ihn machen sollen *(worry about)*, und er hat sich entschlossen, ein Jahr lang um die Welt zu reisen – allein. Nichts könnte ihn dazu veranlassen *(cause)*, seine Meinung zu ändern.

b What would your parents or friends like you to do after school? Write a short paragraph.

3 Get it right subject in infinitive constructions   ▶ 127b/c

a Rewrite the sentences using the construction noun/adjective/verb + *for* + object + *to*-infinitive.

1 We shouldn't have come here. It was a mistake …
2 Sheila isn't usually so careless. It's unusual …
3 John's going to take us to the station. I have arranged …
4 I can't finish this essay in such a short time. It's impossible …
5 We're going to the cinema, but my brother hasn't finished his homework yet.
I'm waiting …
6 Everyone should know the procedure in case of fire. It's important …

b Translate into English using the same construction as in a) above.

1 Es ist nicht nötig, dass du heute einkaufen gehst.
2 Ich musste warten, bis meine Schwester nach Hause kam.
3 Ich habe es so organisiert *(arrange for)*, dass ein Taxi uns um 8.30 abholt.
4 Es ist notwendig *(essential)*, dass junge Leute heutzutage gute Qualifikationen haben.
5 Ich habe ein paar Brote gemacht, die du auf der Fahrt essen kannst.

4 We don't know where to stay   question word + *to*-infinitive   ▶ 128

a When you visit a city for the first time, it's a good idea to go to the tourist information office. Make a list of things that you can find out there, using a question word + *to*-infinitive. Write eight things. You can use the following words:

question words: what ▪ where ▪ which + noun … ▪ how

nouns: places ▪ sights ▪ hotels ▪ restaurants ▪ tours ▪ transport

verbs: ask ▪ eat ▪ find ▪ go ▪ get to ▪ see ▪ shop ▪ stay ▪ take ▪ visit ▪ use

What can you find out at the tourist information office?

Examples: *You can find out **where to stay, which** tours **to take** …*

Continue:

b Imagine that an American student stops you on the street and asks you for information about your town. What would you tell him/her to do or not to do? Use question words as in a).

Examples: *I would tell him/her **where to find** the best shops.*
*… **where not to go** shopping.*
*… **how to find** the youth hostel.*

5 *Spot the mistakes* **infinitive: mixed exercise** ▶ **122-124, 126, 129, 132-134**

Three of the following sentences are correct. Spot the mistakes in the others and correct them.

1 I would rather not to take the early flight. The later one would suit me better.
2 Does your maths teacher make you to learn formulas by heart?
3 Tim hopes to go to university after school for to study law.
4 I wanted to give Liz a bit of advice, but she refused to listen to me.
5 Susan would like be chosen for a part in the school play. She loves acting.
6 Let's stay at home and cook pasta rather than to go out for a meal.
7 You really ought to see the film. It's too good to miss.
8 If Leo thinks his moped has been stolen, he had better to report it to the police.
9 I read a lot about the company in order to make a good impression at the interview.
10 Do they let you to take photos in the museum?
11 It's a very difficult problem to solve. It appears that there is nothing to do.
12 Was that the door? I thought I heard someone to come in.

The gerund

6 *What I like* **gerund as object** ▶ **139a/b**

a Say what you like doing (generally) and what you would like to do, etc. at some time in the future. Complete the sentences with ideas from the box below or your own ideas. Put the verbs in the gerund or to-infinitive form. Sometimes you can use both. Think carefully about the meaning.

Examples: *I **like making** new friends. Or: I **like to make** new friends.*
*I **wouldn't like to lose** my best friend.*
*I **don't mind being alone/lending** my friends money.*

1 I like …	5 I hate …
2 I don't like …	6 I would hate …
3 I would like …	7 I enjoy …
4 I wouldn't like …	8 I don't mind …

make new friends	take risks
lose my best friend	leave school and start work
fly to Los Angeles	have a good time
do tests	go to university
go to the cinema	spend money
learn English	wait in queues
be alone	live on a farm

b How well do you know your best friend? Write four sentences that are true for him/her. Use the ideas in a) or your own ideas.

Example: *My best friend's name is … I know that he/she **wouldn't like to live** on a farm.*

c Now finish these sentences with your own ideas. Use the correct form, gerund, *to*-infinitive or both if possible.

1 Next weekend I would like …
2 At Christmas I always love …
3 At the weekend I always enjoy …
4 Next summer I would love …
5 I would hate … on my birthday.
6 I don't mind … on Sundays.

7 *Which form is correct?* **verbs with different meanings: gerund or *to*-inf.** ▶ **139c**

a Complete the sentence pairs with a gerund or with a *to*-infinitive. Think carefully about the meaning.

1 I meant (call) … you to tell you about the party, but I forgot. Sorry.
   We missed the last train home, so it meant (call) … a taxi.
2 I'll never forget (buy) … my first car. It was so exciting.
   Don't forget (buy) … some snacks from the supermarket on your way home.
3 I can't remember (give) … Rob the money that I owed him, but he says I did.
   You must remember (give) … Pat my message. It's important.

4 Doug Peckham has stopped (answer) … fan-mail because he gets about a thousand letters a week.
I was running for the bus, but I had to stop (answer) … my mobile. So I missed the bus and arrived late.
5 I regret (say) … that our team have lost every game this season.
I regret (not – say) … sorry to Jane for my mistake. It was my fault, not hers.
6 We can go on (discuss) … this subject all day. There's so much to be said.
After the main points on the agenda, we went on (discuss) … a few other matters.

b Translate the sentences using the following verbs + gerund or *to*-infinitive.

forget ▪ go on ▪ remember ▪ stop ▪ try

1 Max fuhr fort, stundenlang über sein neues Auto zu reden, obwohl niemand daran interessiert war.
2 Mein Vater hat aufgehört, Japanisch zu lernen.
3 Ich darf nicht vergessen, David eine Geburtstagskarte zu schicken.
4 Denke bitte daran, die Sachen von der Reinigung *(cleaner's)* zu holen *(collect)*.
5 Ich habe dreimal versucht, die Bank anzurufen, aber die Nummer ist besetzt *(engaged)*.

8 *A job advert* **adjective + preposition + gerund** ▶ **141**

This job advert asks if you are the right kind of person for the job. Complete it with the correct preposition + gerund. If you are not sure which preposition is correct, look up the adjective in the *CEG* or in a dictionary.

Example: *Are you **tired of doing** routine work?*

at ▪ in ▪ of ▪ on ▪ to

1 Are you good … (organize)?
2 Are you interested … (make) new contacts?
3 Are you keen … (travel) abroad?
4 Are you tired … (be) just one of a team?
5 Are you clever … (solve) problems?
6 Are you used … (take up) a challenge?
7 Are you sick … (do) what others say?
8 Are you bad … (wait) in line?
9 Are you afraid … (miss) your big chance?
10 Are you fond … (do) things your way?
11 Are you used … (take) important decisions?
12 Are you interested … (work) for us?

If your answers to our questions is YES, phone us now (020 7661 8340).

BMS BUSINESS MANAGEMENT SYSTEMS

Working au pair noun + preposition + gerund ▶ 142

Have you ever thought about being an au pair after school? There are advantages and disadvantages. Read the text and answer the questions.

After school, young people often have the choice between working or studying. Others take the opportunity of spending a year abroad as an au pair. The most popular host country is the USA.
The reasons for going abroad are usually the following: young people like the idea of
5 travelling, or they go in the hope of learning the country's language perfectly. But more often than not, they want the experience of doing things on their own, away from home. But it isn't easy and there are disappointments.
First, there's often difficulty in getting a suitable place. Not everybody gets the chance of living in San Francisco or New York. You may find yourself in a small wildwest town, or in a
10 boring village in the mountains.

a Make a list of noun + preposition + gerund in ll. 1-10 and note which prepositions follow which nouns.

   Example: *the **choice between working** or **studying**, …*

b Complete ll. 11-24 adding a preposition and the correct form of the verb in brackets.

   Then there's always the problem (1 communicate) …, even if you were the best in your English class at school. Most students have difficulty (2 make) … themselves understood at first. There's also the possibility (3 get) … stuck with a family that you don't like, and the risk (4 not – be) … happy in your new environment. Unfortunately, there's always the
15 danger (5 be) … used as cheap labour. There are other reasons (6 not – get on) … too. The way the family does things may not be your way (7 do) … things. Then there's the problem (8 not – have) … enough free time for yourself – you may find that you are a 24-hour babysitter.

   It's clear that many young people have their doubts (9 go) … so far
20 away from home. On the other hand, the opportunity (10 spend) … a year in the States is usually welcomed.
   What do you think are the advantages (11 live) … in an English-speaking country for a year? If you had the choice (12 go) … to the States as an au pair or starting a job at home, what would you do?

c Write two paragraphs (6-8 lines each) about the advantages and disadvantages of taking a job abroad. Use the structure noun + preposition + gerund as often as possible. If you wish, you can take ideas and vocabulary from the text.

   Example: *I think one disadvantage is the **risk of being** homesick.*

10 *A boat trip*   **preposition + gerund**   ▶ 144

Read the story and change the underlined sentences. Make two sentences into one by using a suitable preposition + gerund. Sometimes there is more than one possible way of combining the two sentences.

after ▪ before ▪ by ▪ in spite of ▪ instead of ▪ on ▪ without

Examples: *Steve parked the car. Then he showed Cheryl the way to the marina.*
After parking *the car, Steve showed Cheryl the way to the marina.*
Cheryl saw how rough the water was. She felt nervous.
On/After seeing *how rough the water was, Cheryl felt nervous.*

Steve said, 'It's just a bit of wind. Don't worry, I'm a good sailor.' But Cheryl was worried.
1 Steve jumped on the boat. Then he started the engine.
'It's going to be great fun,' he shouted. Cheryl didn't feel too sure about that.
2 She looked up at the dark clouds again. Then she got on the boat.
Cheryl felt really nervous.

3 Then she heard thunder[1] in the distance. She started to panic.
Surely Steve would decide not to take the boat out. The wind was getting stronger and the thunder was getting louder.
4 Steve saw that a storm was coming. But he still wanted to take the boat out.
5 He didn't turn off the engine. He just laughed.
'You'll love it. Just wait and see,' he called. But how could she love being on the lake in a storm? Steve was just about to leave the marina.
6 Suddenly Cheryl climbed off the boat. She didn't say a word. She was angry and disappointed in Steve.
7 Steve turned off the engine. He ran after Cheryl. He stopped her and asked her what was wrong.
8 Cheryl thought for a few seconds. Then she answered.
9 She tried to hide the fact that she was afraid. She said it was too cold.
Such a macho wouldn't understand her feelings anyway. He would probably laugh at her. Cheryl realized that Steve only wanted to show off[2] with his father's car and his father's boat. He didn't care how she felt at all.
10 Cheryl didn't say another word. She ran to the main road and took the next bus home.

---

1 thunder *Donner*   2 show off *angeben*

11 *Class gossip*   **subject in gerund constructions**   ▶ **149**

a   Make one sentence out of two, using a gerund with its own subject, i.e. with a pronoun/noun before it.

Examples: a Beth's boyfriend has passed his driving test. She's proud of that.
   *Beth is proud of **her boyfriend passing/having passed** his driving test.*
   b But he drives too fast. She hates that.
   *But she hates **him driving** too fast.*

1 a Brian's friends borrow all his CDs. He doesn't mind that.
   b But sometimes they borrow his mobile. He doesn't like that.
2 a Nick's new girlfriend always arrives late. He's not very pleased about that.
   b Sometimes she wears too much make-up. He hates that.
3 a Jenna's parents tell her when to come home. She objects to that.
   b But they give her lots of pocket money. She doesn't mind that.
4 a Sharon has got a place at university. Her parents are proud of that.
   b But she's going to study in London. They aren't keen on that.
5 a Sarah's little brother sometimes uses her computer. She's not fond of that.
   b And he leaves all his stuff in her room. She's tired of that.

b   What are you sometimes tired of people doing? What don't you mind people doing? What do you object to people doing? Write three sentences.

12 *Jeff's old car*   **other structures instead of a gerund**   ▶ **141, 144, 149, 150**

a   Jeff has bought an old car. In sentences 1– 5 there is a gerund.
Can you write each sentence in a different way without the gerund?
Change the underlined parts, but do not change the meaning.
Sometimes there is more than one way.

Examples: Jeff was very happy about getting the car so cheaply.
   *Jeff was very **happy to get** the car so cheaply.*
   *Jeff was very **happy that he had got** the car so cheaply.*

1 The man who sold it to Jeff said <u>he had difficulty in starting it</u>.
2 Jeff's friends thought it was stupid <u>buying</u> a car that wouldn't start.
3 They suggested <u>buying</u> a new one.
4 But Jeff decided <u>against buying</u> a new one.
5 The reason <u>for Jeff buying</u> an old car was the cheap price.

b   Now write sentences 6-10 with a gerund, but do not change the meaning.

6 Before <u>he bought</u> the car, Jeff had a good look at the engine.
7 Jeff loved <u>to repair</u> things.
8 He was glad <u>that he had</u> something to do in the evenings.
9 After <u>he had put in</u> some new parts, he had a car that was like new.
10 And his friends didn't mind <u>if he drove</u> them about in it …

13 *Interview with a band*   gerund: mixed exercise   ▶ **138, 139a/c, 141-145**

The British new metal band *Night Express* gave a TV interview for a music channel. Here are some of the interviewer's questions. Complete the answers using suitable verbs in the gerund form and adding prepositions and other words where necessary.

Examples: Int.:   Before you started the band, had any of you played or sung professionally?

Greg: No, we had no experience of ***playing*** or ***singing*** *professionally*.

Int.:   You have had two top-ten hits in the British charts. Who writes the songs?

Rod: Well, we all enjoy ***writing*** *songs*. We just put our ideas together.

1 Int.:   And what about the lyrics? Who writes them?

 Greg: That's Guy's job mostly. He's good … A good lyricist is important.

2 Int.:   How did you get your big break? Did you play support for other bands first?

 Mick: Yes, of course. Most small bands become known … for well-known bands. So did we, for two years, in fact.

3 Int.:   When did you sign your first recording contract? Do you remember?

 Rod: Of course. We'll never forget … That was about a year ago.

4 Int.:   You travel around quite a lot – European tours, concerts, TV shows.

 Guy: That's true. But we don't mind … It's part of the job. We love it.

5 Int.:   Your job's not easy. You have to work late hours. Do you find it unpleasant?

 Mick: No, that's our life. We're used … We sleep during the day.

6 Int.:   You give a lot of interviews now. Is it just routine work for you?

 Greg: Oh, no. … is always fun. We enjoy it.

7 Int.:   Now about your concert plans. You go to New York next week. Is that correct?

 Rod: Yes, that's right. We're looking forward … It will be our first visit.

8 Int.:   New metal is big in the States. But what about British-style new metal? Do you think you'll be successful?

 Guy: Well, of course there's always the risk … (not) successful in the States, but we're optimistic. We get fan mail from American teenagers. They seem to like us.

9 Int.:   Well, playing in New York is every band's dream. You must be excited.

 Greg: You bet! We're so excited … in New York that we talk of nothing else.

10 Int.:   One last question. Your new album is going to be released very soon. When will it be in the shops?

 Mick: In just three weeks. And it's well worth … So buy it, everybody!

▶ 122, 132, 133, 139a, 143, 145-147

14 *Write a dialogue* **gerund or infinitive**

Two pupils are working on a project together. One of them doesn't feel like working at all. The other thinks they should at least make a start with the project. Write a suitable dialogue, using the 15 structures given + gerund or infinitive (with or without *to*). You can use the structures in any order.

Examples: A: It isn't much fun **having** to work, is it?
B: Well, let's **go** to the cinema instead.
A: But surely it would be better **to stay in** and **do** something.

Continue:

1 Why not ...?
2 I suggest ...
3 ... won't let me ...
4 I hope ...
5 You had better ...
6 I am looking forward to ...
7 How about ...?
8 ... can't make me ...

9 It's best ...
10 I would rather ...
11 There's no point ...
12 ... rather than ...
13 I'm busy ...
14 I feel like ...
15 It's no use ...

15 *Your star sign* **gerund or infinitive** ▶ 124, 126, 127b, 128, 138, 139a-c, 141, 143

a First, read the star sign descriptions and complete them with the correct verb in the gerund or *to*-infinitive form. If you think both are possible, write both.

Examples:
Aquarius
(20 January – 18 February)   *make   work   do*

You are a practical person who likes **working/to work** hard. You enjoy **doing** exciting things and find it easy **to make** friends.

Pisces
(19 February – 20 March)   *help   be   organize   paint*
You prefer (1) ... on your own rather than in a group, but you enjoy (2) ... others. You are fond of artistic things like (3) ..., but you're not very good at practical things like (4) ...

Aries
(21 March – 19 April)   *compete   lose   do   win*
You are adventurous and fond of (1) ... energetic sports. You love (2) ... with others and you always try (3) ... You hate (4) ...

Taurus
(20 April – 20 May)   *accept   draw   listen   do* (2×)
You avoid (1) ... things that are energetic. You prefer (2) ... things slowly and carefully. Your hobbies are quiet things, like (3) ... to music and (4) ... You don't mind (5) ... rules.

Gemini

(21 May – 21 June)   ***get on with   work   do   discuss***

You are an active person, better at (1) … with your head than your hands. You enjoy (2) … interesting topics with friends, but you quickly get bored with (3) … the same things. You are easy (4) …, but perhaps a little too talkative.

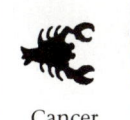

Cancer

(22 June – 22 July)   ***collect   swim   take   help***

You enjoy (1) … and water sports, but also (2) … things. You are always willing (3) … friends and you are not afraid of (4) … risks.

Leo

(23 July – 22 August)   ***get   be   do*** (2×)   ***tell***

You have lots of energy and are used to (1) … the centre of attention[1]. You like (2) … others how (3) … things. In fact, you often insist on (4) … what you want, and you usually succeed in (5) … what you want.

Virgo

(23 August – 22 September)   ***spend   say   know   rely on***

You are quiet and helpful and nice (1) … You don't mind (2) … time and energy on others. Friends know that you are someone (3) … You often find it difficult (4) … no.

Libra

(23 September – 23 October)   ***be   argue   waste   travel***

You love (1) … time. You dislike (2) … and are good at (3) … diplomatic. (4) … is one of your favourite activities.

Scorpio

(24 October – 21 November)   ***solve   do   be   make***

You are creative and ambitious[2], but you sometimes try (1) … the impossible. You love (2) … puzzles. You find it easy (3) … friends because you are an extrovert and fun (4) … with.

Sagittarius

(22 November – 21 December)   ***follow   play   be***

You are active and good at (1) … all kinds of sports. You hate (2) … forced to do things you dislike. It's difficult for you (3) … a routine.

Capricorn

(22 December – 19 January)   ***concentrate   be   do   work***

You are capable of (1) … hard and you don't find it difficult (2) … for long periods of time. You don't mind (3) … alone, but you also look forward to (4) … things with friends.

b Read the description of your star sign. Do you think it is true for you? If not, why?
Write a short paragraph using gerunds and/or *to*-infinitives. Then write a second paragraph about your best friend, brother or sister. Is the description true for him/her?

Example: *My star sign Aquarius says I like to **work/working** hard, but that's not true because I often enjoy **doing** nothing. I used to find it difficult **to make** friends when I was younger, but now I don't.*

---

1 centre of attention *im Mittelpunkt*   2 ambitious *ehrgeizig*

Complete the text with a gerund or with an infinitive (with or without *to*). If you think two forms are possible, write both. Remember that some forms may be passive.

In the past, vast forest areas in Europe and North America were the first (1 clear[1]) …, making room for settlers (2 set up) … farms and towns. Deforestation is still taking place in western countries, but tropical rainforests in the less developed countries near the equator are the only ones (3 disappear) … at such an alarming rate. An area the size of a football field is destroyed every second.

(4 clear) … tropical rainforests causes problems to the rainforest ecosystem, which survives by (5 store) … its nutrients in the trees and plants, not in the soil[2]. When an area of forest is cleared, the nutrients are soon washed away. The soil erodes and becomes useless for (6 farm) … after only a few years. So why are rainforests destroyed?

Trees are felled for their valuable tropical hardwood, such as teak and mahogony, used for (7 make) … furniture. A further reason is (8 provide) … land for cattle-ranching. Some idealists have stopped (9 eat) … hamburgers because fast food chains have had rainforests cleared (10 ranch) … cattle for their products.

It is interesting (11 note) … that, although most people would agree that it is irresponsible (12 go on) … (13 destroy) … rainforests, many governments do not seem (14 be) … too concerned. People in general are not indifferent to the fate of rainforests. Environmentalists have been trying for years (15 persuade) … people (16 change) … their attitude towards rainforest destruction by (17 make) … them (18 realize) … the potential that is being destroyed. Rainforests are needed for scientists (19 carry out) … valuable medical research. The value of such research is easy (20 prove) … In recent years a drug has been developed (21 fight) … leukemia, from a tropical rainforest plant. Yet not even one per cent of rainforest plants have been tested for their medical properties.

Surely we cannot afford (22 miss) … the chance of (23 find) … a cure for AIDS or cancer. Governments of the world should not let multinational companies (24 take away) … this chance. Politicians should not continue (25 allow) … big business (26 make) … enormous profits by (27 sacrifice) … nature's gifts.

Conservationists[3] are succeeding in (28 make) … people (29 realize) … the seriousness of the problem. They want governments (30 bring in) … strict laws against the exploitation[4], but unfortunately business concerns often prevent them from (31 do) … so.

Tropical rainforests are too valuable (32 destroy) … and their loss is too serious (33 ignore) … It is easy (34 destroy) … rainforests, but impossible (35 replace) … them. Surely they are worth (36 fight) … for.

Adapted from 'Physical Geography' by Keith Grimwade

---

1 clear *roden*   2 soil *Boden*   3 conservationist *Naturschützer/in*   4 exploitation *Ausbeutung*

Read the articles about the dolphin deaths off England's South West coast.

Tuesday, 31 December, 2002

RSPCA[1] urges action over dead dolphins

The RSPCA is calling for urgent action from the government and EU to prevent the deaths of hundreds of dolphins in commercial fishing nets off the South West coast every year.
During December, 31 dead dolphins were found washed up on the Cornish coast alone.
5 […] During 2002, a total of 180 of the sea mammals were victims of fishing off Cornwall. 'These healthy animals die a grisly[2] death,' said Laila Sandler, an RSPCA marine wildlife officer. 'Some thrash around[3] violently in an effort to escape suffering cuts, broken teeth and even jaws before eventually running out of oxygen.'
Early in 2003 the government is due to release its strategy to tackle the problem – and for
10 the first time ever the European Commission is considering including[4] plans to deal with the issue[5] in its Common Fisheries Policy. […]

'We will never know exactly how many dolphins die this way off UK shores each year. We expect the government and the EU to adopt tough new measures to stop the killing. Any action is too late to save this year's victims but we cannot let this situation drag on, year
15 after year,' said Ms Sandler.

Wednesday, 22 January, 2003

Dolphins 'in danger of dying out'

Dolphins off the South West coast are in danger of being wiped out, environmentalists have warned. They say increasing numbers are being killed, after getting caught in huge fishing nets
20 used by trawlers. Since the beginning of this year the bodies of more than 40 dolphins have washed up on Devon and Cornwall beaches. […]

Conservationists[6] believe pair trawling is to blame – where a huge net is strung between two
25 boats. And they are calling on the European Union to put independent observers on fishing boats to monitor the situation. […]

Fishing representatives say the local fleet is not responsible and have blamed industrial foreign
30 vessels[7] […] Many dead dolphins have been found mutilated, some have knife wounds.

[…] MP Matthew Taylor urged the government to adopt a clear strategy to prevent further unnecessary dolphin deaths. In a Westminster debate, Mr Taylor told minister Elliot
35 Morley that he had to save the dolphins before there were none left to save.

From *BBC News Online*

---

1 RSPCA: Royal Society for the Prevention of Cruelty to Animals   2 grisly: cruel   3 thrash around: *um sich schlagen*
4 include *einschließen*   5 issue: question, matter   6 conservationist *Naturschützer/in*   7 vessel (here): large boat

a   In the first article, look for examples of:

1   a verb + gerund
2   a preposition on its own + gerund
3   an adjective + *to*-infinitive

b   In the second article, look for examples of:

1   a passive gerund
2   a noun + preposition + gerund
3   an infinitive of purpose
4   a verb + object + *to*-infinitive

c   1   Translate the sentence 'We expect … killing.' into German. (ll. 12-13)
2   Replace the construction with *let* with a construction with *allow*. (l. 14)

d   Rewrite the underlined sentence parts using a gerund construction with a preposition.

before ▪ by ▪ for ▪ in spite of ▪ instead of ▪ without

1   The fishing industry believes that they can catch more fish if they pair trawl.
2   Fishing boats use trawling nets to catch fish, but do not consider the fate of the dolphins.
3   Unfortunately, the number of dolphin deaths is increasing, not decreasing.
4   Conservationists are fighting hard, but they have not been able to protect the dolphins.
5   Dolphins caught in nets suffer injuries before they die from lack of oxygen.
6   RSPCA workers think culprits[1] should be punished because they kill or harm dolphins.

e   Continue or complete the sentences suitably using an infinitive or gerund construction. Use your own words as far as possible.

1   Environmentalists believe that dolphins are in danger …
2   The RSPCA wants the government …
3   The government should not let …
4   Conservationists expect the EU …
5   Environmentalists are fighting hard to prevent …
6   When caught in a net, the dolphins do not know how …
7   MP Matthew Taylor is trying …
8   Mr Taylor wants minister Elliot Morley …
9   I couldn't help … when I read these articles.
10   In my opinion, the best way … would be …

f   Explain the meaning of the following words, using a gerund or an infinitive in your definitions.

Examples: *Pair trawling is a method of* **catching** *fish. It works by* **stringing** *a huge net between two boats.*

1   a conservationist   2   a trawler   3   the RSPCA

---

1 culprits: guilty people

The participle

A ▶ **Complete the sentences with present or past participles.**

1. Most of the churches (destroy) … in the Great Fire of London were rebuilt by Christopher Wren.
2. My sister has two children, both badly- … (behave), I'm afraid.
3. With the weather (get) … worse, it may be wise to postpone our climbing trip.
4. Visitors (not – hold) … EU passports must fill in immigration forms.
5. I noticed a huge dog (run) … towards me, so I ran into a garden and closed the gate.

B ▶ **Change the underlined sentence parts using suitable participle constructions. Make any additional changes that are necessary.**

6. <u>Because she is a nurse</u>, Laura knew what to do at the scene of the accident.
7. 'I'll be back in half an hour', said Layla <u>as she ran out of the office</u>.
8. <u>The manager was highly satisfied with Max</u>, so he extended his contract.
9. <u>After he had completed the project</u>, Dixon decided to take a week's holiday.
10. <u>As he had arrived early for the interview</u>, Ed had time to read some information brochures.
11. The man <u>who is interviewing Barbara</u> is the head of the personnel department.
12. <u>Since temperatures had fallen below zero in the night</u>, morning traffic was delayed owing to icy roads.
13. <u>As Dad has lost his job</u>, we can't afford to go on holiday.
14. <u>Since she doesn't speak much Italian</u>, Pat is having problems with her new job in Rome.
15. <u>When he heard his exam results</u>, he shouted out in surprise.

C ▶ **Translate the German sentence parts, using participle constructions.**

16. James sat at his window on the tenth floor *(und beobachtete die Menschen auf der Straße.)* …
17. *(Als er aus dem Taxi stieg)* … he slipped on some ice and fell.
18. *(Da er als Student in London gelebt hatte)* … it was easy for him to do business there.
19. *(Nachdem die Pressekonferenz beendet war)* … the journalists were allowed to ask questions.
20. David saw a ten-dollar bill *(die auf der Straße lag.)* …
21. Janice ran into her old headmaster *(als sie in die Bank hineinging.)* …
22. *(Obwohl er in Frankreich geboren war)* … he always had bad marks in French at school.
23. Jane looked down at the dead bird, *(und lächelte traurig.)* …
24. The cake will stay fresh longer *(wenn er im Kühlschrank aufbewahrt wird.)* …
25. At first I wanted to let my hair grow, but then I decided *(sie kurz schneiden zu lassen.)* …

D ▶ **Spot the mistakes. There is one mistake in each sentence or sentence pair.**

26. Increasing profits for the last five years, the company is now in a strong financial position.
27. Being under reconstruction, traffic is not allowed to use the bridge.
28. Does Tim still work for a software company or is he self-employing now?
29. James noticed a new Indian restaurant walking up Carlton Road.
30. Shall we let a pizza delivered?
31. I noticed a young man read a newspaper in the hotel lobby.
32. I heard the telephone ringing. Just once. It must have been a wrong number.
33. James has just bought a new house. He must have a well-paying job.
34. Having been held for questioning, the police released the suspect yesterday.
35. With prices risen at an increasing rate, consumers are spending less and saving more.
36. We saw John in his new car coming down the escalator outside the shopping mall.

The participle

? ▶ **Correct yourself**

A ▷ 1: *destroyed*   2: *badly-behaved*   3: *getting*   4: *not holding*   5: *running*

B ▷ 6: *Being a nurse, Laura …*   7: *… said Layla running out of the office.*   8: *The manager being highly satisfied with Max, he …*   9: *Having completed the project/The project completed, Dixon …*   10: *Having arrived/Arriving early for the interview, Ed …*   11: *The man interviewing Barbara is …*   12: *Temperatures having fallen below zero in the night, morning traffic …*   13: *With Dad having lost his job, we …*   14: *Not speaking much Italian, Pat …*   15: *Hearing his exam results, he …*

C ▷ 16: *… watching the people on the street.*   17: *Getting out of the taxi, …*   18: *Having lived in London as a student …*   19: *The press conference having finished/being over, …*   20: *… lying on the street.*   21: *… when going into/when entering the bank.*   22: *Though born in France …*   23: *…, smiling sadly.*   24: *… if kept/stored in the fridge/being kept in the fridge.*   25: *… to have it cut short.*

D ▷ 26: *Having increased profits for the last five years, the company …*
27: *The bridge being under reconstruction, traffic is not allowed to use it.*
28: *Does Tim still work for a software company or is he self-employed now?*
29: *James noticed a new Indian restaurant when walking up Carlton Road. / Walking up Carlton Road, James noticed a new Indian restaurant.*
30: *Shall we have a pizza delivered?*
31: *I noticed a young man reading a newspaper in the hotel lobby.*
32: *I heard the telephone ring …*
33: *… He must have a well-paid job.*
34: *The suspect having been held for questioning, the police released him/her yesterday. / Having held the suspect for questioning, the police released him/her … / Having been held for questioning, the suspect was released yesterday.*
35: *With prices rising at an increasing rate, consumers …*
36: *We saw John in his new car when coming down the escalator …*

▶ **Exercise finder**

Sentences	CEG	Exercises
1, 4, 11, 20	▶ 153c	▶ 4, 10, 11, 12
2, 28, 33	▶ 153b	▶ 1, 12
3, 13, 35	▶ 162b	▶ 8
5, 31, 32	▶ 154a, 134	▶ 2, 11
6, 10, 14, 18, 26	▶ 159	▶ 4, 9, 10, 11, 12
7, 16, 23	▶ 160	▶ 4, 10, 11, 12
8, 12, 19, 27, 34	▶ 162a/c	▶ 7, 9, 10
9, 15, 17	▶ 158	▶ 4, 10, 11, 12
21, 29, 36	▶ 161a	▶ 5, 6, 9
22, 24	▶ 161b	▶ 5, 10, 12
25, 30	▶ 156	▶ 3

1 *Making adjectives*   participles used to form a compound   ▶ **153b**

a How would you describe the things and people in the pictures? Combine the words in boxes 1 and 2 to make suitable adjectives. Then choose the corresponding noun from box 3.

1

tight
hard
well (2×)
badly
fun
good
French

2

speaking
looking
loving
working
fitting
paid
written
dressed

3

job
secretary
girl
jeans
teenagers
schoolgirl
~~jacket~~
application
man

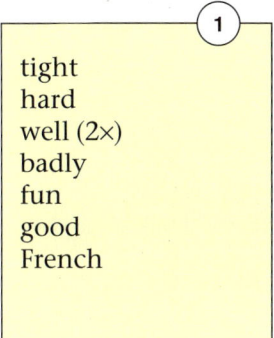

Example: *a **badly-fitting** jacket*

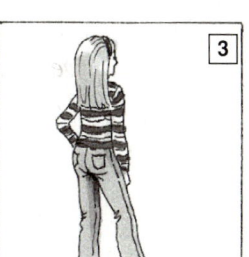

b Write a story using the adjective-noun combinations in part a). Use at least five people, etc. from the pictures. For example, write about where they all are, who they are, how they meet.

Example: *One day at Heathrow Airport, John, a **well-dressed** man with …*

An eye-witness account   **verbs of perception + obj.+ pres. part. or inf.**   ▶ **154a, 134**

a Complete the eye-witness's report of the fire, using the notes.

Examples: (see – smoke – come) (notice – people – run)
I **saw smoke coming** from a building a few streets away, and I **noticed people running** towards the paper factory.

'I opened the kitchen window and then I (1 smell – something – burn) … as well. I (2 see – flames – come) … from the paper factory. Just then a neighbour arrived, so we decided to go and see what was going on. As we got closer, we (3 hear – people – shout)… When we got to the factory we (4 see – big crowd – stand) … in front of the gates. We (5 hear – fire brigade – come) … When they arrived we (6 watch – firefighters – set up) … their equipment. My neighbour (7 notice – two people – climb) … down a fire escape[1]. We (8 see – cat – run) … along the roof. I (9 notice – woman – wave) … from a window on the fourth floor. She must have been terrified. We (10 smell – wood – burn) … and there was thick smoke everywhere. It was awful.'

b Sometimes an infinitive is used after the verb of perception. Here are some more eye-witness statements which use a present participle or an infinitive. Correct the ones that you think are wrong.

1 I saw the robber suddenly pulling a gun out of his pocket. I almost died of fright.
2 I noticed a dark-haired man with a beard wait in the get-away van.
3 My wife and I saw the woman jump out of the window and run away.
4 Through my rear mirror I noticed the car behind me crashing into a tree.
5 We could smell rubber burn. At first we thought it was our car brakes. But then we saw the fire at the tyre factory and phoned the police.
6 I overheard two men in a pub talk about a break-in that they were obviously involved in.
7 We saw the van run into the dog. The poor thing was dead immediately.
8 I felt something hitting my car. My wife looked back and saw a large stone on the motorway and two teenage boys on the bridge.
9 I noticed a man lie on the pavement. At first I thought he was drunk, but he was dead.
10 Two men ran out of the café. A minute later we suddenly heard the bomb exploding.

---

1 fire escape *Feuerleiter*

a What are the people in the pictures having done? What have they had done? What are they going to have done? Use the verbs in the box.

~~develop~~	repair	cut
take	deliver	wash
test	manicure	clean

Example: *He **has had** some photos **developed**.*

b Translate into English. Think carefully about tenses.

1 Wo kann ich diese Hose kürzen *(shorten)* lassen?
2 Warum lässt du dir nicht die Haare färben *(dye)*?
3 Dr. Sutton hat ein neues Computer-System installieren lassen.
4 Wo ist Jack? – In der Werkstatt *(garage)*. Er lässt seine Reifen *(tyres)* wechseln.
5 Die Pakete sind sehr schwer. Wir können sie schicken lassen.

c What have you or members of your family had done, repaired, tested, etc. recently? Write four sentences.

4 *Romeo and Juliet* part. expressing time, reason, etc., rel. clauses ▶ **153c, 158-160**

Read the story of Shakespeare's *Romeo and Juliet*, then shorten the text by using participle constructions where suitable instead of 1) relative clauses 2) subordinate clauses of time and reason 3) clauses linked by *and* expressing accompanying circumstances. In ll. 1-12 the clauses are underlined. In the remaining text (ll. 13-33) you must look for suitable clauses yourself. There are 16 possibilities. Rewrite eight of the 16 clauses using participle constructions.

Examples: <u>Since it is the first of Shakespeare's great – tragedies –</u> and perhaps the most beautiful – *Romeo and Juliet* is the work <u>that is best known to young people</u>.
***Being** the first of Shakespeare's great tragedies – and perhaps the most beautiful – 'Romeo and Juliet' is the work **best known** to young people.*

<u>As it has become the symbol of love and youth</u>, the story of Romeo and Juliet is timeless. The background to the story is the city of Verona, <u>which is troubled by fighting between the Capulet and Montague families</u>. At a feast in the Capulets' house, Romeo, <u>who is wearing a mask</u> so as not to be recognized, sees Juliet dancing. <u>As he is fascinated by her beauty</u>,
5 Romeo falls in love with her immediately. <u>Because he does not know who Juliet is</u>, he asks her nurse. <u>When he discovers that Juliet is a Capulet</u>, the daughter of his father's enemy, Romeo forgets the family quarrels. He can think of nothing else but Juliet.

Later in her room, <u>because she cannot sleep</u> Juliet goes onto the balcony <u>which overlooks the orchard</u>. <u>When he passes Juliet's window on the way home</u>, Romeo decides to climb
10 over the wall into the orchard <u>as he hopes to see her again</u>. What follows is the famous balcony scene, in which the two young lovers declare their undying love. This scene has become perhaps the most famous love scene in the whole of literature.

Because he has decided to marry Juliet without delay, Romeo pays a visit to his old friend Friar Laurence to ask him to marry them. The old priest, who thinks that the two families
15 will put aside their quarrel if their children are united in marriage, agrees to marry them that same afternoon. The marriage takes place in secrecy.

Later in the day, Romeo, who has killed Juliet's cousin Tybalt in a provoked duel, is banned from Verona on threat of death. Romeo and Juliet can spend only one night together before Romeo has to escape to Mantua.
20 Desperately unhappy, Juliet is told by her mother that she is soon to marry Paris, the husband who has been chosen for her by her father. Juliet refuses. Since she has no one to talk to, she turns to Friar Laurence and asks him to help her. After he has told her his plan, he gives her a potion of herbs which will put her into a death-like sleep. He promises to send a letter to Romeo, which will tell him that Juliet is not dead but only sleeping. Romeo will
25 then take her from the family tomb to Mantua, where they can live happily in safety. Juliet trusts Friar Laurence's words and drinks the potion. Since they believe her to be dead, Juliet's grief-stricken family lay her to rest. Unfortunately, Friar Laurence's letter to Romeo was not delivered. When he hears the news that Juliet is dead, Romeo rushes to the tomb. Juliet is still sleeping. Romeo takes her in his arms. In his grief he drinks poison and dies
30 beside her.

When she awakes from the long sleep, Juliet sees Romeo lying dead at her side. Friar Laurence tells her the truth, but cannot comfort her. Because she does not want to live without Romeo, Juliet kills herself with his dagger.

Based on *Stories from Shakespeare* by Marchette Chute

Complete the text about Christmas in England with a conjunction + the correct participle form of the verbs given. Remember that the form *having* + past participle expresses an action which lies in the past. Choose the most suitable conjunction from the brackets.

Examples: **Although living** next door to each other, neighbours exchange Christmas cards – often by post.
After having waited so long, small children are impatient to get their presents.

Christmas preparations in England start long before the event. Christmas trees are put up two or three weeks before and living-rooms are decorated with paper chains, cards, holly[1] and mistletoe[2]. Artificial trees are usual, especially in families with small children. (1 Although/If – cost) … less and (2 be) … safer than real trees, artificial trees are found strange by most Germans. Additionally, mistletoe is hung up over doors or from the ceiling. By tradition, (3 if/though – catch) … standing under the mistletoe, you can be kissed – and you can't refuse.

(4 Although/When – celebrate) … primarily as a religious festival in most countries of Europe, Christmas in Britain is not strictly observed as such. Christmas Eve is not as quiet as in Germany, and it is not for close family only. (5 After/If – go) … to church in the early evening, people often invite friends to their homes or they go out. Young people like to party on Christmas Eve. Presents are not exchanged until Christmas Day. For small children, Father Christmas comes in the night and leaves presents in their bedrooms or under the tree. (6 Before/After – go) … to bed on Christmas Eve, children leave a glass of wine and a mince pie[3] for Father Christmas in the living-room. (7 After/Unless – hang up) … a traditional stocking[4] for presents – or usually a large pillow case[5] –, they go to bed. On Christmas morning, (8 although/unless – sleep) … much less than usual, children wake up early and open their presents. Adults usually find theirs under the tree. (9 While/If – open) … their presents, people play Christmas carols[6] and traditional Christmas songs.

Lunch on Christmas Day is special. Christmas crackers[7] as a table decoration are popular with both adults and children. (10 When/Before – pull) … open, the crackers bang and small surprises fall out, often a paper hat, a joke or puzzle. People wear their paper hats (11 when/although – eat) … the traditional Christmas lunch of roast turkey and Christmas pudding for dessert.

Perhaps you have already celebrated a Christmas in England. If not, perhaps an English penfriend will invite you one day. (12 If/While – give) … the opportunity, you should take it. You will certainly have a 'Merry Christmas'.

---

1 holly *Stechpalme* 2 mistletoe *Mistelzweig* 3 mince pie *mit* mincemeat *gefüllte Pastete* (mincemeat = *Pastetenfüllung aus Rosinen, Äpfeln usw.*) 4 stocking *langer Strumpf* 5 pillow case *Kopfkissenbezug*
6 Christmas carol *Weihnachtslied* 7 Christmas cracker *Knallbonbon*

6 *Get it right*   **participle constructions with and without conjunctions**   **161a**

Some of the following sentences are correct. In others, there should be or should not be a conjunction.
Think carefully about the meaning:
1 If you think the sentence is correct, write 'Correct'.
2 If you think the conjunction *when* should be omitted in the subordinate clause, rewrite the sentence
   without it.
3 If you think *when* is missing in the subordinate clause, rewrite the sentence with *when*.

1 Adrian accidentally met his ex-girlfriend when dating his new girlfriend one evening.
2 Cindy saw her headmaster queuing up at the disco with her friends.
3 Susan met her boyfriend when doing his paper round.
4 Julian bumped into an old lady running for the bus.
5 Jimmy watched his little sister when eating her pizza hungrily.
6 Mick and Andy noticed two deer[1] putting up their tent in the woods.
7 Jenny saw a huge black dog waiting for a taxi.
8 The manager came to an important decision while studying the sales figures.
9 Marie saw her brother at the police station when reporting the theft of his bicycle.
10 Mr Williams noticed a new men's hairdressing saloon walking down Castle Road.

7 *Written English*   **subject in participle constructions**    **162a/c**

a Make the style of the following sentences suitable for written or TV news reports, i.e. more formal. Change
   the adverbial clauses into participle constructions with their own subject. Study the examples carefully.

Examples: As heavy snow had fallen in the night, several roads in the North were closed.
          Heavy snow having fallen *in the night, several roads in the North were closed.*
          Several accidents occurred in the early morning hours because roads were icy.
          Several accidents occurred in the early morning hours, ***roads being*** *icy.*

1 Commuters arrived late to work because several trains were delayed.
2 Since interest rates have fallen, more and more people are now buying homes.
3 As demonstrators were blocking the streets, traffic had to be diverted.
4 Since camera phones cost more than expected, sales are slow.
5 A new price policy will be necessary, as sales have dropped by more than 10%.
6 As more and more teachers are falling ill with influenza, some schools have been
   temporarily closed.

b Correct the following sentences, changing any necessary words. Pay attention to the position of the
   subjects.

1 Having been kept in a dark room for five days, the kidnappers finally released the captive.
2 Being difficult to see in the fog, several drivers missed the new motorway exit.
3 Costing over a hundred thousand pounds, the tenants are not willing to buy the property.
4 Having bitten three people, the owner was forced to have the dog destroyed.

---

1 deer *Reh, Hirsch*

▶ 162b

8 *Street talk*   **participle constructions beginning with *with* + own subject**

Rewrite what Kathy and Tahira say in only one sentence. Begin with *With* … and use a participle construction (either a present participle or a past participle).

Examples:

The concert tickets are so expensive. I can't afford to go with you.

Most of the tickets have already been sold, so we might not get any anyway.

With the concert tickets being *so expensive, I can't afford to go with you.*

With most of the tickets *already **sold**, we might not get any anyway.*

1 Christmas is getting closer, so I've started looking for presents.
2 And now that the exams are finished, we'll be able to enjoy Christmas.
3 But all the shops will be closed over Christmas. There will be nowhere to go.
4 My mum has lost her job, so we haven't got much money for presents anyway.
5 My boyfriend's family lives in Scotland, so I might not see him over Christmas.
6 Train fares are going up, so I can't afford to go to Scotland with him.
7 And petrol costs so much that it's too expensive by car, I expect.
8 Well, my computer has been repaired at last, so I will have enough to do over Christmas.

9 *Spot the mistakes*   **participles: mixed exercise**   ▶ **159, 161a, 162a/c, 163**

In some of the following sentences there is a mistake which has to do with a participle. Tick the correct sentences (✔) and cross the wrong ones (✗). Then correct the mistakes, adding words where necessary.

Examples: Being over, the teachers left the meeting.   ✗
Correct: ***The meeting being over**, the teachers left.*
(The subject of 'being over' is 'the meeting', not 'the teachers'.)
Nicole saw a big, brown dog waiting for the bus.   ✗
(= The dog is waiting for the bus.)
Correct: *Nicole saw a big, brown dog **when/while waiting** for the bus.*
(= Nicole is waiting for the bus.)

1 Feeling hungry, the teenagers stopped for a hamburger on the way home.
2 The youth club having closed, Andy and his friends went to see a late-night film.
3 Being warm and sunny, Angela and John decided to cycle to the coast.
4 Having completed the forms the students gave them in.
5 Being long and boring, the class didn't want to read the book.
6 Thomas saw a herd of bulls cycling along a country road.
7 With costing over a thousand pounds, people didn't buy the new computers.
8 Georgina feeling cold, Nick lent her his jacket.
9 Leaving very early in the morning, Ben and Anna missed their train.
10 His wife having died, Mr Spencer decided to sell the house.
11 Having a big hole in the knee, Pete threw away his favourite jeans.
12 Janet noticed a man with a very long beard eating her lunch at the *Hard Rock Café*.
13 Strictly spoken, this *-ing* form is a participle, not a gerund.
14 Seeing *Scream 6* already at the cinema, we didn't rent the video.

Thomas Alva Edison participles: mixed exercise ▶ **153c, 158-160, 161b, 162a/c**

a Read the statements about Edison, then rewrite them in a formal style, using participle constructions. You can change, shorten or join sentences, sometimes in more than one way. Notice that some participle constructions have their own subject.

Examples: Thomas Alva Edison was born in Ohio in 1847. He was to become one of the world's greatest inventors.
Born in Ohio in 1847, Thomas Alva Edison was to become one of the world's greatest inventors.
As school was uninspiring for a sharp young mind, Edison did not pay attention.
School being uninspiring for a sharp young mind, Edison did not pay attention.

Edison's childhood

1 After only three months the headmaster expelled young Edison from school because he thought that the seven-year-old was too slow to learn.
2 Though he had only three months of formal education, he became one of the greatest inventors and industrial leaders in history.
3 His mother knew full well that her son was intelligent. She began to teach him at home.
4 She noticed that he enjoyed doing experiments, so she encouraged him to read about science.
5 But she was not able to afford books for her son. She realized that she could not help him further.
6 Because he needed money for books, at the age of twelve Edison began selling newspapers on the first passenger trains.
7 Since he had nothing to do while the train stood in the station, he set up his own laboratory in the luggage van.

Edison's later life

8 Because he had great faith in scientific progress, Edison valued long, hard work.
9 He stretched himself to his limits, and he sometimes worked twenty hours a day.
10 After he had invented the light bulb in 1879, Edison went on to develop the phonograph.
11 He made great improvements to the telegraph, telephone and in film-making technology. He also founded the first modern research laboratory.
12 Edison was a clever businessman. He set up companies worldwide to manufacture and sell his inventions.
13 Edison was also a hard businessman, who fought fiercely to defeat his competitors.
14 Because Edison had encouraged Henry Ford to use the gasoline-powered engine for the automobile, the two men became good friends.
15 Edison obtained 1,093 United States patents, the biggest number that has ever been issued to any individual.

Adapted from 'Edison Alva', in: *Oxford Children's Encyclopedia,* Vol. 6 Biography; 'Thomas Edison, American Inventor' by Robin Chew

b Find out some information about the life of a famous person who interests you, perhaps another inventor, a writer, painter or politician. Write a long paragraph about his/her life using participle constructions.

The Great Fire of London   part.: mixed exercise   ▶ **153a/c, 154-155, 158-160**

Read the text about the Great Fire of London, then carry out the tasks.

In September 1666 a fire broke out in London, destroying eighty per cent of the city.

The fire began on the night of 2nd
5   September in the King's bakery in Pudding Lane, started perhaps by the carelessness of a maid or of the baker himself. Awakened in the night, the baker's assistant smelt something
10 burning. Finding the house full of smoke, he alarmed the sleeping family.

Climbing through a window onto the roof, all the people in the baker's household were able to escape the fire – all but the maid. Being too frightened to climb over the roof tops, she was caught in the flames.
15 Accelerated[1] by the strong winds, sparks fell from the burning building onto dry hay in the yard of the *Star Inn*, setting it on fire too. Being built of wood, the houses around easily caught fire. In the narrow streets, the blaze soon spread to an inferno, destroying not only houses but warehouses packed with flammable materials such as oil, spirits[2], coal and straw. The flames were soon half way over old London Bridge. The strong easterly winds kept the
20 flames advancing. They soon left the whole city burning.

The best account[3] of the fire comes from the diaries of Samuel Pepys. Called from his home in Seething Lane, he walked to the Tower and watched the fire from a safe distance high up. Later he recorded the dreadful sight. He saw houses on both sides of the bridge burning. He went down to the river and noticed people trying to remove their goods from their houses.
25 He watched sick people being carried away in their beds. Having been sent for by the King, Pepys told him what terrible scenes he had witnessed. Being greatly troubled, the King ordered houses to be pulled down so that they could not burn. However, having started the demolition too close to the fires, the helpers were too late. The flames ate up the demolished houses too. But water being scarce away from the banks of the river, there was
30 little that could be done to stop the spread of the fires.

The fires burned all day and through the next, Fleet Street, Old Bailey, Ludgate Hill and Newgate, all being reduced to ashes.

For three more days the fire raged through the city, destroying 13,200 houses and 87 churches. Amazingly, only seven deaths were recorded, but the figure was probably much
35 higher. The city known by Shakespeare was devastated[4]. Having lost everything, many people were reduced to poverty for years to come. Thousands of people were ruined and the debtor's[5] prisons became overcrowded.

Christopher Wren, the great 17th century architect, built 49 new churches, including St. Paul's Cathedral. When the city was rebuilt, wooden houses dating back to the medieval
40 period were replaced by stone buildings. After the fire of 1666 the face of London had changed forever.

Based on 'The Great Fire of London – 1666', *Anglia Campus*

---

1 accelerate *beschleunigen*   2 spirits: alcohol   3 account: report   4 devastate: damage severely
5 debtor *Schuldner*

a Looking at the language:

1 Write down all the participle constructions used in ll. 1-18 ('In September … straw.') Which are active? Which are passive? Make two lists.
2 Look for examples of participles used as adjectives before a noun.

b Explain the following:

1 The use of the present participle in '… the baker's assistant smelt something burning.' (ll. 8-10). Search the text for further examples of the same and translate them all into German.
2 The use of the present participles in 'The strong easterly winds kept the flames advancing. They soon left the whole city burning.' (ll. 19-20). Translate both sentences into German.
3 The participle construction 'But water being scarce away from the banks of the river, there …' (ll. 29-30).

c Expand these participle constructions into relative clauses, adverbial clauses of time or reason, or a clause linked by *and* expressing accompanying circumstances:

1 Finding the house full of smoke, he … (ll. 10-11)
2 …, setting it on fire too. (l. 16)
3 … warehouses packed with flammable materials … (l. 18)
4 Having been sent for by the King, Pepys … (ll. 25-26)
5 Being greatly troubled, the King … (ll. 26-27)
6 … having started the demolition too close to the fires, … (ll. 27-28)
7 … all being reduced to ashes. (l. 32)
8 For three more days the fire raged through the city, destroying 13,200 houses and 87 churches. (ll. 33-34)
9 Having lost everything, many people were reduced … (ll. 35-36)
10 … wooden houses dating back to the medieval period were replaced … (ll. 39-40)

d Write a short summary of the text (about 100 words). Put in as much information as possible, using suitable participle constructions to keep the text as short as possible.

Like a breeze: *Guy Nègre thinks he has
a cure for urban traffic fumes – an
ultralight car that runs on compressed air.*
By William Underhill

It doesn't take much to test the advantages of auto engineer Guy Nègre's latest invention.
Just put your nose near the tailpipe[1] and sniff: no smell, no fumes, but a lungful of cool,
pure air. In downtown Nice, only a few miles from Nègre's factory where one of his
prototype Air Cars is parked, smog-belching traffic fills the streets. If people switched to
5 Nègre's car, which runs on compressed air, the Riviera might once again be a place of
beauty.
Too good to be true? Nègre doesn't think so. After having worked almost ten years on the
project, he expects to start producing air-powered cars early next year. That would give
Motor Development International, the company he founded to exploit his invention, an
10 early lead in the race to replace the combustion engine[2] with a cleaner alternative. The main
competitor – hydrogen-powered cars that produce zero emission – have won the backing of
the big auto companies, but they won't be ready for the road for five years at the very least.
By then, Nègre hopes to have proved the Air Car's potential. [...]

The Air Car certainly wins points for cheapness of fuel. Fresh air, compressed to 4,500
15 pounds per square inch – about 150 times the pressure which is used for the standard car
tire – is stored beneath the chassis[3]; the pressure is used to drive the engine's pistons[4].
Refueling takes just three minutes from a special air pump at a filling station, or up to four
hours at home using a household plug to provide the energy for the car's own compressor.

[...] When Nègre was an engine designer of Formula One racing cars, he learned how
20 compressed air was used to start engines. He began his attempts to design an air-powered
car in the early 1990s. Since big carmakers weren't interested, he pieced together financing
from 150 private investors. Money is tight: the workforce, including Nègre's own son, still
numbers fewer than forty.

To save the planet, the Air Car will first have to catch on[5]. For all its green charms, its
25 performance is less than dazzling[6]: its maximum speed is only 68 miles an hour, so it won't
leave other cars standing. It also needs refueling every 120 miles, making it essentially a
short-distance city car. [...]

The Air Car is designed for the smogbound metropolis of the 21st century, which needs a
cheap, reliable vehicle that won't add to the street-level pollution. [...] He's already
30 patented the idea. Now all he needs is another small army of investors.

From *Newsweek* Special Edition December 2002 – February 2003, Issues 2003

---

1 tailpipe (AE) *Auspuff*   2 combustion engine *Verbrennungsmotor*   3 chassis *Fahrgestell*   4 piston *Kolben*
5 catch on: become popular   6 dazzling: brilliant

a   Look for examples of the following:

1   a participle which combines with another word to form a compound adjective (ll. 1-13)
2   a participle which replaces a relative clause (ll. 14-18)
3   a participle construction which replaces an adverbial clause of time (ll. 1-13)
4   a participle which replaces a relative clause (ll. 19-23)

b   Explain the meaning of these noun phrases using relative clauses:

1   smog-belching traffic (l. 4)
2   compressed air (l. 5)
3   a hydrogen-powered car (l. 11)

c   Change the language.

1   Replace the relative clause in l. 5 with a participle construction.
2   Change the relative clause in l. 11 into a participle construction.
3   Use a participle instead of a relative clause in ll. 15-16.
4   Look for an adverbial clause of reason in ll. 14-23 and replace it with a participle construction with its own subject.
5   Rewrite the following sentence using a relative clause:
    'It also needs refueling every 120 miles, making it essentially a short-distance city car.'
6   Rewrite the following sentence, using a participle construction beginning with 'Though ...':
    'Hydrogen-powered cars have won the backing of the big auto companies, but they won't be ready for the road for five years at the very least.'

d   Explain the use of the present participle in the following:

1   '... or up to four hours at home using a household plug ...' (ll. 17-18)
2   '... it won't leave other cars standing.' (ll. 25-26)

e   Complete the sentences about the text, using a participle or participle construction in each. There are, of course, many possible answers.

1   An Air Car is a new kind of car ...
2   The main competitor of the Air Car is ...
3   Motor Development International is ...

f   Write a summary about the Air Car (about 8 lines), discussing its advantages and disadvantages. Use participle constructions as much as possible.

The noun

A **Choose the correct form from the brackets.**

1 If you need (some/an) advice about university courses, talk to Mr Johnson.
2 Where have you put (next week's TV guide/the TV guide of next week)?
3 You can't miss the post office. It's at (the street's end /the end of the street).
4 The United States (consist of/consists of) a large number of different ethnic groups.
5 My little brother hates going (to the dentist/to the dentist's).
6 I can't find the scissors anywhere. Has anybody seen (it/them)?
7 I'm just reading a critical (analyses/analysis) of Arthur Miller's plays.
8 (Women's/Womens') tennis has become much more competitive in the last few years.

B **Translate the German sentence parts into English.**

9 *(Die Japaner sind bekannt* [known]*)* ... for their electronics entertainment systems.
10 Christine phoned to say she'll be home late. *(Sie ist bei einer Freundin.)* ...
11 *(Dies ist das Zimmer von Jerry.)* ... It's always a mess, I'm afraid.
12 *(Ich trinke nie mehr als zwei Tassen Kaffee.)* ... I can't sleep if I do.
13 *(Nach* [according to] *welchen Kriterien)* ... are the students' applications assessed[1]?
14 Sarah lives in a village in the Cotswolds. *(Die Umgebung ist sehr schön.)* ...
15 *(Barbaras Freund ist Schweizer.)* ... He comes from Geneva.
16 When you go to the supermarket, remember *(eine Tube Zahnpasta zu kaufen.)* ...
17 *(Die Geschichte Englands)* ... has been strongly influenced by religious quarrels.
18 *(Wo ist die Zeitung von gestern)* ...? I haven't read it yet.
19 *(Goldie ist die Katze unserer Nachbarn.)* ... She doesn't get on very well with our dog.
20 Do you think that *(diese Treppe sicher ist)* ...?

C **Spot the mistakes. There is one mistake in each sentence or sentence pair.**

21 What time are the news on TV?
22 The English teacher doesn't give us as many homeworks as the maths teacher.
23 Does anybody know where my binoculars is?
24 All the rooms' doors were closed, so we couldn't go in.
25 It's my parent's wedding anniversary tomorrow. We're all going out to dinner.
26 Can you give me some informations about language courses in Ireland?
27 Can you tell me which floor childrens' shoes are on, please?
28 I didn't think of selling my old CDs on the Internet. It was the idea of my sister.
29 Your blue pyjamas is in the washing machine, I'm afraid.
30 I bought these cakes at the new baker on the corner of Ash Street.
31 The next village isn't far. It's about a twenty minutes drive from here.
32 Do you like my room's colour? I painted it myself.
33 Physics have always been my favourite subject.
34 The latest economic crises in Britain is a matter of great concern.
35 Could we have a beer and two coffee, please?
36 Is it true that clothes is cheaper in the US than in Germany?

---

1 assess *einschätzen, bewerten*

The noun

? **Correct yourself**

A 1: *some*   2: *next week's TV guide*   3: *the end of the street*   4: *consists of*   5: *to the dentist's*
6: *them*   7: *analysis*   8: *Women's*

B 9: *The Japanese are known …*   10: *She's at a friend's.*   11: *This is Jerry's room.*   12: *I never
drink more than two cups of coffee.*   13: *According to which criteria …*   14: *The surroundings are
very beautiful.*   15: *Barbara's boyfriend is a Swiss.*   16: *… to buy a tube of toothpaste.*
17: *England's history/the history of England …*   18: *Where is yesterday's paper?*   19: *Goldie is
our neighbours' cat.*   20: *… these stairs are safe?*

C 21: *What time is the news on TV?*
22: *The English teacher doesn't give us as much homework as the maths teacher.*
23: *Does anybody know where my binoculars are?*
24: *All the doors of the rooms were closed, so we couldn't go in.*
25: *It's my parents' wedding anniversary tomorrow. We're all going out to dinner.*
26: *Can you give me some information about language courses in Ireland?*
27: *Can you tell me which floor children's shoes are on, please?*
28: *I didn't think of selling my old CDs on the Internet. It was my sister's idea.*
29: *Your blue pyjamas are in the washing machine, I'm afraid.*
30: *I bought these cakes at the new baker's on the corner of Ash Street.*
31: *The next village isn't far. It's about a twenty minutes' drive from here.*
32: *Do you like the colour of my room? I painted it myself.*
33: *Physics has always been my favourite subject.*
34: *The latest economic crisis in Britain is a matter of great concern.*
35: *Could we have a beer and two coffees, please?*
36: *Is it true that clothes are cheaper in the US than in Germany?*

Exercise finder

Sentences	CEG	Exercises
1, 22, 26	▶ 177c	▶ 5, 7
2, 18, 31	▶ 179e	▶ 6, 7
3, 17, 24, 32	▶ 180a	▶ 6, 7
4, 21, 33	▶ 177d	▶ 3
5, 10, 30	▶ 179c	▶ 6
6, 23, 29	▶ 175a	▶ 3, 7
7, 13, 34	▶ 174	▶ 1
8, 19, 27	▶ 179a	▶ 6, 7
9, 15	▶ 173	▶ 2
11, 25, 28	▶ 179b	▶ 6, 7
12, 16, 35	▶ 177b	▶ 4, 7
14, 20, 36	▶ 175b	▶ 3, 7

1 *Words, words, words* **regular/irregular/foreign plurals** ▶ **171, 172, 174**

a Study the following words carefully, then write them in three lists:

Examples: 1 words in the plural: ***bacteria*** …
2 words in the singular: ***city*** …
3 words which are both singular and plural: ***crossroads*** …

> analysis ▪ ~~bacteria~~ ▪ ~~city~~ ▪ crisis ▪ criterion ▪ ~~crossroads~~ ▪ life ▪ means ▪
> media ▪ passers-by ▪ phenomena ▪ roof ▪ series ▪ sheep ▪ spacecraft ▪ species ▪
> studio ▪ teeth ▪ tomato ▪ women

b 1 Write the plural forms of the words in a) which are in the singular.
2 Write the singular forms of the words in a) which are in the plural.

c Complete the sentences with words from a) in the correct form.

1 For me, a car is only a … of getting from A to B. For some people, it's a way of life.
2 What … are used by teachers to assess a pupil's suitability[1] for university study?
3 I don't watch soap operas, but there are a few crime … that I sometimes watch.
4 The students were asked to present a written … of the computer data.
5 At the Air and Space Museum in Washington we saw various … including Apollo 11, Voyager and Skylab 4.
6 The giant panda is unfortunately becoming a rare …
7 We were held up on a narrow country road, waiting for some … to cross.
8 Widespread[2] interest in reality TV has become a … of our modern society.
9 In England, all … were given the right to vote in 1928.
10 In 16th century England, … were hardly used in cooking. They were suspected to be poisonous.
11 Susan's baby has already got two …
12 English country cottages often have thatched[3] …

2 *What nationality were they?* **nationality words** ▶ **173**

a What nationality were the following famous people? Use nationality nouns (e.g. *a German*).
Discuss in class who they were and what they are famous for. If you're not sure, use the Internet.

1 Pablo Picasso	5 Maria Teresia	9 Roald Amundsen	13 Alfred Nobel
2 Marie Curie	6 Maria Montessori	10 Sir Alexander Fleming	14 Emperor Hirohito
3 Indira Gandhi	7 Deng Xiao Ping	11 Nicolas Copernicus	15 van Gogh
4 Maxim Gorki	8 Franz Liszt	12 Socrates	16 James Joyce

---

1 suitability *Eignung* 2 widespread: existing in a large area, among many people
3 thatched: made of dried straw

b What are the people from the following countries famous for? Think of as many things as you can, e.g. culture, music, consumer goods, food, drink. Use nationality nouns in the plural.

1 England	4 Greece	7 Japan	10 Spain
2 France	5 Holland	8 Russia	11 Switzerland
3 Germany	6 Italy	9 Scotland	12 Turkey

Example: **The Germans** *are famous for their beer and their engineering.*

c If you were not a German, which nationality would you like to be? Give your reasons in a short paragraph.

Example: *I might like to be* **an American**. *I think* **the Americans** *have a more relaxed lifestyle than* **the Germans**.

3 *More words*   pair/plural/collective/uncountable nouns   ▶ **175, 176, 177d**

a Put the following words into three groups according to the verb which follows. Must the verb be singular, plural, or can it be either singular or plural?

> band ▪ belongings ▪ cattle ▪ ~~class~~ ▪ ~~clothes~~ ▪ crowd ▪ family ▪ glasses ▪
> goods ▪ government ▪ jeans ▪ maths ▪ news ▪ ~~physics~~ ▪ police ▪ politics ▪
> scissors ▪ shorts ▪ surroundings ▪ team ▪ the USA

Examples: 1 verb always singular: *physics* …
2 verb always plural: *clothes* …
3 verb singular and plural: *class* …

b Look for the 'pair nouns' in a) and write them down using *a pair of*.

c Complete the sentences with the correct form and tense of the verbs in brackets. If you think both singular and plural forms are possible, write both.

1 Who says maths (be) … boring?
2 How much (the jeans in the window – cost) … , please?
3 We're British, but all my family (speak) … French. We lived in Paris for eight years.
4 I read that the USA (have) … serious economic problems at present.
5 I find it hard to believe that (politics – not – interest) … you at all.
6 The concert must be over. Look, the band (leave) … the stage now.
7 My glasses (not – be) … strong enough. I can't read the small print.
8 Apparently the police (already – arrest) … a suspect in connection with the kidnapping case.
9 When (be) … the news on Channel Four?
10 I'm afraid the scissors (not – cut) … paper very well.
11 When I was in Rome, all my belongings (steal) … from my car.
12 The new shorts that I bought (not – fit) very well. I must lose a bit of weight.
13 Clothes (be) … very important to most of my friends, but I spend my money on other things.
14 The government (think) … that Britain's immigration problems can be solved with a new EU law.
15 I think our team (be) … pretty good. We've won all our matches this season so far.

4 *Food and drinks* **uncountable nouns**

 **177a/b**

a Alan and Kate are planning to ask four friends to a barbecue. Complete the dialogue with suitable words and phrases. Use *some*, *a/an*, numbers and countable units (*pound, bottle, can*, etc.). Write as many suitable answers as you can. If it is not necessary to add a word/phrase, write '–'.

Examples: Alan: We'll grill – /*some* sausages, as usual I expect. How **many/many pounds** shall I buy?

Kate: Enough. Leo can eat **a pound of** sausages on his own.

Kate: Get (1) … pork chops too, and (2) … hamburger steaks perhaps. And buy (3) … sauce for the meat. Something spicy and something with chilli or garlic.

Alan: OK. Could you make (4) … tomato salad? Everybody likes that.

Kate: All right. And what about drinks? We'll need (5) … cola. Quite a lot, I expect. And get (6) … orange juice too.

Alan: And how about (7) … ice cream for dessert?

Kate: Good idea. Get (8) … vanilla ice cream and we can have it with strawberries.

b You are in a café in England with a group of friends. Two of you want cola, one wants orange juice, two want coffee, one wants mineral water, two want strawberry ice cream and you would like some tea. Give the waitress the order. Begin with *We'd like two …*

5 *Mini-dialogues* **uncountable nouns**

 **177a-c**

a Which of the following nouns are uncountable? Write them down, then choose the words and phrases in brackets which can be used to complete the dialogues. Sometimes more than one word or phrase is correct.

> accident ▪ accommodation ▪ damage ▪ furniture ▪ information ▪ job ▪
> music ▪ pollution ▪ progress ▪ sun ▪ traffic ▪ travel ▪ trip ▪ weather ▪ work

1 A: Our holiday was great. We had (a very good/some very good) accommodation. The flat was quite big, and all the furniture (were/was) new.
   B: And what about the weather?
   A: Well, we had (an awful/awful) weather for three days, then it improved. We didn't have (a/any/much) sun, but it was warm and pleasant.
2 A: Has Mike found (a/ –) work yet? Or is he still looking for (some/a) job?
   B: Well, you know that he loves (the/ –) music, don't you? He's helping out as a DJ at the moment.
3 A: Dave is thinking about going on (a/ –) trip to the Himalayas, trekking.
   B: Really? (A / Some/ –) travel to that part of the world requires a lot of careful planning. He ought to get (some/a) really reliable information from a good travel agency.
4 A: There was hardly (a/any) traffic in town this morning.
   B: There were (some/a lot of/much) accidents on the motorway last night because of fog. (A lot of/Many) damage was caused.
5 A: Karen does voluntary work for an environmental group, doesn't she?
   B: Yes, she does. She says there's still (a lot of/a/many) pollution locally, but her group has made (a good/some good/good/many good) progress.

b In English, please. Sometimes more than one translation is possible. Use uncountable words and the phrase *a bit/piece of* … where suitable.

Example: Ich brauche eine zuverlässige Auskunft.
*I need **some** reliable **information**. /
I need **a bit/piece of** reliable **information**.*

1 Ein Freund gab mir einen guten Ratschlag.
2 Diese Hausaufgaben sind schwierig.
3 Ich habe eine gute Nachricht für dich.
4 Ich bekam viele nützliche Informationen.
5 Die Polizei hat neue Beweise gefunden.

6 *What's the name of the store?* possessive form, *of*-phrase ▶ **179, 180a/b**

a Use the word(s) in brackets in the correct form or order to make a possessive form or the *of*-phrase. Change endings or add words where necessary.

Kate: It's (1 birthday – my brother) … tomorrow. I'd like to get him a leather belt.

Emma: Oh, I saw some really nice ones last week, not expensive, but I can't remember (2 name – store) … where I saw them. Actually, I was on the way to a (3 friend) …

Kate: Well, do you know (4 name – street) … where you were shopping?

Emma: No, but I think I could take you there. The store's next to a (5 hairdresser) … and it's opposite an Italian restaurant, I think.

Kate: And what was (6 Italian restaurant – name) …?

Emma: I'm not sure, but it was at (7 street – end) … It could have been (8 Luigi) … or something like that. The belts were in the (9 department – men) … on the second floor. I bought a few things in the (10 ladies – department) … , a blouse, a T-shirt and some trousers. You won't believe (11 blouse – price) … It was really cheap. Just £10.99. They had a whole range of styles in (12 colours – this season) … There was a (13 chemist) … quite close too. I bought some sunscreen. Well, I'm going to my (14 aunt) … now. I hope you'll find the store. See you later.

b Translate the German phrases into English using the possessive form or the *of*-phrase. If you think both are possible, write both.

1 der beste Freund von James
2 die Wirtschaft Irlands
3 die Kinder von Freunden, die in Leeds wohnen
4 die Bewerbungen der Studenten
5 die Entscheidung der Regierung
6 die Zeitung von heute
7 Frauenzeitschriften
8 der Sohn der Leute, die nebenan eingezogen sind
9 die Adresse von Lisa und Patrick
10 die Bedeutung dieses Wortes
11 Kinderbücher
12 mein Taschengeld vom letzten Monat

Read the text and carry out the tasks which follow.

Elizabeth I was the daughter of King Henry VIII and his second wife, Anne Boleyn. She reigned for 45 years and has even been called a great queen because the country enjoyed progress
5   throughout most of her reign (1558-1603).

England's population was mainly rural[1]. People worked as farmers or craftsmen[2]. Cities with their crowded, dirty, narrow streets were unhealthy, and unsafe places after dark. Travel
10 by coach was dangerous at any time. There were no police in Tudor England, but criminals were severely punished. In the small, dark, wooden houses of the time there was not much furniture, only a few stools[3] and a table. The rich built timber-framed houses[4]. The rooms of their houses were spacious[5] with much bigger windows and wood-panelled walls.
15 The children of rich people generally received an education at home, although boys often went to 'grammar' schools, learning mostly Latin grammar, religion and geography. Girls' education took place at home with private tutors. Poor children seldom went to school.

For the rich, looks were very important. Clothes showed status, wealth or high rank. Small children of both sexes wore long dresses. Later they were dressed as adults. At court[6], clothes
20 were heavy, elaborate and impractical. Men wore tights, often jewellery or even make-up – but always a sword. Hair was very important for both men and women. Styles changed with the fashion. Beards were kept in fashion too, carefully trimmed in many different shapes. Men spent hours at the barber's being powdered, perfumed or dyed. Wigs were fashionable. Elizabeth was thought to have lost her hair when ill with smallpox[7]. She wore a red wig.

25 Ordinary people ate mainly meat and bread. The potato, first brought to Britain by Sir Walter Raleigh from America, was still new. Rich people ate a variety of foods, including fish, deer[8], wild boar, fruit and vegetables. Cakes and puddings were sweetened with honey. Imported goods such as sugar were very expensive. Tea and coffee were still unknown. The taste of chocolate was bitter, so it was drunk only as a medicine, and very rarely.

30 Society saw the growth of the merchant[9] class, and with it a spread[10] in culture. Art, music and dancing, theatre and poetry were cultivated. Plays were acted in rich people's houses, and later in London's theatres. Rich and poor enjoyed games and festivities. Christmas was a particularly merry time. On the other
35 hand, people watched cruel sports such as cockfighting and bear-baiting, which even Elizabeth was said to enjoy. People believed in the supernatural, in ghosts, witches, elves and fairies.

40 This was Elizabeth's and also Shakespeare's England.

Based on 'Life in Elizabethan England' by Maggie Secara

---

1 rural: living in the country   2 craftsman: skilled person who makes things by hand   3 stool *Hocker*
4 timber-framed houses *Fachwerkhäuser*   5 spacious: large   6 court *Hof*   7 smallpox *die Pocken*
8 deer *Hirsch/Reh*   9 merchant *Kaufmann*   10 spread *Verbreitung*

a 1 Write the plural form of the following nouns from the text. Remember that some nouns have the same form in the plural.

  child ▪ city ▪ coach ▪ deer ▪ dress ▪ elf ▪ fairy ▪ furniture ▪ potato ▪ witch

 2 Which of these words is called a 'pair noun'? How many others do you know? Write them down.

  clothes ▪ looks ▪ goods ▪ tights

 3 Write a sentence each using the words *hair* and *hairs*.

b 1 Make a list of uncountable nouns used in ll. 1-14.
 2 Write the following 'food' nouns as countable nouns with a suitable phrase such as *a kilo of …*, etc. There is more than one possibility.

  bread ▪ coffee ▪ honey ▪ meat ▪ sugar

c 1 Write down the possessive forms used in the text, then rewrite them using the *of*-phrase.
 2 Look for the *of*-phrases in the text. Only one of them could be expressed with a possessive form.
   Which one? Explain why the other possessive forms cannot be expressed with an *of*-phrase.

d Translate into English.

 1 Am Hof war das Aussehen sehr wichtig.
 2 Die Kleidung war kompliziert und aufwendig *(elaborate)*.
 3 In Hofkreisen *(court circles)* waren die Haare für Männer und Frauen sehr wichtig.
 4 Elisabeth war schlank *(slim)* mit blasser *(pale)* Haut und roten Haaren.
 5 Das Benehmen entsprach *(correspond to)* nicht immer unserer Vorstellung *(idea)* von guten Manieren *(manners)*.
 6 Während der Herrschaft Elisabeths wurden viele soziale und wirtschaftliche Fortschritte erzielt *(make)*.

e In your own words, write what you know about clothes, fashion and hair at the court of Elizabeth I. Compare these aspects with those of today's society.

f Would you like to have lived in Elizabethan times? Write a few paragraphs, saying why or why not. Consider such aspects as education, work, social class, food, housing, travel, etc. Use information from the text and from any other sources.

The article

A **Complete the sentences with *a/an* or *the* where necessary.**

1 I expect you're planning to go to … university next year, aren't you?
2 My sister plays four instruments, so she would like to take up music as … career.
3 … pollution has become one of modern society's greatest problems.
4 My new boyfriend is … non-smoker, so I'm going to stop smoking now.
5 Sherlock Holmes is supposed to have lived in … Baker Street in London.
6 … school I go to is old and traditional, but it has high academic standards.
7 My best friend plays … violin in the County Youth Orchestra.
8 Most of my friends who left school before A-levels are without … job.
9 I can't go faster than 50 miles … hour in my old Mini.
10 … tradition has prevented many societies from developing modern values.
11 We always go on holiday in … August – when it's crowded everywhere.
12 The postman comes about 9.30 as … rule, but he's much later today.

B **Translate the German sentence parts in brackets into English.**

13 *(Die meisten Bewerber* [applicants]*)* … for a place at Oxford University are from private schools.
14 *(Was für eine Überraschung!)* … I haven't seen you for months.
15 My father isn't at home yet. *(Er ist noch bei der Arbeit.)* …
16 Layla would like to work *(als Ingenieurin)* … in a developing country for a few years.
17 Susan called, but she couldn't stay long. *(Sie war in Eile)* …, as always.
18 *(Mein Bruder studiert Physik an der Universität.)* … He's in his second year.
19 My sister doesn't eat much. *(Mein Bruder isst die zweifache Menge* [amount]*.)* …
20 Zip-off cargo pants *(sind in Mode gekommen.)* … Everybody's wearing them.
21 Don't go out *(ohne Jacke.)* … The forecast says temperatures are going to drop today.
22 I've got a cousin in New York *(der in der Nähe vom Central Park wohnt.)* …
23 My sister came to visit us yesterday. *(Die beiden Kinder kamen auch.)* …
24 *(Wie viele Zigaretten rauchst du am Tag?)* … Not more than ten, I hope.

C **Spot the mistakes. There is one mistake in each sentence or sentence pair.**

25 The accident happened on Saturday before my birthday.
26 The advanced technology has made our lives more comfortable than ever.
27 Our English teacher has written a quite interesting article for the local paper.
28 My sister goes to an African dance class twice the week.
29 My boyfriend is member of the local cricket team. He's a good player.
30 Sir Edmund Hillary and Sherpa Tensing Norgay climbed the Mount Everest in 1953.
31 The bed and breakfast place we booked was great. We had a such nice room.
32 I heard on the news that the petrol prices are expected to go up again early next month.
33 My father always reads the morning paper during the breakfast, so nobody says much.
34 Our holiday was fantastic, but unfortunately all good things come to end.
35 When we were in London, we visited the Buckingham Palace and did the tour.

The article

? ► **Correct yourself**

A ► 1: –   2: *a*   3: –   4: *a*   5: –   6: *The*   7: *the*   8: *a*   9: *an*   10: –   11: –   12: *a*

B ► 13: *Most (of the) applicants …*   14: *What a surprise!*   15: *He's still at work.*   16: *… as an engineer …*   17: *She was in a hurry …*   18: *My brother is studying physics at university.*   19: *My brother eats twice/double the amount.*   20: *… have come into fashion.*   21: *… without a jacket.*   22: *… who lives close to/near Central Park.*   23: *Both the children came too.*   24: *How many cigarettes do you smoke a day?*

C ► 25: *The accident happened on the Saturday before my birthday.*
26: *Advanced technology has made our lives more comfortable than ever.*
27: *Our English teacher has written quite an interesting article for the local paper.*
28: *My sister goes to an African dance class twice a week.*
29: *My boyfriend is a member of the local cricket team …*
30: *Sir Edmund Hillary and Sherpa Tensing Norgay climbed Mount Everest in 1953.*
31: *… We had such a nice room.*
32: *I heard on the news that petrol prices are expected to go up …*
33: *My father always reads the morning paper during breakfast, …*
34: *Our holiday was fantastic, but unfortunately all good things come to an end.*
35: *When we were in London, we visited Buckingham Palace and did the tour.*

► **Exercise finder**

Sentences	CEG	Exercises
1, 6, 18	► 184	► 2, 5, 7
2, 8, 21	► 191	► 4, 5, 6, 7
3, 10, 26, 32	► 183	► 1, 4, 5, 6, 7
4, 16, 29	► 190	► 4, 5, 6, 7
5, 22, 30, 35	► 185	► 3, 4, 5, 7
7, 15, 20	► 188	► 2, 3, 4
9, 24, 28	► 192	► 4, 5, 7
11, 25, 33	► 186	► 3, 4, 5
12, 17, 34	► 195	► 4
13, 19, 23	► 187	► 4, 5
14, 27, 31	► 194	► 4, 5

1 *Mini-dialogues*   *the* **with abstract/material nouns and nouns in the plural**   ▶ **183**

Complete the mini-dialogues using the word in brackets with or without *the*.

Examples: A: ***Poetry*** doesn't really interest me, but I like ***the poetry*** of Robert Frost.
B: So do I. I like the way he makes you think about ***nature***.

1 A: (crime) is one of the biggest problems in cities, so I suppose we can be glad that we live in a small town
.

B: True. (crime) we get locally is mainly vandalism and car thefts. I don't like (city life). (pollution), (traffic), (noise) – all things that we can do without.

2 A: Joe has a very unconventional lifestyle, but he doesn't care what (people) think of him.

B: I don't think (people) in our neighbourhood think much about others at all. (life) is too full of problems.

3 A: (pizza) you bought at the supermarket was really good.

B: Yes, but (pizza) is best when you bake it yourself, fresh from the oven. Mum always makes it herself, but (cooking) isn't really my thing. (food) I make isn't all that bad, though, is it?

4 A: I read that (industry) is producing less economic growth than expected in Europe.

B: That's not true of all branches. (tourist industry), for example, is expecting to have a boom year.

5 A: My parents hate (music) my brother plays, and he plays it all day. They're always complaining about (noise).

B: It's the same at our house. (music) is my brother's favourite hobby too.

6 A: (coffee) is quite expensive now. Prices have gone up again recently.

B: Have you tried (coffee) they serve at the café in Barnes Road? It's great and not expensive. I don't usually eat (cake), but (cakes) they make there are delicious too.

7 A: (paper) is something we take for granted, isn't it?

B: You're right. Did you know that it takes about six trees to make (paper) that each of us throws away every year?

A: I'm not surprised. (waste) we produce in (developed countries) is scandalous.

8 A: Many EU governments are gradually fading out (nuclear power). I suppose that means that (electricity) will be more expensive in future.

B: Not necessarily. In future, more of (electricity) that we use in Europe will come from renewable sources in the form of (wind power), (wave power) and (solar power).

a   What's missing? Complete the sentences with the missing phrase, i.e. with the correct preposition and noun (*hospital, university, prison, court,* etc.), with or without *the*.

Example: I overslept this morning. When the school bus passed our house, I was still *in bed*.

1   My best friend had a bad accident last week. He had to be taken …
2   Dad hasn't come home yet. There's a lot to do at the office, so he will still be …
3   I don't read a daily newspaper. I always watch the news …
4   When I'm driving long distances, I usually listen to the traffic reports …
5   Next year Trish would like to study microbiology …
6   Dave lost his driver's licence and he hates flying, so he always goes from London to Edinburgh …
7   We always watch the latest films on video or DVD. We seldom go …
8   I don't go out much in the week. I usually have too much homework. So I just stay …
9   Doug Jenkins has been arrested for theft four times. Next time he will be sent …
10 The police think Smith committed the robbery, but there isn't enough evidence to take the case …
11 Shall we go to see a Shakespeare play at the Globe? – Good idea. Let's go …
12 How did you manage to get a flat right in the heart of London? You're so lucky to live …

b   Choose the correct phrase from the brackets.

1   (The school/School) is sometimes out earlier on Fridays. We all go to (the school/school) in Blackmoor Road. It's the big comprehensive next to (the church/church).
2   When my sister had her appendix[1] out, I had to take piles of books to (hospital/the hospital) every day. She was in (the hospital/hospital) on Queen's Road.

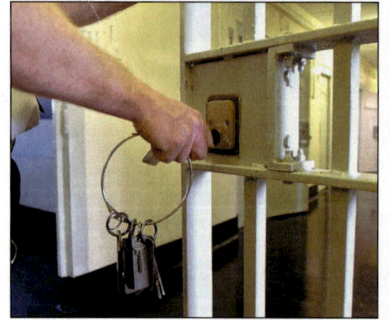

3   If I pass all my exams, I'll leave (the university/ university) next summer and get my first job.
4   Our neighbour works in (prison/the prison). He's a chef[2] in the kitchen.
5   Janet goes to (college/the college) not far from the town hall. It's a secretarial college, I think.

c   Make up a short story about someone's life using the words *school, class, university/college, church, hospital, court, prison* with and without an article. Use your imagination. Your story can be humorous, if you wish.

---

1 appendix *Blinddarm*   2 chef *Koch*

a Heike is planning a trip to London. Her English friend Emma is giving her some tips.
Complete the dialogue with *the* where necessary.

Emma: Well, you've got a lot of options. There's so much to do by (1) … day and at (2) … night. You're going in (3) … July, so take my advice, don't go sightseeing at (4) … weekend. It's terribly crowded. My American boyfriend was in London in (5) … July of 2001. He came to visit me one weekend from (6) … Friday to (7) … Monday. He said it looked as if London's 25 million annual visitors were all there at the same time. I suppose you will do the usual sights first, like a tour of (8) … Buckingham Palace, for example. Set off early in (9) … morning. For (10) … breakfast at the hotel you should take (11) … full English breakfast, that means eggs, bacon, sausages and lots more. You won't want much for (12) … lunch after that.
So, you can go by (13) … tube to (14) … Green Park. You come out not far from (15) … Ritz Hotel. Then go up (16) … Mall, that's the long avenue leading up to the Palace. You must have seen it on (17) … TV. Don't miss (18) … Changing of the Guard at 11.30. After that you could walk through (19) … Hyde Park, then take a bus. I can't remember which number, but it will take you past (20) … Marble Arch, down (21) … Oxford Street, to (22) … Piccadilly Circus and up to (23) … Trafalgar Square. You could get off and walk around there. If you stay on the same bus route, you'll see (24) … Old Bailey and (25) … St. Paul's Cathedral. And from there you can get to (26) … Tower of London and (27) … Tower Bridge. You can see (28) … Houses of Parliament and (29) … Westminster Abbey another day. And you must take a boat trip on (30) … Thames, past (31) … London Eye, etc. It's great if the weather's nice.

Heike: I'll have to write all that down. And what shall we do in (32) … evening?

Emma: Well, I think you'll be glad to fall into (33) … bed.

b Have you ever been to London? What sights did you see? Write a short paragraph.

c Write a list of the famous sights and places in New York. Remember to include parks, streets, hotels, rivers, museums, etc. Don't forget *the* where it is part of the name. Check your list with a partner or with the class.

4 *Correct the mistakes* **definite/indefinite article: mixed ex.** ▶ **183, 185-188, 190-192, 194, 195**

Only two of the sentences or sentence pairs are correct. Which are they? There is one mistake in each of the others. Study the sentences carefully and correct them.

1 Do scientists really know how the life began?
2 My brother's going to change his job. He's been offered the double salary with a firm in Leeds.
3 I'm helping out at a petrol station three nights the week for some extra cash.
4 Peter works as systems analyst for ACB, I think.
5 Have you ever looked round the British Museum in London? It's fascinating.
6 As result of the train strike in Italy, many tourists were stranded and couldn't get home.
7 Winchester is a quite nice town with a very interesting history.
8 All the pupils have got offers of university places in England, with exception of Peter, who wants to study abroad.
9 My sister is very musical. She plays guitar and the keyboard and she writes songs as well.
10 Jenny's invited all the class to a party on the Saturday.
11 Psychologists fear that some children may confuse cyber figures in computer games with real life.
12 The most pupils in my class have got their own bank account and their own mobile.
13 In New York we had hash browns, eggs Benedict, even blueberry muffins for the breakfast.
14 I'll lend you twenty pounds on the condition that you give me the money back by next Saturday.
15 Which famous person lives on the Pennsylvania Avenue in Washington?
16 We didn't really enjoy our touring holiday in the US. The half time we were sitting in the bus.

5 *Going to university* **definite/indefinite article: mixed ex.** ▶ **183-187, 190-192, 194**

a Beth is visiting an aunt in Scotland. Complete the conversation with *a/an* or *the* in the correct place. If you think no article is necessary, write '–'.

Aunt: What are you going to do after (1) … school?

Beth: I'd like to go to (2) … university. With Mum being (3) … dentist and Dad (4) … doctor, they would like me to go into (5) … medicine too. But I hate hospitals. In (6) … April last year I broke my arm and had to go to (7) … hospital for a few days. What (8) … unpleasant experience! I'm (9) … such … coward.

Aunt: Does your dad still work at (10) … hospital next to (11) … church?

Beth: That's right. At (12) … St. James's in (13) … Bristol Road. He's always very busy. He usually works seven days (14) … week, even if he's not on duty[1].

Aunt: So what do you want to be?

Beth: I'd like to take up engineering as (15) … career.

---
1 on duty *im Dienst*

Aunt: Really? Isn't that unusual for a girl?

Beth: No, not any more. (16) … most of … girls I know want to study languages, history or sociology, but (17) … quite … large number are interested in maths and physics too. Medicine would take longer than engineering. You have a lot of practicals to do.

Aunt: So you'll be finished in (18) … half … time if you do engineering.

Beth: Well, no, not quite. (19) … both … subjects are hard work, but (20) … life at university will be lots of fun, I'm sure. Just imagine, (21) … freedom, (22) … choice, (23) … responsibility – all the things that you never really have as (24) … pupil living at home.

b Answer the following questions in a paragraph, using some of the words given in brackets. Pay attention to the use of *a/an* and *the*.

- What would you like to be one day? What course of study will be necessary?
- How many pupils in your class would like to go to university?
- What do the boys want to study? What do the girls want to study? *(quite – half – all – most of)*
- What aspects of university life do you expect to find most attractive? (Refer to Beth's last sentences for ideas.)

6 *The 'American Dream'* definite/indefinite article: mixed ex. ▶ **183, 190, 191**

a The text explains the background to the concept of the 'American Dream' and its influence on American values. Complete the text with *a/an*, *the* or '–'.

The United States has always been considered (1) … country of unlimited possibilities, a place where a dishwasher could become (2) … millionaire. Famous examples are Henry Ford, John D. Rockefeller, Thomas Edison, Andrew Carnegie and many others. This belief in (3) … material success has come to be known as the 'American Dream'.

Its origins date back to (4) … Puritan settlers of the 17th century, who believed in (5) … predestination[1]. To be born as one of God's 'chosen people' meant to receive salvation[2], and (6) … material success in (7) … life was considered evidence of this. (8) … hard work, a virtuous[3] life and (9) … struggle against (10) … poverty and (11) … temptation[4] were the Puritan values. These values produced a work ethic that regarded (12) … material success as (13) … reward for being virtuous.

American literature has often taken (14) … critical interest in this subject. In *The Grapes of Wrath* (1939), Steinbeck portrays[5] (15) … farming families of the American Midwest who lost their lives and their livelihood in (16) … great drought[6] of the 1930s. [...]
Scott Fitzgerald's *The Great Gatsby* (1925) looks critically at the other side of the American Dream, namely (17) … lives of the rich. Here, Fitzgerald depicts[7] (18) … corruption and (19) … moral decline that often accompany (20) … material success.

The American Dream and (21) … hope it offers of a better future and of personal and economic improvement, remains a positive motivating force for working Americans of all social classes.
In the business world, the United States continues to be a land of (22) … opportunity where (23) … hard work can be rewarded with profit and success. This belief in (24) … success has helped make the United States synonymous with (25) … progress and (26) … innovation in the areas of (27) … science and technology and (28) … business.

From *Economics in the Modern World* by M. Krämer & Dr. H. Mühlmann

b Discuss the concept of the 'American Dream' in class. Then write a short paragraph on your understanding of it. Think of more examples of persons who made the 'American Dream' come true, e.g. Arnold Schwarzenegger. Take care with the use of the article when using abstract nouns.

---

1 predestination *Schicksalsbestimmung*   2 salvation *Erlösung*   3 virtuous *tugendhaft*   4 temptation *Versuchung*   5 portray *darstellen*   6 drought [draut] *Dürre*   7 depict *schildern*

Read the text, then carry out the tasks.

The life of Shakespeare is comparatively well documented. He was born in 1564, in Henley Street, Stratford-upon-Avon. His father was a glove maker and a wool dealer. Wool had become an important commercial product. John
5 Shakespeare had a good run of success as a merchant and he later became the mayor of Stratford.

We know that William went to school from the age of 7 to 14. The school he attended was the 'grammar school', where classes concentrated on Latin grammar and the
10 ancient classics of Greece and Rome. Later Shakespeare had to be taken from school due to his family's financial difficulties. He never completed his education, which makes his subsequent accomplishments[1] all the more remarkable.

15 At the age of 18 Shakespeare married Anne Hathaway. The marriage may have been forced, as Anne was pregnant[2] with a daughter, Susanna. This first child was followed by twins, Hamnet and Judith, in 1585. Hamnet died as a child.
The next seven years of Shakespeare's life are a mystery, though he is thought to have worked as a school teacher. Some time before 1592, Shakespeare left his home and family to
20 lead the life of an actor in London.

London's theatres were closed in January 1593 due to an outbreak of the plague[3], and many players left the capital to tour the provinces. Shakespeare preferred to stay in London, and it was during this time that he began to gain recognition as a writer, mainly of poetry.

When the theatres reopened in late 1594, Shakespeare was no longer a simple actor, but a
25 playwright as well, writing and performing for the theatre company. Shakespeare became an investor in the company, and made his fortune. For the next 17 years he produced an average of two plays a year.

The company constructed a new circular theatre on the south bank of the River Thames, called the Globe. The Globe remained London's premier theatre until it burned down in
30 1613 during a performance of Shakespeare's *Henry VIII*. A cannon shot set the thatched roof[4] of the gallery on fire.

Life in Shakespeare's day was hard for the common people, but the life of an actor or playwright could be financially rewarding. Shakespeare held a share in the profits from the Globe, which gave him an excellent annual income. He bought New Place, the house in
35 Stratford to which he retired[5] around 1611. Shakespeare died in April 1616 and was buried in Holy Trinity Church, Stratford.

Visitors to London should see a Shakespeare play at the present Globe Theatre which was completed in 1996, very close to the original site[6]. The theatre is reconstructed as it was in Shakespeare's time, that is, with wooden benches for spectators in the galleries, an open
40 yard without a roof, and a stage without a curtain.

Adapted from 'The Shakespeare Biography' by David Ross

---

1 accomplishment: achievement   2 pregnant: expecting a child   3 the plague *die Pest*   4 thatched roof *Strohdach*
5 retire: stop working and live a quieter life   6 site: place where a building is or was situated

a 1 Look for examples of *a/an* in ll. 1-19 where the use of the indefinite article is different from German. Write the examples and their translations.

   2 In the sentence 'Wool had become …' (ll. 3-4), explain why there is no definite article before 'wool'.

   3 Explain the two uses of the word 'life' in l. 32. Why is it used without and then with the definite article?

   4 Write down the two examples of 'school' in ll. 7-8. Explain why one is used without the definite article and the other with.

b Search the text for examples which demonstrate the following rules:

   1 'We use the indefinite article before jobs, etc.' There are several examples in the text.
      Write down the first three.
   2 'The indefinite article means the same as *per*.' Search the complete text.
   3 'The indefinite article comes after *as (= als)* and *without* + a countable noun in the singular.'
      Write down all the examples.
   4 'In contrast to German, many place names in English are without the definite article.' Look for examples in the text where this applies, then look for examples where it does not apply, i.e. proper names with *the*.

c Complete the sentences with or without *a/an* or *the*.

   1 Shakespeare spent the greater part of his life as … actor and producer on … London stage.
   2 All classes of people went to … theatre to see Shakespeare's plays, not only the rich.
   3 … music and power of Shakespeare's language and … beauty of his imagery were enjoyed by all, even if they could not read or write.
   4 Shakespeare had a deep understanding of … human nature. This makes his plays timeless.
   5 He gives his audiences a picture of … life and of … human emotion in all their variety.
   6 The actors in Shakespeare's company loved him as … writer and as … human being.
   7 In 1611 Shakespeare retired from … public life to … New Place, the largest house in Stratford.
   8 In England, Shakespeare's plays are taught in … school as 'required reading'.

d In your own words, write a short paragraph each about 1) Shakespeare's birth and parentage, 2) his education and family, 3) his working life and financial position, etc. Check your use of the articles.

The adjective and the adverb

A ▸ **Use the comparative or superlative form of the adjectives. Add words where necessary.**

1 Jane is the (intelligent) … of the three sisters, but also the (lazy) … in my opinion.
2 Maths has always been a hard subject for me, but now it's getting harder and (hard) …
3 The new DVD-player was even (expensive) … my computer.
4 Pat got a bad mark in history, but Jeff's mark was even (bad) …
5 I have just heard the (late) … unemployment figures on the news.
6 London is one of the (cosmopolitan) … cities in the world.
7 The more you practise at the keyboard, (good) … you will become.
8 Which is London's (famous) … landmark? Big Ben, Tower Bridge or St. Paul's?

B ▸ **Add a word where necessary. Choose from: *people, boy/girl/etc., thing, one(s).***

9 In theory, there are more job opportunities for the disabled … nowadays. But in practice?
10 Jan has got two dogs. Toby is a labrador. I can't remember what the little … is.
11 There's a blind … in our street. She told me all about the special school she goes to.
12 The strange … is, why didn't Jason tell you about the missing money?
13 All the apples look good. We needn't buy the most expensive …
14 Several young … have been invited to a discussion with our local MP.
15 The American education system promotes the gifted … more than the German system.

C ▸ **Translate the German sentence parts in brackets into English.**

16 The first question was *(schwieriger als die zweite)* …, but the third was *(die schwierigste.)* …
17 When the mountain rescue team found the injured climber, *(war er noch am Leben.)* …
18 *(Wenn Sie weitere Fragen haben)* …, send an e-mail to Customer Service.
19 *(Das Beste)* … about school holidays is not having to get up early.
20 *(Hast du die neuesten Nachrichten gehört?)* … Who has won the cup final?
21 Our new flat has got three bedrooms, *(ein großes und zwei kleinere.)* …
22 We've got a French assistant at our school now, so my pronunciation is getting *(immer besser.)* …
23 Our youth group is collecting money for a mini-bus for *(Behinderte.)* …
24 Can I borrow your history notes? *(Deine sind nicht so unordentlich wie meine.)* …
25 *(Je kleiner das Handy, umso teurer ist es.)* … But I think some of them are too small.
26 Your car is *(umweltfreundlicher als meins)* …, but I can't afford to buy a new car yet.

D ▸ **Spot the mistakes. There is one mistake in each sentence.**

27 The worst about school is that it doesn't really prepare pupils for the world of work.
28 Jane's older brother studied medicine, but it's the younger that's really intelligent.
29 I thought your cough was getting better, but it seems to be getting always worse.
30 What are the last developments in the French rail strike?
31 A crowd of unemployed had gathered outside the townhall, demonstrating with banners.
32 The afraid boy didn't give the policeman an answer. He just ran away.
33 Everybody agrees that even a small tax reduction is better as nothing.
34 The worse thing about dieting is the psychological pressure and stress that's involved.
35 I think Sally is about twenty, but her boyfriend is quite a bit elder.
36 The bigger the flat, so more expensive it will be.

The adjective and the adverb

? **Correct yourself**

A 1: *most intelligent, laziest*   2: *harder*   3: *more expensive than*   4: *worse*   5: *latest*   6: *most cosmopolitan*   7: *the better*   8: *most famous*

B 9: *–*   10: *one*   11: *girl*   12: *thing*   13: *ones*   14: *people*   15: *–*

C 16: *… more difficult than the second (one), … the most difficult (one).*   17: *… he was still alive.* 18: *If you have (any) further questions, …*   19: *The best thing …*   20: *Have you heard the latest news? …*   21: *… a big one and two smaller ones.*   22: *… better and better.*   23: *… disabled people/physically handicapped people.*   24: *… Yours are not as/so untidy as mine.*   25: *The smaller the mobile, the more expensive it is …*   26: *… more environment-friendly than mine, …*

D 27: *The worst thing about school is that …*   28: *… but it's the younger one that's really intelligent.*   29: *… but it seems to be getting worse and worse.*   30: *What are the latest developments in the French rail strike?*   31: *A crowd of unemployed people had gathered …* 32: *The frightened boy didn't give the policeman an answer …*   33: *… a small tax reduction is better than nothing.*   34: *The worst thing about dieting is the psychological pressure …* 35: *… but her boyfriend is quite a bit older.*   36: *The bigger the flat, the more expensive it will be.*

Exercise finder

Sentences	CEG	Exercises
1, 6, 8	▶ 197	▶ 2, 13
2, 22, 29	▶ 200d	▶ 2
3, 16, 24, 26, 33	▶ 200a	▶ 2, 13
4, 34	▶ 198	▶ 2, 13
5, 18, 20, 30	▶ 199	▶ 3
7, 25, 36	▶ 200e	▶ 2
9, 15	▶ 202a	▶ 4
10, 13, 21, 28	▶ 201	▶ 4
11, 14, 23, 31	▶ 202b	▶ 4
12, 19, 27	▶ 202d	▶ 4
17, 32, 35	▶ 196c/d	▶ 1

The adjective and the adverb *The adverb; adjective or adverb*

A ▶ **Change the form in brackets where necessary.**

1 John is working as an artist in Bristol, apparently very (successful) …
2 Leo feels (bad) … about the trouble at the office. He thinks it was his fault.
3 Sylvia worked very (hard) … to get a scholarship to Oxford.
4 What's wrong with the school band these days? They're playing far (badly) … than usual.
5 Trish says she passed her driving test (easy) … the first time.
6 The films of Tolkien's *The Lord of the Rings* have proved to be (immense) … popular.
7 Jonathan says his interview went very (good) …, so he thinks he will get the job.
8 Simon's in hospital. From what his mother told me, his condition sounds (serious) …
9 Why does Marion behave (shy) … when she meets people? She isn't shy at all.
10 I'm afraid I don't work much, but Sarah works less, and Liz works the (little) …

B ▶ **Which form is correct?**

11 Jake kicked the ball as (high/highly) as he could, but the goalkeeper managed to save it.
12 Karen is feeling (sad/sadly) because her dog was killed in a road accident.
13 Denise is taking an exam next week, but she has (hard/hardly) found time to do any work.
14 Your pizza smells (delicious/deliciously). Can I have a piece?
15 You really must read the new Helen Fielding novel. It's (high/highly) amusing.

C ▶ **Translate the words in brackets into English.**

16 *(Hoffentlich)* … the club's financial situation will soon improve.
17 It snowed *(gestern Nacht im Westen Schottlands.)* …
18 I don't always understand what our chemistry teacher means. *(Er spricht zu schnell.)* …
19 I always get up *(früher als mein Bruder.)* …
20 *(Vermutlich)* … the present government will remain in power after the next election.
21 You could be really good at the keyboard. *(Du solltest regelmäßiger üben.)* …
22 Which branch of skilled workers earns *(am wenigsten)* … in Britain?
23 It's *(extrem wichtig)* … for Jason to get the transfer that he applied for.
24 If Sarah wants to have a worthwhile career, she ought to take school *(ernster.)* …
25 Sandra's father *(hat früher für die United Nations in New York gearbeitet.)* …
26 Doing sport once a week isn't enough to get fit. *(Du musst täglich trainieren.)* …

D ▶ **Spot the mistakes. There is one mistake in each sentence or sentence pair.**

27 David is flying tomorrow to Berlin on business for his new firm.
28 The story is hard to believe, but I assure you, it's perfect true.
29 Jeff is great on the guitar. He plays really good.
30 We discovered never how the accident actually happened.
31 The museum's not expensive, and children under twelve are admitted freely.
32 The Crown Plaza is an old, traditional hotel, but it's been total renovated.
33 We didn't know how much the price was in pounds, but we had luckily a pocket calculator.
34 Sophie looks miserably. What's wrong with her?
35 A good sales assistant always addresses customers politely and friendly.
36 We go often to a nice little Italian restaurant in Duke Street.

The adjective and the adverb *The adverb; adjective or adverb*

? Correct yourself

A 1: *successfully* 2: *bad* 3: *hard* 4: *worse* 5: *easily* 6: *immensely* 7: *well* 8: *serious*
9: *shyly* 10: *least*

B 11: *high* 12: *sad* 13: *hardly* 14: *delicious* 15: *highly*

C 16: *I hope …* 17: *… in the west of Scotland yesterday/last night.* 18: *… He speaks too fast/quickly.* 19: *… earlier than my brother.* 20: *I suppose …* 21: *You ought to/should practise more regularly.* 22: *… (the) least …* 23: *… extremely important …* 24: *… more seriously.*
25: *… used to work for the United Nations in New York.* 26: *… You must/have to train daily.*

D 27: *David is flying to Berlin tomorrow on business for his new firm.* 28: *The story is hard to believe, but I assure you, it's perfectly true.* 29: *Jeff is great on the guitar. He plays really well.*
30: *We never discovered how the accident actually happened.* 31: *The museum's not expensive, and children under twelve are admitted free.* 32: *The Crown Plaza is an old, traditional hotel, but it's been totally renovated.* 33: *We didn't know how much the price was in pounds, but luckily we had a pocket calculator.* 34: *Sophie looks miserable. What's wrong with her?* 35: *A good sales assistant always addresses customers politely and in a friendly manner/way.* 36: *We often go to a nice little Italian restaurant in Duke Street.*

Exercise finder

Sentences	CEG	Exercises
1, 5, 7, 9, 29, 35	▶ 206	▶ 5, 10, 11, 12
2, 8, 12, 14, 34	▶ 209	▶ 10, 11
3, 18, 26	▶ 207	▶ 6, 12
4, 10, 22	▶ 212	▶ 7, 12, 13
6, 23, 28, 32	▶ 203b	▶ 5, 10, 11, 13
11, 13, 15, 31	▶ 208	▶ 6, 10, 13
16, 20, 25	▶ 216	▶ 9
17, 27, 30, 33, 36	▶ 215	▶ 8, 13
19, 21, 24	▶ 211	▶ 7, 12, 13

1 *Find the mistakes* **predicative adjectives** ▶ **196c/d**

a Only four sentences are correct. Remember that some adjectives cannot stand in front of nouns. Others can only stand in front of nouns. Find the mistakes and correct them.

Example: The asleep baby woke up when the dog started to bark. *(Wrong)*
Correct: *The **sleeping** baby …*

1 The frightened little boy ran to his mother.
2 The ill child had to stay in bed.
3 The asleep man didn't hear the doorbell.
4 You needn't be afraid of mice.
5 The glad girl ran down the street singing.
6 The police found the missing boy alive and well.
7 The afraid children started to cry.
8 Simon's mother says that he will soon be well again.
9 My sister is younger than me, but my brother is elder.
10 Gaelic is still an alive language in Scotland.

b Complete the sentences with the correct adjectives.

1 Gina and Beth look … And they often wear … clothes.
2 You shouldn't wake a/an … baby. – But she isn't …
3 The police questioned the … children, telling them that they needn't be …
4 When the ambulance arrived, the injured man was still …
5 The … girl is thought to have eaten poisonous berries.

| similar • alike |
| asleep • sleeping |
| afraid • frightened |
| |
| living • alive |
| ill • sick |

2 *School subjects* **sentences with comparisons** ▶ **197, 198, 200**

a Give your opinion about the following school subjects. Compare them with …*-er than* or *more … than* and the adjective given. Start with *I think/don't think …*

1 art, sport (enjoyable)
2 English, German (hard)
3 Latin, French (useful)
4 chemistry, biology (interesting)
5 maths, music (boring)
6 geography, physics (easy)
7 history, maths (difficult)

	MORNING	AFTERNOON
MON	10.00 – 11.30 English Literature (Rm.6A – Ms.Jones)	1.00 – 2.00 German Language (Rm. 4B – Mr.Seidel)
TUES	9.30 – 11.00 German Language (Rm. 4B – Mr.Seidel)	2.00 – 3.30 Biology (Practical) (Laboratory – Ms.Gardiner)
WED	11.00 – 12.30 Biology (Theory) (Rm. 2A – Ms.Gardiner)	SPORTS + CLUBS (No Lessons)

b Write a list of your school subjects. Compare them in a short paragraph (about 50 words), using comparative and superlative forms of *good, bad, important, challenging, practical.*

Examples: *I think the **best** subject is maths. In my opinion it's **more challenging than** the others. I would say that music is perhaps the **least important** subject for me. My **most practical** subject is probably English, because …*

c In English, please. Translate the comparisons, putting in school subjects which are true for you.

1 Mein bester Freund/Meine beste Freundin ist besser als ich in *(at)* …
2 Aber sie/er ist nicht so gut wie ich in …
3 Meine Noten in … werden immer besser/schlechter.
4 Mein(e) Freund(in) ist weniger interessiert an *(in)* … als ich.
5 Weniger *(fewer)* Schüler lernen … als …, weil … nützlicher ist.
6 Das Abitur rückt *(get)* immer näher.
7 Je mehr ich an die Prüfungen denke, desto nervöser werde ich.
8 Aber die Schule wird bald aus *(over)* sein. Je früher, desto besser!

3 *Mini-dialogue* **adjectives with two forms of comparison** ▶ **199, 196d**

Tom and Simon are looking at cameras. Complete the conversation with the correct word from the brackets. If you think both words are possible, write both.

Tom: Ed, my (1 older/elder) brother has got a good camera. It's Japanese.
Simon: Do you know what make it is?
Tom: It's a *Sony*, I think. One of the (2 last/latest) models. Digital, of course.
Assistant: We've got the *Sony* range over here.
Simon: The (3 last /latest) shop we were in had this model on offer. It was cheaper.
Assistant: Yes. That model's a bit (4 older/elder). We had it on offer last week too.
Simon: Let's look at some others first and compare prices, shall we? Where's the
            (5 nearest/next) camera shop? We've only been in two so far.
Tom: Well, there's one on Charles Street and there are two on Bank Street.
Simon: Which is the (6 next/nearest)?
Tom: Dixon's, I would say. It's on Bank Street, a bit (7 further/farther) than the Odeon.
Assistant: Well, you'll find our prices are very competitive, so if you need any
            (8 farther/further) information, you can come back or call me on this number.

4 *Add a word* **one/ones after adjectives; the adjective used as a noun** ▶ **201, 202a/b/d**

Add a word where necessary. Choose from: *people, man/men, woman/women, thing, one, ones.*
If you think two words are possible, write both.

1   In Britain's cities there are at least 200,000 homeless … living on the streets.
2   Have you got an English dictionary? – Yes, I have, but just a pocket-sized …
3   The worst … about holidays is that they pass so quickly.
4   Do you think that the very rich … donate money to charities?
5   I spoke to a deaf … on the bus. She could lip-read perfectly.
6   There were some young … on the train playing music and making a lot of noise.
7   An unemployed … told me that he had been looking for a job for three years.
8   The crazy … about James is that he's highly intelligent but just as lazy.
9   Humanitarian aid doesn't always reach those who need it most – the weakest …
10 Do you prefer quiet holidays or more adventurous …?
11 The less fortunate … in life are often treated with much less respect than they deserve.
12 I stopped to help two blind … to cross the road because the traffic light wasn't working.
13 You'll have to use the small photocopier. The big … is out of order, I'm afraid.
14 The funny … about the film is that the story doesn't end the same way as the book.
15 The committee discussed the main issues and left the less important … for the next
    meeting.

5 *My ideal teacher* **adjective or adverb**  **203, 206**

a What do you think an ideal teacher should be like? Write a list of five suitable adjectives.

Examples: He/She should be **understanding**, **fair**, …

b How do you think an ideal teacher should do things? Write a list of five things using suitable adverbs.

Examples: He/She should explain things **simply**, talk to pupils **in a friendly manner**, …

c Complete the pupils' conversation with the correct form of the word given, adjective or adverb.

Marie: I like Mr Marsh best. He's never (1 boring) … He's got a good sense of humour too.
Jason: That's true. And he always listens (2 patient) … when Sharon asks (3 stupid) … questions.
Marion: And he's not often (4 angry) …, not even when some of the boys behave (5 idiotic) …
Jason: Not like old Johnson. He starts shouting (6 angry) … even if you just forget your homework. And when Jake and the others at the back are (7 noisy) …, he gives everybody extra work. That's really (8 unfair) … And he doesn't take our questions (9 serious) … either. There's no wonder that he's not very (10 popular) …
Sean: I agree. I think Mr Marsh explains things (11 good) … and (12 clear) … And he doesn't go too (13 fast) … I never knew how (14 interesting) … physics can be. Mr Marsh doesn't have favourites either, like some teachers.

6 *Get it right* **adverbs with the form of adjectives; adverbs with two forms** ▶ **207, 208**

a Compare the sentence pairs and complete them with the correct form of the word given. Think carefully. Some adverbs have the form of adjectives, other adverbs have two forms.

1 **cheap:**
   It's almost impossible to live … in London.
   Do you like my car? I got it … from a dealer in Islington.
2 **daily:**
   My brother has just gone for his … jog in the park.
   It's no good jogging once a week. You have to do it …
3 **long:**
   I had a … wait for the bus this morning.
   There weren't many people at the doctor's, so I didn't have to wait …
4 **high:**
   Carol sings solo in the school choir. She can sing really …
   Apparently the music teacher thinks very … of her abilities.
5 **early:**
   I don't mind getting up … I'm used to it.
   If you took the … train, you would be in Cardiff by lunchtime.
6 **pretty:**
   We stayed at a lovely, old country hotel. The rooms were decorated very …
   Unfortunately, it was … expensive too.

7 **hard:**
   Steve said that he worked very … to improve his marks in maths.
   But I can … believe that Steve did more work than usual.
8 **right:**
   Have I got the date … , or is the meeting tomorrow?
   No, as you quite … remembered, the meeting is today.

b Write pairs of sentences as in a) using the adverb forms *wrong/wrongly* and *late/lately*.

7 *How to be a winner*   **regular and irregular comparison**    **211, 212**

a Tony wants to play tennis professionally, but his club coach tells him how hard it is. Complete the text with the correct adverb form (positive, comparative or superlative) of the adjectives given.

Examples: *You can't become a Pete Sampras or a Lleyton Hewitt overnight. To play **better than** others, you have to be prepared to work **harder** and train **more regularly**.*

'To compete in high-risk, high-reward tennis, you have to train (1 intensive) … than ever before. You have to be top fit, not only (2 physical) … but also (3 mental) … Tennis is also played in your head. You have to believe (4 firm) … in yourself and your abilities. In professional tennis it's the ones who take their job (5 serious) … that win the trophies. And it's the ones who play (6 confident) … that play (7 successful) … Today's power-tennis has little to do with luck. In a match you have to concentrate (8 full) … on every single ball. You have to play (9 aggressive) … than your opponent. You have to cover the court (10 fast) … than him, serve (11 hard) … and play your shots (12 skillful) … than him. You have to take the ball (13 early)… than he does, and play (14 good) … at the net. Some days you will play (15 bad) … than others, but you must always think (16 competitive) … and find your form again. A tennis professional needs a lot of self-discipline. You have to sleep (17 long) … than usual during tournaments, so no late-night parties. You must eat (18 sensible) … than you would normally do, and eat (19 little) … than you would perhaps like to. Even just one kilo overweight causes you to move (20 slow) … than you would do otherwise. And what's more, you have to keep a cool head, always. If you play (21 nervous) …, your opponent will use your weakness to his advantage. So it's quite simple. If you want to be the best, you have to play (22 good) … It's up to you. There's not much time for fun and friends on the way to the top. Now, Tony, do you still want to be a professional tennis player?'

b An athlete's career depends on his or her physical health and skill. In what ways does a professional athlete have to live his or her life differently from a 'normal' young person? Write a few sentences using adverb comparisons.

8 *A disappointing weekend* **position of various types of adverbs** ▶ **215**

Put the adverb phrases in their usual, non-emphatic position or order. If there are
two adverb phrases of time or place, remember that the more exact one usually comes first.

(1) The exams would be starting (soon). (2) Paul had been working (every evening/very
hard/at home). (3) He felt that he needed a break (really). (4) So he asked his girlfriend
if she'd like to go (for the weekend/in Cornwall/to his brother's cottage). (5) They had
had a great time (the year before/there). (6) The cottage was empty because Paul's brother
had gone to work (for six months/in the States). (7) Cathy welcomed the idea, so Paul
arranged to collect her (at about five /the next day/from the office). (8) The journey to
Tintagel took about three hours (usually), (9) so they expected to arrive (on Friday
evening/at about eight/at the cottage). (10) Paul was looking forward to having a swim
(in the sea/before breakfast) (11) and to taking a walk (in the afternoons/on the beach).
(12) And perhaps a barbecue (on Saturday evening/in the garden).
(13) Paul had trouble with his car on the way (unfortunately). (14) They managed to find
a garage (luckily/easily), (15) but the mechanic told them that he was closing
(politely/just). (16) He said they could collect the car (the next day/at about lunchtime).
So they had to spend the night at a hotel. The car repairs weren't cheap either. (17) Paul
didn't have enough money to pay the bill (in fact). He had to borrow from Cathy.
(18) They arrived (at four/in the afternoon/at the cottage), only to discover that Paul had
forgotten to take the keys with him.

9 *Living in London* **English verbal expressions for German adverbs** ▶ **216**

Heike has studied and lived in London for some years. In an e-mail she tells a friend about the cost of living
in London.

German adverbs are
often translated by
English verbs or
expressions. Match the
lists, then use the
English expressions to
translate the German
parts of Heike's letter to
her friend in Wales.

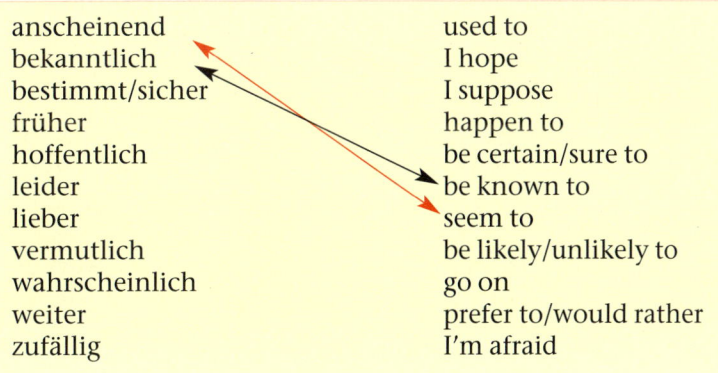

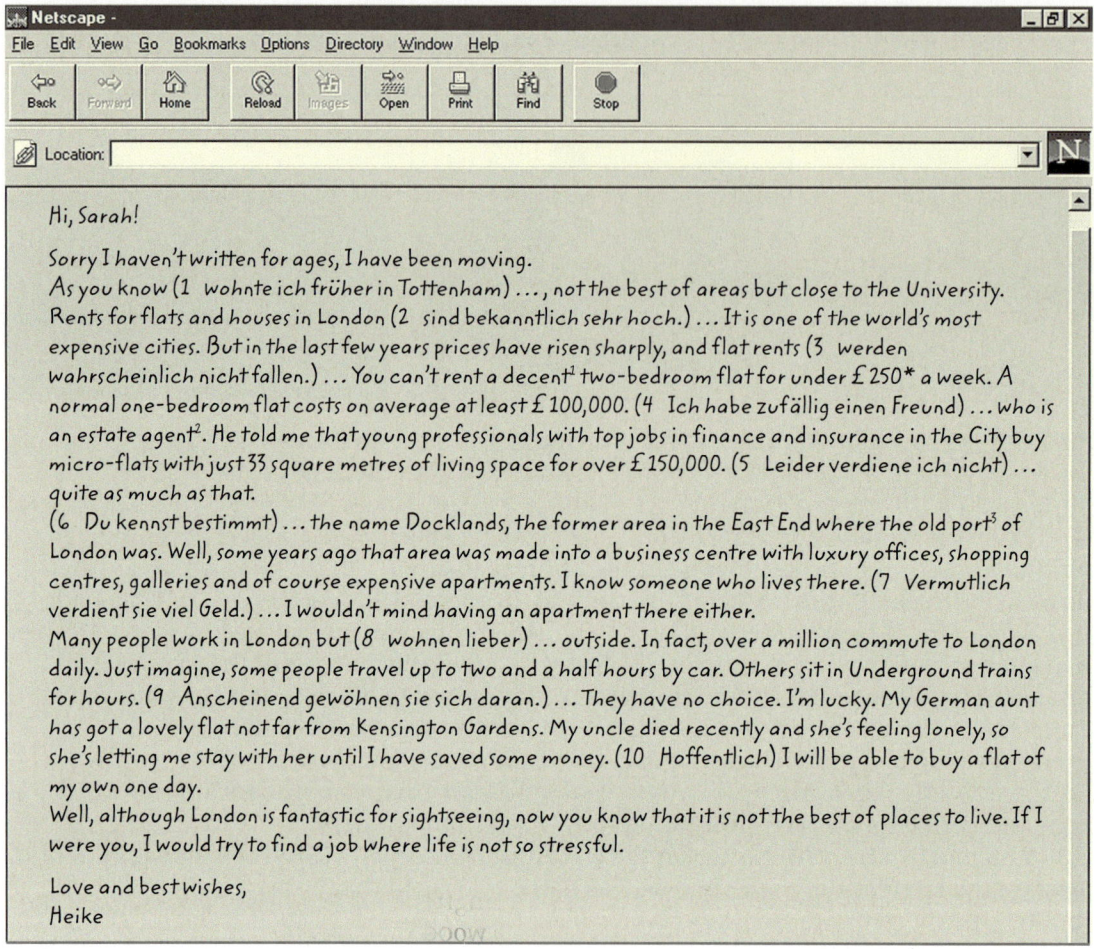

Netscape -

File   Edit   View   Go   Bookmarks   Options   Directory   Window   Help

Back   Forward   Home   Reload   Images   Open   Print   Find   Stop

Location:

Hi, Sarah!

Sorry I haven't written for ages, I have been moving.
As you know (1 wohnte ich früher in Tottenham) ..., not the best of areas but close to the University.
Rents for flats and houses in London (2 sind bekanntlich sehr hoch.) ... It is one of the world's most
expensive cities. But in the last few years prices have risen sharply, and flat rents (3 werden
wahrscheinlich nicht fallen.) ... You can't rent a decent[1] two-bedroom flat for under £ 250* a week. A
normal one-bedroom flat costs on average at least £ 100,000. (4 Ich habe zufällig einen Freund) ... who is
an estate agent[2]. He told me that young professionals with top jobs in finance and insurance in the City buy
micro-flats with just 33 square metres of living space for over £ 150,000. (5 Leider verdiene ich nicht) ...
quite as much as that.
(6 Du kennst bestimmt) ... the name Docklands, the former area in the East End where the old port[3] of
London was. Well, some years ago that area was made into a business centre with luxury offices, shopping
centres, galleries and of course expensive apartments. I know someone who lives there. (7 Vermutlich
verdient sie viel Geld.) ... I wouldn't mind having an apartment there either.
Many people work in London but (8 wohnen lieber) ... outside. In fact, over a million commute to London
daily. Just imagine, some people travel up to two and a half hours by car. Others sit in Underground trains
for hours. (9 Anscheinend gewöhnen sie sich daran.) ... They have no choice. I'm lucky. My German aunt
has got a lovely flat not far from Kensington Gardens. My uncle died recently and she's feeling lonely, so
she's letting me stay with her until I have saved some money. (10 Hoffentlich) I will be able to buy a flat of
my own one day.
Well, although London is fantastic for sightseeing, now you know that it is not the best of places to live. If I
were you, I would try to find a job where life is not so stressful.

Love and best wishes,
Heike

---

10   *Anke's English*   **adjective or adverb: mixed exercise**   ▶ **203b, 206, 208, 209**

a   Anke has just taken a job as a translator with a London firm, but she wants to improve her everyday
English. She talks about her language problems. Complete what she says with an adjective or adverb.

Examples: I can read English very **well**, but my spoken English isn't always **good**. There are a
lot of words that I don't pronounce **correctly**.

I understand written texts (1 easy) ..., but when people speak everyday English too (2 fast)
..., I don't always understand them (3 proper) ... I still don't speak (4 fluent) ..., I'm afraid.
I often feel (5 stupid) ... when I say something that sounds (6 strange) ... or even (7 funny)
... to English people. I often pronounce a word (8 bad) ..., or I say something that seems
(9 unusual) ... in the situation. Then everybody smiles at me (10 friendly) ... and says
nothing. If I'm with friends and I say something (11 wrong) ... which they find (12 high)
... (13 amusing) ..., they laugh at me. I don't mind that so much. But at work, especially on
the phone, I sometimes get (14 extreme) ... (15 nervous) ... I would like to do a course in
English, but it's usually (16 fair) ... (17 late) ... when I leave work and I feel too (18 tired)
... There's (19 hard) ... enough time at weekends. I'll just have to work (20 hard) ... at my
English on my own. What I (21 real) ... need is an English boyfriend who is (22 particular)
... patient.

---

* about € 375   1 decent *anständig*   2 estate agent *Makler*   3 port *Hafenanlage*

b   What kind of problems do you have with English? Think of understanding, speaking, reading and writing. Write a short paragraph about the things you would like to improve, using adjectives and adverbs. Read what Anke says again. It may help you.

Example: *I speak **slowly** because I can't think of the right grammar **quickly** enough. I often feel **shy** and **embarrassed** when I speak.*

c   Translate into English.

1 Anke spricht Englisch ziemlich gut.
2 Am Anfang fand sie die Grammatik furchtbar kompliziert.
3 Sie fand das *'th'* extrem schwierig auszusprechen.
4 Sie übte vor dem Spiegel. Ihr kleiner Bruder dachte, sie sei total verrückt.
5 Sie kaufte eine englische Grammatik, aber sie fand sie schrecklich langweilig.
6 Nach sechs Monaten in London war ihr Englisch erheblich *(considerable)* besser.

11   *A camping trip*   **adjectives, adverbs: mixed ex.**   ▶ **196, 197, 199, 203, 206, 209**

Florian talks to some English friends about his first camping trip when he was a boy. Find his mistakes and correct them. Are there 21, 23 or 25 mistakes?

Florian:
'I remember quite clear the first time I went camping. I was just thirteen. My friends Sebastian and Andreas were twelve. We weren't very good prepared for the trip. The tent was my Dad's – not the last model and extreme awkward to put up. Admitted, we could have put it up more easier if we had practised at home, but we felt excitedly about our first time in a tent, and tried not to get angrily just because a few tent pegs were missing.

At seven o'clock it started to get dark. We all felt hungrily, so we decided to make a fire and cook something to eat. Unfortunately, most of the wood we collected was damp, so the fire started smoking terrible, making us all cough. As soon as it was burning properly, we warmed up our cans of chilli con carne. Actually, it smelt awfully and it tasted even worse. But we ate it hungry.

Just as we were getting into our sleeping bags, Basti heard a strange noise. It sounded fairly closely, in the bushes right behind our tent. We felt pretty frightened, because it seemed to be getting more close. We lay in our tent staring into the darkness, not daring to speak loud. One of us switched on a torch. I looked at the two afraid faces – but I probably looked just as nervously myself. I told the others that we were perfect safe, and to prove it I got up, took my torch and went outside to look.

Everything seemed calm. I felt my way careful through the bushes and I felt proudly of myself for having overcome my fear. But then, it was high unlikely that I would meet a dangerously animal in our local woods.

Anyway, we felt great relieved, and at some time in the early hours we must have fallen asleep.'

12 *The London 'Tube'* **adjective or adverb: mixed ex.** ▶ **197, 198, 206, 207, 211, 212**

a   Complete the text with the most suitable adjective forms or with adverb forms of the words given.

The London 'Tube' is the (1 old) … underground in the world. It is (2 public) … run but was (3 private) … built, much of the network being over 100 years old. This means that repairs and renovations are being carried out (4 continual) … , but they progress (5 slow) …, causing congestion[1] and delay. However, riding the Tube is still the (6 fast) … and (7 popular) … way of getting around London. Not (8 surprising) …, about three million journeys are made on the Tube every day. There are 275 stations on 11 lines, operating on 408 km of railway, both above and below the ground.

Most people have to travel during the rush hour, but within that period there are times when the Tube is (9 crowded) … than others. Arriving at your station ten minutes (10 early) … or (11 late) … can make the difference between sitting (12 comfortable) … or standing for the whole journey. With good timing it is possible to make your journey a little (13 stressful) … Even during peak travel periods[2] some times are (14 quiet) … than others. So use them.

London Underground figures on station passenger density[3] in the rush hour show that it is (15 good) … to try to arrive at the really busy stations on the hour[4], when passenger numbers (16 temporary) … ease off[5]. Here's an example. At Victoria, the Tube's (17 busy) … station, at 8.45 in the morning there are on average 16,000 passengers. Just 15 minutes later there are about 14,000 and at 9.15 there are almost 17,000. So the station is (18 crowded) … at nine o'clock.
Commuters make their journeys in and out of the central city in waves, and travelling at the bottom of a wave is (19 convenient) … than at the top. Especially for the trip home, an extra five minutes' walk may take you to a much (20 congested[6]) … station.

There are six zones on the underground – Zone 1 being Central London. A one-way underground journey in Zone 1 costs £1.50 for adults and 60p for children. The (21 far) … you travel, the more expensive the journey, so if you are changing zones, it's (22 cheap) … to buy a Travelcard.

Despite the size of the Tube, everything runs (23 fair) … (24 smooth) …, and the stations aren't full of grafitti and rubbish like many other undergrounds. It's also said to be (25 safe) … than, for example, the Paris Metro.

Based on *London Transport Information*

b   Read the text through once more, then close the book. In your own words, write down as much as you can remember about the Tube, using comparisons.

c   Tell a partner when it's best to travel on the Tube and why. Use comparisons.

---

1 congestion: overcrowding   2 peak periods: busiest times   3 density *Dichte*   4 on the hour *zur vollen Stunde*
5 ease off: decrease   6 congested *verstopft, überfüllt*

13 *The triumph of English*   adjective, adverb: mixed ex. ▶ **197, 198, 200, 203b, 204, 208, 211, 212, 215**

Read the text carefully, then carry out the tasks.

The world language seems to be good for everyone – except for native English-speakers perhaps.

You hear it and you see it everywhere. Some 380 million people speak it as their first language and perhaps two-thirds as many as their second. A billion are learning it, and by
5   2050, it is predicted[1] that half the world will be using it competently. It is the language of globalisation, of international business, politics and diplomacy. It is the language of computers and the Internet. Truly, English has come a long way.

How come? Not because English is easy. True, genders are simple, but the grammar is bizarre and the match between spelling and pronunciation is a learner's worst nightmare[2]. English
10   is now so widely spoken in so many places that several versions have evolved, some so peculiar that even 'native' speakers may have trouble understanding each other.

As a language with many origins – Romance, Germanic, Norse, Celtic and so on – English was bound to be[3] a mess. But its elasticity makes it messier, as well as stronger. New words are readily received by English. The past decade, for instance, has produced a flood of
15   Internet, computer and phone terms ('browsers', 'downloading', 'texting' and so on). English is highly flexible and infinitely tolerant. English, in other words, moves with the times.

The success or failure of a language has to do with the power of the people who speak it. This is particularly true of English, as it is spoken by the people of the United States, a world
20   power. But languages are not only a medium of communication. They are also repositories[4] of culture and identity. And in many countries the advance of English threatens to damage or destroy much local culture. This is sometimes lamented[5] even in England itself, for although the language that now sweeps the world is called English, the culture carried with it is American.

25   Now that EU members also include Denmark, Finland and Sweden, whose peoples often speak better English than the British, English is the EU's dominant language. Indeed, over 85% of all international organisations use English as one of their official languages.

Unfortunately, native English-speakers are becoming lazier at learning other languages. Given that everyone else is learning English, it is perhaps not surprising that the British are
30   less highly motivated. Some 66% of them speak no foreign language at all, compared to the EU's average of 47%. Luxembourgers are the cleverest linguists: only 2.2% of them are monoglottal[6]. The Dutch are quite brilliant too; over 80% of them speak English more or less fluently.

Thus the triumph of English also isolates native English-speakers from the literature, history
35   and ideas of other peoples. It is, in short, a thoroughly dubious[7] triumph. But then who's for Esperanto?

Adapted from *The Economist* print edition, 20/12/2001

---

1 predict: say what will happen in the future   2 nightmare: frightening dream   3 bound to be: sure to be
4 repository: place where sth. is stored   5 lament: feel sadness, disappointment
6 monoglottal: speaking only one language   7 dubious: doubtful

a Look for examples of the following in the text:

1 comparative forms of adjectives
2 superlative forms of adjectives
3 an adverb that modifies an adjective
4 adverbs of manner
5 sentence adverbs
6 focusing adverbs

b Write the opposites of:

1 less highly motivated
2 lazier
3 cleverest
4 worst

c Complete the sentences using suitable adjective comparisons. There may be more than one answer.

1 According to the text, English has become the world language because it is spoken in the … country in the world. (ll. 19-20)
2 Genders in English are … in most other EU languages. (l. 8)
3 A lot of learners think that English grammar is bad enough, but English pronunciation is even … (ll. 8-9)
4 The English seem to be … of European nations as far as language learning is concerned. (ll. 29-31).

d Put in the correct form of the word given.

1 English may (right) … be called the world language.
2 All over the world, pupils (most) … learn English as their first foreign language.
3 The language skills of several EU peoples are (high) … developed.
4 People from Luxembourg and Holland are apparently (pretty) … good linguists.
5 People from small countries often work especially (hard) … to learn English.
6 Perhaps the British are (wrong) … accused of being poor at learning languages.

e Put the adverbs into their usual, non-emphatic position in the sentence.

1 English is understood in most countries in the world. (usually)
2 English doesn't seem difficult for people from EU countries. (particularly)
3 Foreigners speak better English than the British. (often)
4 66% of British people do not speak a foreign language at all. (unfortunately)

f Explain in your own words why the author thinks that '… the triumph of English … is a thoroughly dubious triumph.' (ll. 34-35). Write a short paragraph using comparisons.

Quantifiers

A ▶ Complete the sentences with *some* or *any*. If you think both are possible, write both.

1 I've just bought … delicious peaches. Would you like one?
2 The night buses only run at the weekend. There aren't … in the week.
3 If you would like … more biscuits, there are plenty left.
4 I'm at home most evenings, so you can call …. time.
5 Dad won't be here next week. He's going to … conference or other. It's in Rome, I think.
6 Sorry, but I haven't had … time at all to do the shopping.
7 The concert was great. There must have been … two thousand kids there.
8 I think smoking is a really dangerous habit. … doctor will advise you to stop.

B ▶ Choose the correct form from the brackets. More than one form may be possible.

9 I won't be long. I only need (few/a few) minutes to get ready.
10 (All the/All) young people I know are interested in music and sports.
11 Shall I come at four or at seven? – Actually, (no/neither/none) time is suitable. Come tomorrow instead.
12 Uncle David has (a few/few) friends. He likes to be alone with his books and his dog.
13 Which shirt shall I buy, the white one or the blue one? – They both look good. Buy (any/either).
14 This is your room. If you need (any/some) more towels, just let me know.
15 We get (much/a lot of) snow here in winter.
16 You can have (any/either/some) of these three CDs. Just choose.

C ▶ Translate the German sentence parts in the brackets.

17 (Ich werde morgen etwas Geld von der Bank holen) …, then I'll be able to pay you back.
18 How many groups are there and how many students (gibt es in jeder Gruppe) …?
19 (Möchtest du noch etwas Salat?) … There's plenty left.
20 (Keiner der drei Jungen) … knows the way. So we'll have to ask someone else.
21 It was hard to decide who should get the job. (Fast jeder Bewerber hatte gute Qualifikationen.) …
22 Bill Johnson's wife is French. (Die beiden Söhne sind zweisprachig [bilingual].) …
23 (Jeder von uns) has a car, so you can drive with me or with my brother.
24 Did your brother or your boyfriend give you this ? (Keiner von beiden.) … I bought it myself.

D ▶ Spot the mistakes. There is one mistake in each sentence or sentence pair.

25 Which of the two anoraks do you like? – None of them. I'd like a black one.
26 Nobody of the pupils in my class has heard from Barry since he moved to Portsmouth.
27 There are only a little potatoes left, but there are lots of vegetables.
28 Have you seen any of those two boys before? One of them seems familiar to me.
29 All pupils in my class have got their own mobiles and their own bank accounts.
30 Can I have some more orange juice, please? – Sorry, there's no left.
31 Unfortunately, a little is known about rainforest plants.
32 The lecture went on too long, so there was few time for questions afterwards. Pity.
33 The both girls are studying medicine. They both want to go into medical research.
34 There was much traffic on the motorway. That's why we're late.
35 Could you lend me any money until tomorrow? Five pounds would be enough.
36 Why don't you try some of the strawberry cake? There's still little left.

Quantifiers

? **Correct yourself**

A 1: *some* 2: *any* 3: *some/any* 4: *any* 5: *some* 6: *any* 7: *some* 8: *Any*

B 9: *a few* 10: *All the* 11: *neither* 12: *few* 13: *either* 14: *any/some* 15: *a lot of* 16: *any*

C 17: *I'll fetch/get some money from the bank tomorrow …* 18: *… are there in each group?*
19: *Would you like some more salad?* 20: *None of the three boys …*
21: *Almost/Practically/Nearly every applicant had good qualifications.* 22: *Both (of the) sons are bilingual.* 23: *Each of us …* 24: *Neither (of them/of the two).*

D 25: *… – Neither of them. I'd like a black one.*
26: *None of the pupils in my class has heard from Barry since he moved to Portsmouth.*
27: *There are only a few potatoes left, but there are lots of vegetables.*
28: *Have you seen either of those two boys before? …*
29: *All the pupils in my class have got their own mobiles and their own bank accounts.*
30: *… – Sorry, there's none left.*
31: *Unfortunately, little is known about rainforest plants.*
32: *The lecture went on too long, so there was little time for questions afterwards …*
33: *Both (of the) girls are studying medicine …*
34: *There was a lot of traffic on the motorway …*
35: *Could you lend me some money until tomorrow? …*
36: *… There's still a little left.*

▶ **Exercise finder**

Sentences	CEG	Exercises
1, 17	▶ 218b	▶ 1, 4
2, 6	▶ 218c	▶ 1
3, 14	▶ 218c Anm.	▶ 1
4, 8, 16	▶ 220b	▶ 1, 3, 4
5, 7	▶ 218d Anm.	▶ 1
9, 27, 36	▶ 219d	▶ 2, 4
10, 29	▶ 221	▶ 3, 4
11, 24, 25	▶ 222c	▶ 3
12, 31, 32	▶ 219e	▶ 2, 4
13, 28	▶ 222b	▶ 3
15, 34	▶ 219c	▶ 2
18, 21, 23	▶ 220a	▶ 3, 4
19, 35	▶ 218d	▶ 1
20, 26, 30	▶ 223c	▶ 3, 4
22, 33	▶ 222a	▶ 3, 4

1 *Mini-dialogues*   *some, any,* and compounds; *somebody/anybody* + *they/them/their*   ▶ **218a-d, 220b, 224a/b, 225**

Complete the mini-dialogues between Andy and his sister Beth. Put in *some, any* or compounds such as *something, anybody, somewhere,* etc. Remember that the pronouns *they/them/their* are used with *somebody/anybody.* If you think *some* or *any* is possible, write both.

1 Beth: There's (1) … potato salad in the fridge. Or shall I make you (2) … sandwiches?
  Andy: No, don't bother. I'm really hungry. I'll eat (3) … at all – as long as it's quick, even your potato salad. Are there (4) … bananas?
  Beth: I'm not sure. I haven't bought (5) … Where's Jason? He hasn't done (6) … homework today.
  Andy: He's out again. He met (7) … girl at the disco and he's out with her every evening. He's done hardly (8) … for school for over a week.

2 Beth: Oh, I see you've got (1) … new posters.
  Andy: Yes, I got them from Dave. If you'd like to have (2) … of them, just say so.
  Beth: Well, which one can I have?
  Andy: (3) … of them. Just choose. Dave got them cheap from (4) … man or other. He's got a market stall (5) … in town. So if you need (6) … more, I'll ask Dave where it is.

3 Andy: How was Jane's barbecue?
  Beth: Nice, but there was hardly (1) … there that I knew. There must have been (2) … fifty people or so. (3) … asked about you, but I can't remember (4) … name.
  Andy: Well, were (5) … male or female? You must remember that, surely.
  Beth: Let me think. Oh, yes. A girl. Good-looking. But I've lost the telephone number.
  Andy: Great.

4 Andy: I'm back. Did (1) … phone for me while I was out?
  Beth: Yes, (2) … from school. Jerry, I think his name was.
  Andy: What did he want? (3) … special?
  Beth: He said (4) … had left (5) … schoolbag on the bus. So if you know who it is, tell (6) … to call him.
  Andy: I've got to go out again. I'm meeting Jason. He's got (7) … problem or other. If (8) … phones for me, tell (9) … that (10) … can get me on my mobile. Bye!

2 *There isn't much left*   *a lot of, much, many, (a) little, (a) few*

a   Some teenagers have been celebrating an 18th birthday party. What's left at the food buffet?
Use *a lot of*, *a little* and *a few*.

Examples: *There's **a lot of** chocolate cake. There are **a lot of** grapes.*
*There's **a little** cheese. There are **a few** sandwiches.*

b   Imagine you were one of the guests at the party. Tell a friend what you had to eat and drink.
Use *a lot of*, *not much*, *not many*.

Examples: *I ate **a lot of** sandwiches, but I did**n't** eat **much** noodle salad.*
*I did**n't** have **many** sandwiches, bit I had **a lot of** ice cream.*

c Do you prefer healthy food or junk food? How much do you eat of all these things? Write a short paragraph using *(quite) a lot of, (very) little, (very) few*. Pay attention to countable and uncountable nouns.

vegetables ▪ fruit ▪ fish ▪ red meat ▪ chicken ▪ sweets ▪ salad ▪
low-calorie products ▪ chocolate ▪ yoghurt ▪ eggs ▪ fries ▪ burgers ▪
convenience food[1] ▪ milk ▪ fruit juice ▪ diet cola

Examples: *I usually prefer healthy food. I eat quite **a lot of** vegetables, but **little** chocolate.*
*I like fries, but I eat very **few**, only with my friends when we're in a fast food restaurant.*

---

3 *Get it right*   *every, each, any, all, both, either, neither, no, none*   ▶ **220-223**

Choose the correct word from the brackets.

1 It isn't true that (all/all the) British people drink tea.
2 Do you like the blue T-shirt or the white one? – I don't like (any/either/both) of them.
3 (Both the/The both) boys have passed their driving test, but only one has bought a car.
4 What shall we order? Chicken or steak? – (Each/Any/Either). I really don't mind.
5 (All/All the) pupils in my class want to stay on at school to do A-levels.
6 How much money have you got with you? – (No/None), I've forgotten my purse.
7 Sue thought I wasn't listening, but I heard (every/each) word she said.
8 Maria and Megan are in a sports club, but (neither/none) of them is very good at sports.
9 You can try to phone Sandra (any/all/either) time of the day. She's never at home.
10 There are four children in the family, and (each of them/every of them) plays an
    instrument.

---
1 convenience food *Fertiggerichte*

11 You have to answer five questions, and there are twenty points for (each/every) answer.
12 (Every/Each) Christmas Day, Dad starts playing carols[1] on the piano.
13 It was quite cold in the restaurant, but (none/no/nobody) of the guests complained.
14 Choose a card, (either/any/every) card from the whole pack.
15 Chris and Tony made a mess in the kitchen, but (none/neither/either) of them offered to clean it up.
16 (Both of the/The both) books are exciting. They're well worth reading.
17 Do you know Rod Stewart's song '(Every/Each) beat of my heart'? It was a big hit in the 80's.
18 All the buses to town pass this way. (Either/Each/Any) will take you to the centre.
19 There's (none/no) butter left. Remind me to buy some, will you?
20 Do you want to come on Monday or Wednesday? – (Any/Either/Each) day would suit me.

4 *Young people vote against politics*   quantifiers: mixed exercise    218-223

The Electoral Commission is so concerned[2] by the apathy of young voters that it is running a campaign to sell the message that 'Votes Are Power'. Two members of the Electoral Commission are visiting schools to encourage young people to talk about their view of politics.

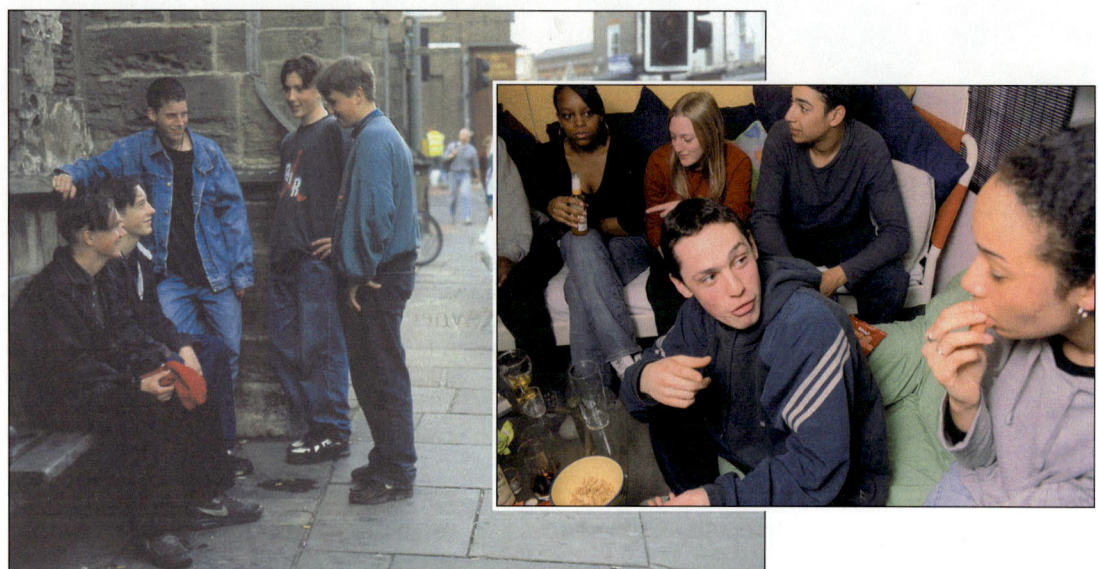

All young people in Britain can vote at the age of eighteen, but only one in ten under the age of 24 is expected to vote in this year's local elections. More votes were registered for *Pop Idol* than for the last general election. Why don't young people bother to vote?

Each young person interviewed was asked to list reasons why they should or should not
5   vote. The reasons given by a group of 17- and 18-year-old pupils in north-west London are not good news for anyone involved in the political process. Many politicians are seen as untrustworthy. One girl said no politicians could be trusted to keep their promises. 'Take any of them, they are all the same,' she continued. 'Tony Blair said he would improve the health service and do something about crime. But little has been done.' A lot of young
10 people had concerns about unemployment among school-leavers, but the government had not done much to improve the situation.

---

1 carol *Weihnachtslied*   2 concerned: worried

All the sixth formers interviewed at Queen's Park Community School in Brent showed a deep cynicism towards their elected representatives. Although ready to talk about issues[1] affecting their lives, the youngsters could see little connection between their own
15 experiences and the world of Westminster. What was most striking[2] was not the pupils' antipathy towards politicians and their parties, but their complete indifference[3]. They showed little knowledge of 'Who's who in politics'. When asked who the leader of the Conservatives was, most pupils didn't have any idea. A few pupils knew the answer, but in practice they could draw few distinctions[4] between Tony Blair and Iain Duncan Smith – and
20 they recognised hardly any differences between the parties.

Some sixth formers were quite aware[5] of the benefits[6] of voting. They were quick to list the idea that voting was a way of getting an opinion heard, and that it was a way of applying pressure. A few suggested that voting through text messages could perhaps make elections more accessible[7], but not many youngsters were convinced that it would be worth paying
25 the 10p.

Both members of the Commission agree that such widespread indifference towards politics is a problem to be taken seriously. The reasons could be a declining sense of civic duty, or the lack of allegiances[8] to political parties, suggests Tabitha Cunniffe, or perhaps the fact that both the major parties have similar political aims. They are too much alike.

30 The head of sixth at Queen's Park Community School, Jennifer Akhurst, says that the school makes every possible effort to get pupils interested in politics, but it may take a little time. None of the pupils interviewed expects to vote at this year's local elections. Few will be first-time voters at the next general election, but most students are more likely to be first-time abstainers[9].

From 'Young people vote against politics' by Sean Coughlan, *BBC News Online*, 28/01/2003

---

1 issue: topic, problem   2 striking *auffallend*   3 indifference: total lack of interest   4 distinction: clear difference
5 be aware of sth.: know, realize sth.   6 benefit: advantage   7 accessible: easy to reach, use, do   8 allegiance: continued, unquestioned support   9 abstainer: a person who chooses not to vote

a   Underline all the quantifiers in ll. 1-20.

b   Look at the language.

    1   Explain the use of *all* and *all the* in 'All young people in Britain …' (l. 1) and 'All the sixth formers interviewed …' (l. 12).
    2   How would you translate *any* in 'Take any of them …' (ll. 7-8) ?
    3   What is the opposite of 'A lot of young people …' (ll. 9-10)?
    4   Explain the use of *little* and *a little* in 'They showed little knowledge …' (ll. 16-17) and '… it may take a little time.' (ll. 31-32).
    5   '… they recognized hardly any differences between the parties.' (l. 20)
       The verb 'recognized' is positive. Explain why *any* is used after it and not *some*.

c   Express the following sentences in a different way without changing the meaning. Use different quantifiers or a different structure.

    Example: In Britain, few young people under 24 bother to vote.
               *In Britain, **not many** young people under 24 bother to vote.*

    1   British sixth formers show little interest in politics.
    2   Few can name the leader of the Opposition.
    3   The government has not done much to improve the job situation for school-leavers.
    4   Most pupils didn't have any idea who their local MPs are.
    5   Pupils showed little knowledge of politics.
    6   A few pupils knew the answer.
    7   Each young person interviewed was asked to list reasons for voting or not voting.
    8   The youngsters could see little connection between their world and the world of Westminster.
    9   They could draw few distinctions between Tony Blair and Iain Duncan Smith.
   10   The school makes every possible effort to get the pupils interested in politics.
   11   None of the pupils interviewed expects to vote.
   12   Both the major parties have similar political aims.

d   In your own words, state the main reasons that the sixth formers give for not bothering to vote. (ll. 6-15)

e   In a short paragraph, describe the situation of first-time or young voters in your country. Do you think it is similar to the situation in Britain, or do you believe that 18-year-olds in your country are more politically interested and better motivated to vote? Use quantifiers where possible.

f   Do you consider voting in a general election to be a 'civic duty'[1]? State your main reasons for wanting to vote or for not wanting to vote. Use quantifiers.

---

1 civic duty   *Bürgerpflicht*

Pronouns and question words

A ▶ Put in the missing pronouns or determiners: *you, they, his, her, our, mine, yours, each other*

1 How do … spell 'Mississippi'? Is that right?
2 Maria and I have known … since we were in kindergarten together.
3 Nick is 28 and he still lives with his parents. It's time he got a flat of … own.
4 … say that the council is going to approve the plans for the new shopping centre.
5 I'd like you to meet Tony. He's an old friend of …
6 Sue put the money in … pocket. I saw her do it.
7 Thanks for the advice. That's a very good idea of …
8 Mum likes us to take off … shoes when we come in, because we've just got a new carpet.

B ▶ Put in a reflexive pronoun (*myself*, etc.) where necessary or *each other*.

9 From what age do you think children are able to look after …?
10 Try to concentrate … better on what you are doing.
11 We didn't really enjoy … at the new disco. There weren't many people there.
12 Do you and your classmates sometimes help … with homework?
13 You're going out with Angela tonight, aren't you? What time have you arranged to meet …?
14 Don't blame … for the accident. I really don't think it was your fault.
15 I remember the dentist saying, 'Now just relax … This won't hurt.'
16 How often do you and your penfriend write to …?
17 Don't move … There's a wasp on your neck.

C ▶ Translate the German sentence parts into English.

18 *(Janet hat sich den linken Arm gebrochen.)* … She fell off a ladder picking apples.
19 How can Michael buy a car? He hasn't got any *(eigenes Geld.)* …
20 There's some money lying on the table. *(Wofür ist es?)* …
21 *(Wen hast du auf der Party kennen gelernt* [meet]*?)* … Anybody I know?
22 I haven't met Justin before. *(Ist er ein Nachbar von euch?)* …
23 *(Man sagt, Vickys Vater sei sehr reich.)* … He's thought to own a lot of property.
24 *(Rachel hat ein eigenes Zimmer)* …, but her two little sisters share a room.
25 *(Wie ist das Wetter?)* … Is it warm enough to go swimming?

D ▶ Who, whom, what, which?
Choose the missing question word and use the correct form of the verb *given* (in 29,31).

26 … of the pupils have registered for the advanced course in IT?
27 I heard that you had failed your driving test again. – … idiot told you that? I passed it.
28 … did you give the money to?
29 … you (phone) last night at midnight? I heard you talking and laughing.
30 … is your favourite kind of music?
31 … (phone) you in the middle of the night? The phone woke everybody up.
32 I heard that one of you had managed to get a place at Cambridge. … of you is it?
33 … of these magazines would you like to borrow?
34 To … should we address the complaint?
35 … did Sue say that for? It wasn't a very nice thing to say.

Pronouns and question words

? Correct yourself

A 1: *you*   2: *each other/one another*   3: *his*   4: *They*   5: *mine*   6: *her*   7: *yours*   8: *our*

B 9: *themselves*   10: *–*   11: *ourselves*   12: *each other/one another*   13: *–*
14: *yourself/yourselves*   15: *–*   16: *each other/one another*   17: *–*

C 18: *Janet has broken her left arm.*   19: *… money of his own.*   20: *What is it for?*   21: *Who did you meet at the party?*   22: *Is he a neighbour of yours?*   23: *They/People say that Vicky's father is very rich.*   24: *Rachel has a room of her own/her own room …*   25: *What's the weather like?*

D 26: *Which …*   27: *What …*   28: *Who …*   29: *Who did you phone …*   30: *What …*
31: *Who phoned you …*   32: *Which …*   33: *Which …*   34: *… whom …*   35: *What …*

Exercise finder

Sentences	CEG	Exercises
1, 4, 23	▶ 229	▶ 1
2, 12, 16	▶ 234	▶ 5, 6, 7
3, 19, 24	▶ 231b	▶ 2, 6
5, 7, 22	▶ 231d	▶ 2, 6
6, 8, 18	▶ 231c	▶ 2, 6
9, 11, 14	▶ 233a	▶ 3, 4, 5, 6, 7
10, 13, 15, 17	▶ 233b	▶ 3, 4, 6, 7
20, 25, 35	▶ 245	▶ 9
21, 26, 32	▶ 243	▶ 8, 9
27, 30, 33	▶ 244	▶ 9
28, 29, 31, 34	▶ 242	▶ 8, 9

1 *The German 'man'* *you, one, they* ▶ **229a/b**

a Choose the most suitable pronoun from the brackets to translate German *'man'*. Sometimes more than one answer is suitable, depending on the situation.

Examples: (One/You/***They***) said on the news that there's been another bus crash in Spain.
(***One/You***/They) should not criticize others until all the facts are known.

1 The post office is closed. Where else can (they/you/one) get stamps?
2 I heard that (they/you) are building a new car park in Albion Street.
3 (You/One/They) should never expect help from others. Remember that.
4 (You/They) say that William might become the next king, not Charles.
5 (You/They) speak Spanish in Andorra, I think.
6 Are (they/you) allowed to take photos here?
7 Nobody is happy all the time – (they/you) have to take the rough with the smooth.
8 Where did you get these nice glasses? – (You/They) are giving them away at the supermarket. You just have to buy a six-pack of cola.
9 Don't be too trusting. (One/You/They) can never know.
10 Why don't you do the competition? (You /They) can win a holiday in Spain.
11 (One/You/They) should always be prepared. That's the boy scouts' motto.
12 Take an umbrella. (You/One) can never know how the weather will turn out.

▶ b Work with a partner. Write three German sentences with the word *'man'* and ask your partner to translate them.

2 *A flat of her own* **possessive pronouns and determiners: mixed ex.** ▶ **230, 231**

a Some possessive determiners (*my, your*, etc.) and possessive pronouns (*mine, yours*, etc.) are missing from the text. Put them in and remember that with *own* you sometimes need an *of*-phrase.

Alison is a good friend of (1) … I've known her since school. She never had (2) … own room at home, because she had to share with her sister. Then she went to university, and again she had to share a bedsit[1] with another student, Joanne. She really wanted to have a place (3) … own at last, just something small and inexpensive, but private. She simply wanted something that was (4) … alone. She had shared things all (5) … life. She wanted to be able to say to her friends: 'This is (6) … flat' – not 'This is (7) … bedsit.'

One day she heard about a flat not far away that had suddenly become vacant[2]. She got the address and phone number from a neighbour of (8) …
The flat was small and not very well furnished. The carpet on the stairs was worn – it even had holes in it, but the rent was very reasonable. 'If you want it, it's (9) …,' the landlord had said, taking the contract from (10) … pocket. Alison had immediately put on (11) … glasses, read it through and signed. 'All right. Now it's (12) … ,' she had said with a smile.

Unfortunately, as she ran down the stairs, she caught (13) … foot in a hole in the carpet, tripped[3] and fell badly, breaking (14) … right leg and right arm. When she came out of hospital last week, she went back to the bedsit with Joanne. At the moment Alison is very glad that she is not alone.

---

1 bedsit: a rented room where you live and sleep   2 vacant: empty
3 trip: catch your foot in/on sth. and lose your balance

6 *Mixed bag*   possessive pronouns and determiners; reflexive pronouns, non-reflexive verbs; *each other*   ▶ **231b-d, 233, 234, 236**

What is missing? Choose the correct word/phrase from the brackets. Only one answer is correct.

1 At Christmas relatives and friends usually give (themselves/each other) presents.
2 Rob went to Austria skiing and broke (the/his) left leg.
3 We all enjoyed (ourselves/us) when we were on holiday in Italy last year.
4 Jan and I don't see (us/ourselves/each other) as often as we used to.
5 Jim and I first met (ourselves/us/–) at a party when we were at university.
6 My brother never goes to the hairdresser's. He always cuts his hair (himself/oneself).
7 My sister has known Sean for years. He's a classmate (of her/of hers).
8 There were so many people at Joan's party that we could hardly move (ourselves/us/–).
9 Tom always has to borrow his father's car. He would like to have (an own car/his own car).
10 Liz burnt (her/the) right hand with cooking oil from a hot pan.
11 Nick always says what others say. He's got no (own ideas/ideas of his own).
12 Jenny's got four of my books. She's got some videos (of me/of mine) too.

7 *Being Australian*   reflexive pronouns, *each other*: mixed exercise   ▶ **233, 234**

What does being Australian mean to young people who are children of first-generation immigrants?
A teacher from the McQuarrie High School in Sydney said:

'They all feel Australian, but they also feel very much part of their own cultures. Those born in Australia feel more Australian than their parents, which creates a problem for them. We encourage them to be proud of themselves and of their cultural backgrounds. We don't encourage them to think of themselves as Australians, but as Arabic-speaking Australians or
5   as Greek-speaking Australians or whatever, and to value their heritage[1].'

In the1970's and 1980's, waves of migrants brought people from China, Vietnam, India and Indonesia, among many others. Some students talked about their values[2] and those of their parents, many of whom have still not adapted[3] to the language and customs of their new country. All agree that their parents tend to associate only with members of their own
10   communities. But the younger generation mixes freely with Australians.

Maria says of her Chinese-born parents: 'They still strongly identify themselves with China. I try to identify myself with the Chinese culture too, but I consider myself an Australian

---

1 heritage: history, culture, traditions of a country   2 values: beliefs about what is important, right or wrong in life
3 adapt: change one's thinking or behaviour to something new or different

with a Chinese background. My father knows a little English, my mother tried to teach herself some English, but they can't express themselves in English as I can.'

15 Anna with Indonesian-born parents: 'My parents want me to keep their tradition and I want to mix with Australians too. Sometimes it's hard. I can't imagine living in Indonesia. It's a strange world for me. My parents and I differ[1] in the way we think. This is my home'.

Amanda says of her Lebanese-born parents: 'They always remember how it was at home and they think of things that remind them about their home country. They mix only with
20 the Lebanese community. They find it hard to adapt to the customs of this country and their opinions will not change. I have a lot of Australian friends. We meet after school. We help each other with homework. We go out together and we lend each other things – just like friends do. I sometimes wonder what would happen if I fell in love with an Australian. I don't think my parents would ever recover from the shock. They would like me to settle
25 down with someone from the Lebanese community one day. I sometimes worry about my future.'

Adapted from 'The Future of Multiculturalism' by Kerry-Anne Walsh, in: Dr. B. Klewitz, *Australian Encounters*

a Search the text for the equivalents of the following German verbs:

1 auf sich stolz sein 2 sich ausdrücken 3 sich vorstellen 4 sich unterscheiden
5 sich betrachten als 6 sich einig sein 7 an sich denken 8 sich mit etwas identifizieren

b Study the last paragraph. Can you find ten verbs which are non-reflexive in English but reflexive in German? Write them down with their translations.

c Complete the sentences with a reflexive pronoun where necessary or *each other*.

1 Anna and her parents differ … in the way they think about their Indonesian background.
2 Anna finds it hard to identify … with the customs, traditions and language of Indonesia.
3 Teachers want their students to see … as Arabic-speaking Australians, or whatever.
4 Children of immigrants and young Australians mix … freely.
5 They help … and borrow things from …, as friends do.
6 The students' parents do not seem to consider … Australians.
7 If you cannot express … in a foreign language, it is hard to feel … at home.
8 Different cultural attitudes between generations often cause parents and children to quarrel with …

d In your own words, answer the questions on the text in a short paragraph each.

1 How do the Australian teachers try to encourage their students to think of themselves?
2 What do all three girls say about their parents' attitude towards their 'old' and 'new' countries?
3 How does Maria see herself, as a Chinese or as an Australian?
4 Why is Amanda worried about her future? Outline the problem.
5 'Accepting a new culture can be a problem for first-generation immigrants.' Explain.

e What are your thoughts on the subject of multiculturalism? Do you have friends who come from a cultural background which is different from your own? Write a short essay about your knowledge or experience.

_____

1 differ: be different from sb.

8 *At the scene of the crime*   **who, which, what**    **242-244**

a   After a football match a fan was found injured in the changing rooms. The police are asking the players some questions. Translate them into English.

 1 Wer kennt den Verletzten *(injured man)*?
 2 Was haben Sie auf dem Weg zu den Umkleideräumen gesehen *(did … see)*?
 3 Wen haben Sie beim Weglaufen gesehen *(running away)*?
 4 Wer von Ihnen kann die Männer beschreiben?
 5 Wie sahen sie aus?
 6 Was hatten sie an *(wear)*?
 7 Wer hat einen Schlüssel zu den Umkleideräumen?
 8 Wer könnte einen Schlüssel gehabt haben?
 9 Welcher Spieler kam zuerst in die Umkleideräume?
10 Wer fand den Verletzten?
11 Wer von Ihnen hat die Polizei angerufen?
12 Mit *(to)* wem haben Sie darüber *(about this)* gesprochen?

b   Imagine the following situation. You arrive at school one morning and hear that all the new computers have been stolen from the computer room overnight. The police are asking questions. What questions do you think the police would ask the pupils and the teachers? Write as many sensible direct questions as you can think of, beginning with question words, as in a) above.

9 *Find the mistakes*   **question words: mixed exercise**    **241-245**

Only two of the sentences or sentence pairs are correct. Which are they? There is one mistake in each of the others. Study the sentences carefully and correct them.

 1 Who of you would like to go to a concert in Bath with me?
 2 Who's CDs are these? They're not mine.
 3 Which of these videos would you like to borrow? This or that?
 4 What discovered Alexander Fleming in 1928?
 5 Which kind of book are you looking for?
 6 That was a stupid thing to do. What for did you do it?
 7 Who of the pupils hasn't made any mistakes?
 8 To who did you give the information?
 9 What of these paintings do you like best?
10 What for is this metal ring?
11 What do you call this in German?
12 How is the weather like in Berlin today?

Conditional sentences

A ▸ **Fill in the correct tenses/forms of the verbs in brackets.**

Marcus: I'm taking my driving test tomorrow. I'm starting to get nervous already.

Layla: Don't worry. If you (1 keep) … calm, you (2 be) … all right. But I can imagine how you feel. If I (3 have to) … take my driving test tomorrow, I (4 feel) … nervous too.

Marcus: This is my second try. All my friends (5 laugh) … at me if I (6 fail) … again.

Layla: Not all your friends. Anyway, as I remember, you were ill the first time you took your test. You had a virus, didn't you? You (7 not – fail) … the first time if you (8 not – be) … ill.

B ▸ **Translate the German sentence parts into English.**

9 *(Wenn Ruth in Bristol wäre)* …, she could come and visit us.
10 If I lived in the US, *(könnte ich Auto fahren.)* …
11 If you don't want anyone to know about this, *(sage ich nichts.)* …
12 *(Wenn ich du wäre)* …, I would take the job.
13 Would you go out more *(wenn du nicht so viele Hausaufgaben machen müsstest?)* …
14 *(Wenn du ankommst, ruf mich bitte an)* …, so that I won't worry about you.
15 If the van driver hadn't been driving so fast, *(hätte der Unfall verhindert werden können.)* …
16 Steve could have passed his driving test easily *(wenn er nicht so nervös gewesen wäre.)* …
17 *(Wenn ich mehr Geld verdienen würde)* …, I would buy more books.
18 I would simply tell the truth *(wenn ich Sheila wäre.)* …

C ▸ **Spot the mistakes. There is one mistake in each sentence or sentence pair.**

19 Jenny might possibly be at the barbecue. When I see her, I'll give her your message.
20 If Sam doesn't come soon, we eat without her.
21 If John would earn a lot of money, he would tell everybody, I'm sure.
22 If I would have known about the meeting, I wouldn't have stayed at home.
23 If you will fly to Miami with British Airways before 15th May, it will cost £215.
24 You can't access the files in case you know the password.
25 If I had known that there was plenty of time, I hadn't run all the way here.
26 Claire would tell me how to work the machine if she would know.
27 Marie wouldn't have asked you for money if she would have enough herself.
28 I'll give you a key unless I'm not at home when you arrive.
29 If you arrive in York, I'll meet you at the station. Don't worry, I'll be there.
30 It's a secret, but I'll tell you when you promise not to say anything to anybody.

Conditional sentences

? Correct yourself

A 1: *keep*   2: *will be*   3: *had to*   4: *would feel*   5: *will laugh*   6: *fail*   7: *would not have failed*   8: *had not been*

B 9: *If Ruth was/were in Bristol, she could come and visit us.*   10: *If I lived in the US, I could drive (a car).*   11: *If you don't want anyone to know about this, I won't say anything/I'll say nothing.* 12: *If I were/was you, I would take the job.*   13: *Would you go out more if you didn't have to do so much homework?*   14: *When you arrive, phone me, please, so that I won't worry about you.* 15: *If the van driver hadn't been driving so fast, the accident could/might have been prevented.* 16: *Steve could have passed his driving test easily if he hadn't been so nervous.*   17: *If I earned more money, I would buy more books.*   18: *I would simply tell the truth if I were/was Sheila.*

C 19: *Jenny might possibly be at the barbecue. If I see her, I'll give her your message.*
20: *If Sam doesn't come soon, we will eat without her.*
21: *If John earned a lot of money, he would tell everybody, I'm sure.*
22: *If I had known about the meeting, I wouldn't have stayed at home.*
23: *If you fly to Miami with British Airways before 15th May, it will cost £215.*
24: *You can't access the files unless you know the password.*
25: *If I had known that there was plenty of time, I wouldn't have run all the way here.*
26: *Claire would tell me how to work the machine if she knew.*
27: *Marie wouldn't have asked you for money if she had had enough herself.*
28: *I'll give you a key in case I'm not at home when you arrive.*
29: *When you arrive in York, I'll meet you at the station. Don't worry, I'll be there.*
30: *It's a secret, but I'll tell you if you promise not to say anything to anybody.*

Exercise finder

Sentences	CEG	Exercises
1, 2, 5, 6, 11, 20, 23	▶ 252a	▶ 2, 7
3, 4, 10, 13, 17, 21, 26	▶ 253a	▶ 3, 4, 7, 8
7, 8, 15, 16, 22, 25, 27	▶ 254	▶ 5, 6, 7, 8
14, 19, 24, 28, 29, 30	▶ 251d	▶ 1, 7
9, 12, 18	▶ 253b	▶ 3b

1 *Mini-dialogues*　**conjunctions used in conditional sentences**　▶ **251d**

a Complete the mini-dialogues with *if* or *when*.

1 Leo:　I'll tell you how to get to our house. … you get off the train, take the number 24 bus from the station. It only goes once an hour, so make sure you get the 2.30 bus.

　Lucy:　What shall I do … I miss it?

　Leo:　Well, … the train is on time, you shouldn't miss it. So, … you manage to get the bus, ask for Wilton Road. It takes about half an hour. … you get off, just walk down past the church and turn right into Church Lane. OK?

2 Robin:　I'm going to a party on Saturday. Paul will be there too, so I'll see him.

　Rachel:　Oh. … you see him, say hello to him from me, will you? Will Ann be there as well?

　Robin:　I'm not sure. Perhaps.

　Rachel:　… she is there, ask her to phone me, please. She still has some CDs of mine. … I don't remind her about them, she'll forget to give them back.

b Now complete the dialogues with *unless, in case, as long as* or *supposing*.

1 Mother:　Take my umbrella … it rains.

　Sharon:　I'll take my anorak. I won't need an umbrella … it rains really heavily.

　Mother:　But your anorak hasn't got a hood[1]. Your hair will get wet. … it rains heavily, what will you do?

　Sharon:　I'll stand under a tree.

　Mother:　Trees are only safe … there isn't a thunderstorm.

　Sharon:　Mum, stop worrying about rain and thunderstorms. The sun's shining.

2 Nazreen:　Can I borrow your history notes – … you need them yourself tonight.

　Laura:　No, I don't. You can borrow them … you give them back tomorrow so that I can learn for the test.

　Nazreen:　Well, I might not be at school in time for history tomorrow. I have to go to the dentist's. So I'll give them to my brother … I'm not there. He could meet you at the bus stop at eight.

　Laura:　… he misses the bus, what then?

　Nazreen:　I'll bring them over for you tomorrow night and we can learn history together.

c Write suitable sentence endings. There are, of course, many possibilities.

1　I'll buy some extra food in case …
2　Layla will fail her exams unless …
3　I don't mind you playing your music as long as …
4　Take your mobile in case …
5　We can carry on working unless …
6　I'll lend you some money as long as …

---

1 hood　*Kaputze*

2 *What will happen if …?*   conditional sentence I   ▶ 252a

a   Put in the correct tenses/forms of the verbs in brackets to make conditional sentences type I.

Tony: My brother Mike's trying to sell his old car. I'll be really surprised if he (1 manage) … to find a buyer.

Sue: Why? If the price is right, he (2 sell) … it.

Tony: If he (3 not – clean) … it up, he (4 not – sell) … it at all.

Sue: I need a cheap car myself. How much does your brother want for it?

Tony: I'm not sure. But if you (5 phone) … him, he (6 tell) … you. He (7 let) … you drive it, if you (8 ask) … him – if you don't mind sitting between cola cans and tennis balls.

b   How might the situation continue? Write suitable/probable endings, using conditional sentences type I with either *will/won't* or a modal auxiliary (*can, may, should*, etc.) in the main clause. There are, of course, many possibilities. Remember to use some negative forms.

Examples: If Sue phones Mike, …   *she **will find out** the price of the car.*
                                      *she **can ask** him all about the car.*

           Sue might buy the car …   *if it **doesn't need** a lot of repairs.*
                                        *if it **doesn't cost** too much.*

1   If Mike cleans the car up, …

2   If Sue likes the car, …

3   Sue won't buy the car …

4   Sue should ask Mike …

5   If the car needs repairs, …

6   Sue will probably buy the car …

3 *Problems*   conditional sentence II   ▶ 253a/b

a   Ali and Ben are talking about a problem. Complete the conversation with conditional sentences type II.

Ali: I borrowed quite a lot of money from Robin and now I can't pay it back. I feel terrible. He hasn't said anything yet, but …

Ben: Mmm. Well, if you **had** a job, you **would be able to pay** it back easily.

Ali: That's the problem. I had a job, but I had to give it up because I need the time for schoolwork. If my marks were good, I (1 not – have to) … work so hard. But my marks are bad, so now I spend all my free time learning. It wouldn't matter about my marks if I (2 not – want) … to go to university, but I do. My Dad's out of work, so I can't ask him. If Dad (3 get) … a job, there (4 not – be) … any problems. But he's not very hopeful.

Ben: Well, I (5 help) … you if I (6 have) … some spare money, but I haven't. But I can help you with maths and physics. Then you could probably get your job back again soon. And don't worry about Robin. If he (7 want) … the money back immediately, he (8 ask) … you for it.

b Give advice to friends. Say what you would do if you were in their position. Use the expression
If I were you …

Example: I've lost an expensive watch that my parents gave me. I'm afraid to tell them.
          If I were you, I would tell your parents the truth. They will find out anyway.

1 I'm always tired and I can't concentrate properly in school.
2 My parents are always complaining about the mess in my room. I can never find my things.
3 My girlfriend doesn't want me to go to university away from home, but that's what I really want.
4 I'm always short of money. My pocket money doesn't go very far. I suppose I spend too much.
5 My parents want me to do a language course in Paris, but I would prefer to visit my penfriend in the States. There isn't enough time to do both.

4 *Situations*   **conditional sentence II**    **253a**

a How do you react in difficult or unexpected situations? What would you/wouldn't you do if the following things happened? Use conditional sentences type II with *would* in the main clause – and your imagination.

Example: You are in town with friends. You see someone steal an old lady's bag.
          If I saw someone steal an old lady's bag, I think I would run after the thief.
          I'm sure we would try to help if we saw the thief.

1 You lose your passport in a non-EU country.
2 A stranger asks you to lend him/her 20 euros on the street.
3 You are alone at home and the doorbell rings in the middle of the night.
4 You miss the last bus home. It's too far to walk.
5 Your bicycle has a puncture on a lonely road late at night.
6 A pickpocket steals your wallet/purse (with money, tickets, etc.). You are alone in a strange town.

b What could or might you do in the following situations?
Write a sentence with *could/couldn't* and with *might/mightn't* for each of the following situations.

What could/might you do …

1 … if your parents were rich and famous?
2 … if your family lived in the US?
3 … if you won a car?
4 … if you went to university in the UK?

5 *It wouldn't have happened if …*   conditional sentence III   ▶ 254

a   Some of Pete's friends are forgetful and careless. Look at the facts. Write Pete's comments about the following situations, using conditional sentences type III.

Examples: Jill overslept and was late for her interview. She didn't set her alarm.
   Pete: *If Jill **had set** her alarm, she **wouldn't have overslept** and **been** late for her interview.*
   Mark's camera was stolen. He didn't lock his car.
   Pete: *Mark's camera **wouldn't have been stolen** if he **had locked** his car.*

1   Steve left his rucksack in a café. It disappeared.
2   The maths teacher confiscated[1] Sita's mobile. It rang in his lesson.
3   Rachel lost her walkman. She left it lying about.
4   Tom didn't pay his bill. His mobile phone was de-activated.
5   Emma was driving too fast on her moped. That's why she had the accident.
6   Lucy's university application wasn't accepted. She sent it off too late.

b   In English, please.

1   Wenn Laura ihr Fahrrad abgeschlossen hätte, wäre es nicht gestohlen worden.
2   Julia hätte ihren Fotoapparat nicht verloren, wenn sie besser aufgepasst hätte *(take more care)*.
3   Wenn Alan nicht zu schnell gefahren wäre, hätte er seine Fahrprüfung bestanden.
4   David wäre nicht gestürzt *(fall)*, wenn er nicht mit seinem Snowboard hätte angeben *(show off)* wollen.

6 *A bus accident*   conditional sentence III   ▶ 254

a   Read the newspaper report and complete the sentences on the next page.

Crash on Austrian motorway

At least twenty people were injured when a coach carrying British holiday-makers crashed on the motorway near Jenbach in Austria in the early hours of the morning. The accident was probably caused by a chain of unfortunate events. The coach was heading south to Sorrento in Italy. It had rained heavily in the night and was still dark. The driver of the coach had been on the road for eight hours and was perhaps overtired. The co-driver was asleep at the time of the accident. Because of delays in France due to heavy holiday traffic, the coach was behind schedule. It is thought probable that the driver was travelling too fast, trying to make up time. Police said the coach appeared to have skidded[2] on the wet road surface after trying to overtake another vehicle.

The driver may have lost control of the bus before it swerved[3] and hit the crash barrier. Most passengers were asleep and were not wearing seatbelts. The passengers who remained unhurt had had their seatbelts fastened.

A policeman said, 'It was lucky that there was not much traffic on the motorway. The accident could have been much worse. The driver is in shock, so he can't tell us what happened.'

---

1 confiscate: take away and keep   2 skid: slide in an uncontrolled manner   3 swerve: change direction suddenly

Complete the statements with information from the text. Make conditional sentences type III, positive or negative, with *would*, *might* or *could* according to meaning. Sometimes two modals are suitable.

Examples: *If it **had not been raining**, the roads **would not have been** wet.*
*If the co-driver **hadn't been** asleep, he **might have been able to prevent** the accident.*

1 If there … a lot of holiday traffic in France, the coach … delayed.
2 If the coach … behind schedule, the driver … too fast.
3 The accident … if the driver … overtired.
4 The coach … if it … heavily.
5 The driver … control if the roads … wet.
6 The bus … the crash barrier if it … and swerved.
7 If the passengers … asleep, more of them … seatbelts.
8 If the injured passengers … seatbelts, they … hurt.
9 If there … more traffic on the motorway, the accident … worse.
10 If the driver … in shock, he … the police how the accident happened.

b Describe an accident or something unfortunate that happened to you, someone in your family, a neighbour or a friend. Say what happened, why, and how it could possibly have been prevented. Write a short paragraph using conditional sentences type III.

Example: *My friend broke his leg skiing. He was tired but he wanted to ski down the black slope one more time. If he **hadn't been** tired, he **might not have been** careless and the accident **might not have happened**.*

Some friends are planning a trip to New York after they leave school in summer. Complete their conversation with suitable tenses/forms of the verbs given and choose the correct conjunctions from the brackets. Use conditional sentences (all types).

Emma: If I keep my part-time job until summer, I (1 have) … enough money for the trip.

Phil: If I (2 not – spend) … all my money on a new computer last year, I would have had the money for the trip long ago.

Janet: Well, (3 unless/in case/as long as) something unexpected happens, I will have enough for the whole trip by June.

Phil: You always have enough money, Janet.

Janet: Well, I save. If I (4 spend) … a lot on clothes and CDs, I (5 not – have) … much at all.

Emma: If I (6 not – earn) … good money at the garage, I wouldn't be able to afford the trip. Anyway, when shall we go?

Janet: If we (7 book) … before 15th May, it will cost £ 175. That's the cheapest offer. And if we fly before 16th July, we (8 get) … a discount off all US flights.

Steve: July is too early. What about August?

Emma: If we (9 go) … in August, it might be too hot. It's the busiest holiday month too.

Phil: Well then, September? If university (10 not – start) … until October, we could go in the second half of September.

Emma: (11 Supposing/In case/Unless) you have to resit[1] an exam, what will happen?

Phil: Don't worry. If I do enough work, I (12 not – have to) … resit.

Janet: Now, rooms. I think we should book a hotel (13 in case/when/as long as) the students' hostels[2] are full. What would we do if we (14 not – get) … rooms? Everywhere may be full up in summer. Just imagine how scary[3] it would be if we (15 have to) … sleep in Central Park. If we (16 book) … a tourist hotel through a travel agent, it would be cheaper.

Steve: Good idea. If we stayed in Manhattan, somewhere central, we (17 walk) … everywhere and cut travel costs. And what about food?

Phil: My Dad was in Washington last year. He said if he (18 buy) … sandwiches in the delis[4], he (19 save) … a lot. So if we (20 be) … careful with our money, we should be OK.

---

1 resit [riːˈsit]: repeat, take an exam again after failing   2 hostel: cheap accommodation   3 scary: frightening
4 deli: short for 'delicatessen', shop which sells sandwiches, cold food and salads

Will is a 36-year old, modern, carefree single living in London. His father once wrote a successful pop song, and Will lives from the income. Although he is good-looking and reasonably educated, he does not work and does not want to work. So far he is perfectly satisfied with his life as it is.

Will wondered sometimes […] how people like him would have survived sixty years ago. ('People like him' was, he knew, something of a specialized grouping: in fact, there couldn't have been anyone like him sixty years ago, because sixty years ago no adult could have had a father who had made his money in quite the same way. So when he thought about people
5 like him, he didn't mean people exactly like him, he just meant people who didn't really do anything all day, and didn't want to do anything much, either.) Sixty years ago, all the things Will relied on to get him through the day simply didn't exist: there was no daytime TV, there were no videos, there were no glossy magazines and therefore no questionnaires and, though there were probably record shops, the kind of music he listened to hadn't even
10 been invented yet. […] Which would have left books. Books! He would have had to get a job, almost definitely, because he would have gone round the twist[1] otherwise.

Some weeks later:
If there was a disadvantage to the life he had chosen for himself, a life without work and care and difficulty and detail, […] then he had finally found it: when he met an intelligent,
15 cultured, ambitious, beautiful, witty[2] and single woman at a New Year's Eve party, he felt like a blank twit[3] […] If you were falling in love with someone beautiful and intelligent and all the rest of it, then feeling like a blank twit put you at something of a disadvantage.[…] Because the thing was, that when this Rachel woman sat down next to him at dinner she was interested, for the first five minutes, before she'd worked him out, and in that five
20 minutes he got a glimpse[4] of what life could be like if he were in any way interesting. […] He hated the five-minute window of opportunity[5]. In the end, he thought he would be far happier if she turned round to look at him, just about managed not to vomit[6], and turned her back on him for the rest of the evening.

From *About a Boy* by Nick Hornby

---

1 go round the twist: go crazy   2 witty: clever and amusing   3 blank twit: silly person who knows little
4 glimpse: short look   5 window of opportunity: good time/chance for sth.   6 vomit: be sick

a   Identify the four conditional sentences in ll. 13-23. Write down the tenses in *if*-clause and main clause. Two sentences are 'mixed types'. Are the remaining two sentences type I, type II or type III? What do you notice about the use of the comma between *if*-clause and main clause?

b   Complete the conditional sentences using suitable verbs (positive and negative) in the correct tense/form. Remember also to use the modals *could* and *might* where suitable.

1   Will wondered how he would have survived if he … sixty years ago.
2   If Will's father … a lot of money with a pop song, Will … such an easy life.
3   If Will didn't have income from his father's song, he … get a job.
4   If Will had lived sixty years ago, he … watched videos or daytime TV.
5   He … listened to the kind of music he likes now, if he … sixty years ago.
6   If Will had had to read books to fill up his time sixty years ago, he … crazy.
7   Will thought that Rachel … more interested in him if he … an interesting job.
8   Will thought he … happier if Rachel … away from him for the rest of the evening.

c   When Will meets Rachel, he wishes his life was different. Make sentences beginning with *If only …* to express Will's thoughts:

Example: I'm not interesting for her.
           *If only I **was** interesting for her.*

1   Rachel isn't interested in me.
2   I haven't got a job.
3   I can't think of anything interesting to say.
4   I don't do anything with my life.
5   I haven't learnt anything.
6   She asks awkward questions.
7   I have to lie about myself all the time.
8   I have wasted my life.

d   Write a short paragraph for each of the following questions, using conditional sentences.

1   If you were in Will's position, would you choose to live like him? Explain why or why not.

2   If you had lived sixty years ago, how would you probably have spent your free time?

3   Apart from the things Will mentions (daytime TV, etc.), what else would have been different in his life sixty years ago?

4   When Will meets Rachel, why does he regret that he doesn't work?

5   How do you think the New Year's Eve party might continue? Write a short scenario using conditionals, for example:

     If Will …, Rachel might/could … On the other hand, Rachel … if …

Relative clauses

A ▶ **Put in the missing relative pronouns where necessary. Sometimes two are possible.**

1 The people … have just moved in next door are pretty noisy.
2 The last talk … I went to was on twentieth century poetry.
3 Isn't that the photographer … work was on exhibition at the Town Gallery last week?
4 These are the photos … I took on the study trip.
5 The van driver, … was clearly to blame for the accident, will have to face serious charges.
6 The man … the police are looking for was seen on a train in Manchester two days ago.
7 Flight CX 703, … was delayed for almost four hours, finally took off at lunchtime.
8 You look good in blue. It's a colour … really suits you.
9 The English teacher spoke to the pupils … work was below standard.
10 Shall I show you the shop … I bought those posters?

B ▶ **Translate the German sentence parts into English. Leave out pronouns where possible.**

11 Do you remember the people *(die wir auf dem Campingplatz in Bardolino trafen?)* …
12 My friend Joanne, *(deren Eltern beide Musiklehrer sind)* … , plays three instruments.
13 The new hospital, *(das bis Ende Juni fertig gestellt sein wird)* … , is to be opened by the Queen.
14 This is Jerry, the boy *(mit dem ich jeden Morgen zur Schule gehe.)* …
15 Where are the crisps and snacks *(die ich für die Party kaufte?)* …
16 Mr Wilkins has been made deputy head, *(was uns alle überraschte.)* …
17 That's the man *(dessen Foto heute in der Zeitung ist.)* … He rescued a boy from a burning car.
18 This is the house *(wo wir früher gewohnt haben.)* …
19 *(Der Mann, der über uns wohnt, spielt fast jeden Tag Klavier.)* …
20 I would particularly like to thank Dr Fox, *(ohne den)* … this success would not have been possible.

C ▶ **Add commas where necessary.**

21 Edison who was the father of our modern music industry had only three months' formal learning.
22 The river which runs through the city of Stratford is called the Avon.
23 Alexander Bell to whom we owe the invention of the telephone was born in Scotland.
24 The firm is in financial difficulties which means that workers won't get a pay rise this year.
25 The book which deals with the subject most thoroughly is the one by Professor Beech.

D ▶ **Spot the mistakes. There is one mistake in each sentence or sentence pair.**

26 The woman, who lives next door, writes scripts for TV documentaries.
27 Where's the box in that I keep old photos and letters?
28 Which is the man which gave you the wrong information? Can you point him out?
29 Manchester United, against who the team lost, has won every match this season.
30 Look, on this photo you can see the hotel where we stayed at.
31 Dr Jacobs, that used to lecture at Bristol University, has accepted a post in Edinburgh.
32 John described the route to us very well, what saved us a lot of time.
33 William Wordsworth, by who this poem was written, lived in the Lake District.
34 The company lawyer, which advises the board on contract matters, is very experienced.

Relative clauses

? **Correct yourself**

A 1: *who* 2: *–* 3: *whose* 4: *–* 5: *who* 6: *–* 7: *which* 8: *that/which* 9: *whose*
10: *where/at which* (formal)

B 11: *… the people we met on/at the camping site in Bardolino?*
12: *…, whose parents are both music teachers, …*
13: *…, which will be finished by the end of June, …*
14: *… the boy I go to school with every morning.*
15: *… snacks I bought for the party?*
16: *…, which surprised us all.*
17: *… whose photo is in the newspaper today …*
18: *… where we used to live.*
19: *The man who lives above us plays the piano almost every day.*
20: *…, without whom …*

C 21: *Edison, who was the father of our modern music industry, had …*
22: *The river which runs through the city of Stratford is called the Avon.* (no commas)
23: *Alexander Bell, to whom we owe the invention of the telephone, was …*
24: *The firm is in financial difficulties, which means that workers won't get a pay rise this year.*
25: *The book which deals with the subject most thoroughly is the one by Professor Beech.*
(no commas)

D 26: *The woman who lives next door writes …* (no commas)
27: *Where's the box (that) I keep old photos and letters in?*
28: *Which is the man who gave you the wrong information? …*
29: *Manchester United, against whom the team lost, has won …*
30: *Look, on this photo you can see the hotel where we stayed.*
   Or: *… the hotel (that/which) we stayed at.*
   Or: *… the hotel at which we stayed.* (formal)
31: *Dr Jacobs, who used to lecture at Bristol University, has accepted …*
32: *John described the route to us very well, which saved us a lot of time.*
33: *William Wordsworth, by whom this poem was written, lived …*
34: *The company lawyer, who advises the board on contract matters, is …*

Exercise finder

Sentences	CEG	Exercises
1, 8, 28, 34	▶ 260	▶ 1, 4, 5
2, 6, 14, 27	▶ 264b	▶ 2
3, 9, 12, 17	▶ 262	▶ 4, 5
4, 11, 15	▶ 264a	▶ 4, 5
5, 7, 13, 21, 31	▶ 265a	▶ 3, 4, 5
10, 18, 30	▶ 263b	▶ 4, 5
16, 24, 32	▶ 266	▶ 5
19, 22, 25, 26	▶ 259b	▶ 3
20, 23, 29, 33	▶ 265d	▶ 4b

1 *Definitions*   relative pronoun as subject: *who/that, that/which*   ▶ **260**

a How would you explain the meanings of the following words in English? Use a noun and a relative clause with *who/that* or *that/which* as subject.

Examples: Ausländer/in
It's someone/a person **who/that** comes from/lives in another country.
Wörterbuch
It's a book **that/which** tells you the meanings of words.

> 1 Schauspieler/in   2 Wegweiser   3 Tischler/in   4 Fahrplan   5 Nichtraucher/in
> 6 Einwanderer/-in   7 Anrufbeantworter   8 Verwandte/r   9 Wahrsager/in
> 10 Reiseführer/in

b Work with a partner. Describe three words (people or things) to a partner. Your partner must guess your words in English, so make your description as exact as possible.

Example: It's someone **who/that** takes your order and brings your food in a restaurant.
Answer: *a waiter or a waitress*

2 *The hotel we stayed at*   contact clauses with prepositions   ▶ **264b**

a Patrick Murphy from Ireland is telling a friend about a holiday the family once spent in London, but he can't remember the names of places or where things were. He asks his family. Make questions with contact clauses and put the preposition at the end.

Examples: We stayed at a nice hotel in the West End. What was the name of …?
*What was the name of the hotel ( ) **we stayed at**?*
We didn't fly to Heathrow. It was another airport. Where was …?
*Where was the airport ( ) **we flew to**?*

1 One evening we went to a theatre. What was the name of …?
2 I can remember that we climbed up a big tower. What was the name of …?
3 We drove to a castle just outside London. Where was …?
4 We looked round a big museum. What was the name of …?
5 In the evenings we sometimes used to go to an Italian restaurant. It wasn't expensive.
What was the name of …?
6 But once we ate at an expensive sushi restaurant. Where was …?
7 We went to a musical one night. What was the name of …?
8 We sometimes had a sandwich lunch in a park. Where was …?
9 We often shopped at one of the well-known stores on Oxford Street. What was the name of …?
10 We even rowed a boat on a park lake. What was the name of …?

b Think of your last holiday. Make sentences as in part a) above. Write about four of these things:

1 the place   2 the hotel/guest house/camping site   3 the beach
4 the sea/lake/mountains/etc.   5 the restaurants/shops/etc.

Example: The place **we stayed at** was not far from …/was on the Italian coast.

3 *Places to visit* non-defining relative clauses ▶ 259b, 265a-c

HAWAII

a In the text about Hawaii there are a few defining relative clauses (no commas). The rest are non-defining relative clauses giving extra information. For these clauses you need commas. Can you put them in?

Examples: A place ( ) that most people would like to visit ( ) is Hawaii. (defining)
Hawaii**,** which consists of six main islands**,** is five hours by plane from the Californian coast. (non-defining)

1 Hawaii ___ which is not one island but several ___ became the 50th US state in 1959.
2 The islands were discovered by the Englishman James Cook ___ who also discovered Australia.
3 Cook ___ whom the natives killed in1779 ___ had been warmly welcomed just a year earlier.
4 The capital of Hawaii is Honolulu ___which is situated on the island Oahu.
5 Oahu is the island ___ that most tourists visit.
6 Pearl Harbor ___ which was attacked by the Japanese in 1941 ___ is on Oahu, just north of Honolulu.
7 If you like surfing, Hawaii is the place to go. The beaches ___ where the world surfing championships take place ___ are on Oahu and Maui.
8 Of all the beautiful beaches, Waikiki Beach near Honolulu is the one ___ that is most famous.
9 Spielberg's film *Jurassic Park* was filmed on Kauai ___ which is the greenest of the islands.
10 The island of Hawaii ___ which is also called Big Island ___ is the largest of the group.
11 Hawaii is also the home of Kilauea, the volcano ___ which is known to be the world's most active.
12 *Aloha* ___ which means *Hello* and *Goodbye* ___ is the first Hawaiian word ___ which you learn.

b This text is about the Channel Islands, which are not quite as exotic as Hawaii but are well worth a visit. Combine two sentences, using non-defining relative clauses with *who, whom,* and *which*, as in a).

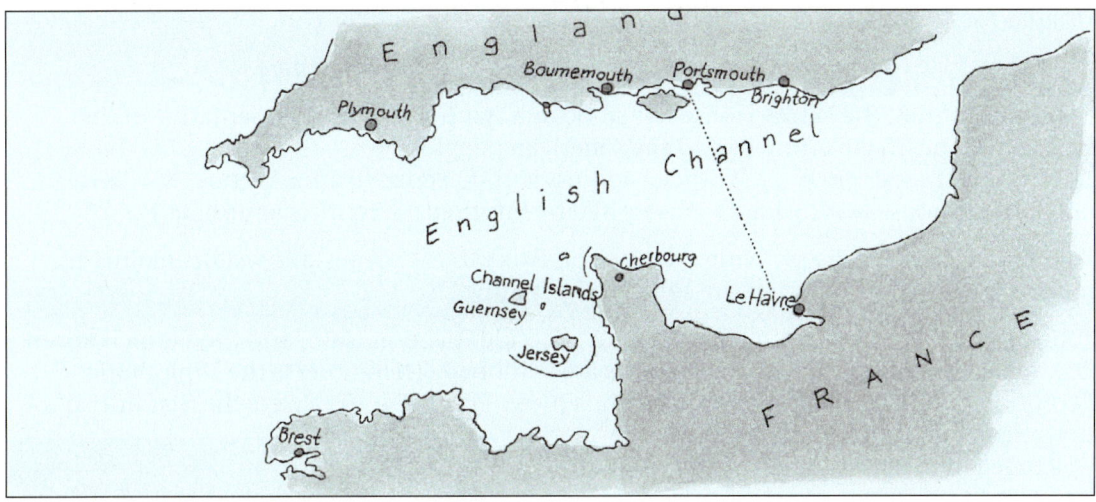

Example: The Channel Islands lie in the English Channel. (They consist of four main islands.)
*The Channel Islands, **which consist of four main islands**, lie in the English Channel.*

1 The Channel Islands are closer to France than to England. (They belong to Britain.)
2 The largest of the four islands is only about 20 kilometres from the French coast. (It is called Jersey.)
3 The nearest island to England is Alderney. (It is 80 kilometres from the English coast.)
4 The Channel Islanders are very friendly. (They speak both English and French.)
5 The island of Sark is only 5.5 square kilometres. (It is the smallest island.) There is no traffic on Sark because cars are not allowed, so the 700 inhabitants go by horse and cart or by tractor.
6 The islands are visited by over half a million tourists every year. (They are known for their mild climate and beautiful beaches.)
7 The tourists are fond of the street cafés and the French cooking. (The tourists come mainly from England.)
8 The English particularly enjoy the southern flair. (The Channel Islanders welcome them warmly.)

a Put in the missing relative pronouns. If a pronoun is not necessary, write '–'.

which ▪ that ▪ who ▪ whose ▪ whom ▪ where

For two centuries, the White House has stood as a symbol (1) … is representative of the Presidency, the US government and the American people.
The President's residence, (2) … official address is 1600 Pennsylvania Avenue, NW, is the only private house worldwide (3) … is visited by hundreds of tourists almost daily.

Tours, (4) … start at the East Wing entrance on Executive Avenue, take visitors mainly to rooms on the State Floor. Here are some of the highlights.

Tourists visit the China Room, (5) … displays presidential porcelain, and the Vermeil Room, (6) … portraits of 20th century First Ladies are exhibited. Then there is the Diplomatic Reception Room. In 1939, King George and Queen Elizabeth, (7) … were the first British sovereigns to visit the White House, were welcomed in this beautiful oval-shaped room.

The Blue Room, (8) … is the centre of the State Floor, is also oval in shape. It is the room (9) … presidents have traditionally received important guests in. From here there is an excellent view of the South Lawn, (10) … today the presidential helicopter lands.

The large East Room is the room (11) … First Lady Abigail Adams (1797-1801) hung the family's washing in. This elegant white and gold room, (12) … was unfinished and unfurnished at that time, is in fact an ideal multi-purpose room, (13) … weddings, funerals, concerts, press conferences and receptions have taken place over the years. It is also the room (14) … Theodore Roosevelt's children used to roller-skate and cycle in, when the weather was bad. Because of its size, it is the room (15) … President Woodrow Wilson turned into a movie theatre.

The Green Room was used as a dining room by President Jefferson (1801-1809) for his dinner guests, (16) … he surprised with new dishes such as ice-cream, wafers and macaroni. President Abraham Lincoln (1861-1865), (17) … the actor and fanatic John Wilkes Booth assassinated at Ford's Theater, mourned the death of his youngest son in this room. It was also the favourite room of President John F. Kennedy.

The Red Room, (18) … small size and deep red decor make it inviting and cosy, was Jacqueline Kennedy's favourite room.

b In formal or written style the preposition is often put before the relative pronoun, not at the end of the clause. Make one sentence out of two, using a preposition before *which* or *whom*.

Example: George Washington never lived in the 'President's House'. The building of the 'President's House' was commissioned **by** him.
*George Washington, **by whom** the building of the 'President's House' was commissioned, never lived there.*

1 The architect James Hoban was born in Ireland. The 'President's House' was built by him.
2 The British set the White House on fire in 1814. The Americans fought against the British in the War of 1812.
3 Theodore Roosevelt was the 26th president of the USA. The White House was officially given its current name by him in 1901.
4 Theodore Roosevelt had six children. The West Wing was built for him as extra working space.
5 The Oval Office is situated in the West Wing. Important presidential speeches are often broadcast from the Oval Office.
6 The White House is 200 years old. There are 132 rooms and 35 bathrooms in the White House.
7 The State Dining Room was enlarged in 1902. 140 guests can be seated in the State Dining Room.

Based on *White House Facts*

5 *Snuffed out*   **relative clauses: mixed exercise**   ▶ **260, 262-266**

The city that never sleeps may soon be the city that never smokes.

New Yorkers whose New Year Resolution is to quit smoking have their mayor, Mike Bloomberg, to thank for making it easier. He signed a bill this week that bans smoking in practically all the city's 14,000 bars and restaurants.

5   […] The new law toughens[1] 1995 legislation that banned smoking in all indoor public areas, required special smoking sections in restaurants seating more than 35 customers. The law forces people to smoke near the windy entrances to skyscrapers, which adds to the risks of their habit.

Surprisingly, the mayor met almost no opposition. Naturally, bar and restaurant owners
10 protested, with some claiming[2] business would drop by 20%. Also unhappy was Philip Morris, the world's largest tobacco company, which happens to have its headquarters in New York.

Mr Bloomberg argued that employees, particularly those who work in restaurants and bars, had to be protected from second-hand smoke breathed in involuntarily. Because there are
15 far more non-smokers than smokers in New York, the public was on his side; but many cigarette-lovers too, […] climbed on board[3].

[…] Smoking will be permitted in outdoor cafés and in the city's seven cigar bars, as well as in any bar that has a special room smokers can use, or which builds a special smoking room that employees do not have to enter.

Adapted from *The Economist,* Jan. 4-10 2003

---

1 toughen: make tougher, more strict   2 claim *behaupten*   3 climb on board: join

a Write down all the relative clauses in the text. In which clauses could a different pronoun be used?

b Look for examples of the following:

1 a relative pronoun that is subject of the relative clause
2 a relative pronoun that is object of the relative clause
3 a non-defining relative clause
4 a contact clause
5 a relative clause which relates to the whole of the previous clause

c Replace the participle constructions with relative clauses.

1 … in restaurants seating more than 35 customers. (l. 6)
2 … second-hand smoke breathed in involuntarily. (l. 14)

d Explain the following using suitable relative clauses:

1 a non-smoker   4 a habit
2 a New Year resolution   5 a cigarette-lover
3 a mayor   6 a smoking room

e Complete the following text with a relative pronoun, or *why*, *where*. If you think two pronouns are possible, write both.

Rudolph Guiliani, Mayor of New York from 1993-2002, (1) … obsession was with cleaning the city of crime, successfully introduced 'zero-tolerance policing', a policy (2) … punishes small crimes in order to discourage serious ones.
Now Michael Bloomberg, (3) … followed Rudolph Giuliani, wants to clean the city's public places of smoke. The introduction of the new anti-smoking law, (4) … means that smokers are banned from all eating places, has not met with serious protest. The only places (5) … smoking is allowed are

outdoor cafés and cigar bars, (6) … forces smokers to stay outdoors in all weathers. As a result, people (7) … businesses are affected expect a sharp fall in profits. The reason (8) … the law has been introduced is to protect non-smokers from second-hand smoke.

f Write a paragraph (about 100 words) giving your opinion about the new anti-smoking law in New York. Compare it with the situation in Germany. Use at least five relative clauses.

Indirect speech

A **Report the sentences, paying attention to pronouns and adverbial phrases.**

1 'Ann, phone the police immediately!' said Janet.
2 'I saw our old French teacher at an exhibition in Leeds yesterday,' Beth told Kim.
3 'We may be moving to Bristol,' Justin said.
4 'I am meeting a few friends this evening, but I'll phone you tomorrow, Liz,' Jeff said.
5 'Can you speak French and Spanish fluently?' the interviewer asked Claire.
6 'A moped was stolen from the school premises two days ago,' the headmaster announced.
7 'Don't buy a car unless you can really afford one,' Nina's father told her.
8 'Do you support my arguments?' the chairman asked the committee members.
9 'I can't confirm the order until I have all the details,' the man said.
10 'Did you phone the dentist?' John's mother asked him.

B **What did they say in direct speech?**

11 Simon told us that he had been offered a job with a mobile phone company.
12 The manager asked if the new secretary smoked.
13 The teacher told Mike not to waste her time asking irrelevant questions.
14 Jenny says she'll be arriving on the 11.30 train from Dover.
15 Moira said she would leave the firm if she was not given a pay rise.

C **Translate into English.**

16 David sagte, er sei nach seinem Fitnesstraining müde.
17 Marion erzählte uns, sie hätte ein neues Auto gekauft.
18 Gina sagte, sie würde mich morgen anrufen.
19 Tom sagte mir, er würde nicht viele Leute in London kennen.
20 Terry sagte, er habe eine neue Freundin.

D **Report the meaning, not every word, using suitable reporting verbs other than *say* and *tell*.**

21 'Let's go to see the new Tom Cruise film, shall we?' said Sheila.
22 'Well, you're right. It's best to do nothing and wait,' said Jason.
23 'Tim, my advice is, don't let others influence you,' Daniel said.
24 'The truth is, it was me who downloaded the wrong files, not Sean,' said Maria.
25 'You see, I really won't have time to attend the conference. I'm too busy,' Ben said.

E **Spot the mistakes. Look carefully. Three sentences are correct.**

26 Our teacher says that learning is never wasted, even though a lot of things seem unnecessary.
27 Nazreen wants to know where does your brother buy all his fantastic film posters.
28 Sarah said that her sister is an active member of *Greenpeace*.
29 Excuse me. Can you say me where the new job centre is?
30 David told me that his maths teacher always gives them piles of homework.
31 Ben said Mary to look for a new job quickly if she felt that she was being bullied.
32 Max said his parents that he had been offered a place to study microbiology.
33 Beth asked her father if she can borrow the car on Friday evening.
34 Sue told to Marie that she was having problems with her computer.

Indirect speech

? ▶ Correct yourself

A 1: *Janet told Ann to phone the police immediately.* 2: *Beth told Kim that she had seen their old French teacher at an exhibition in Leeds the day before.* 3: *Justin said (that) they might be moving to Bristol.* 4: *Jeff told Liz (that) he was meeting a few friends that evening, but he would phone her the next day.* 5: *The interviewer asked Claire if/whether she could speak French and Spanish fluently.*
6: *The headmaster announced that a moped had been stolen from the school premises two days before.* 7: *Nina's father told her not to buy a car unless she could really afford one. / … told her that she shouldn't buy …* 8: *The chairman asked the committee members if/whether they supported his arguments.* 9: *The man said (that) he couldn't confirm the order until he had all the details.* 10: *John's mother asked him if/whether he had phoned the dentist.*

B 11: *Simon said, 'I have been offered a job with a mobile phone company.'* 12: *'Does the new secretary smoke?' the manager asked.* 13: *'Don't waste my time asking irrelevant questions, Mike,' the teacher said.* 14: *Jenny: 'I'll be arriving on the 11.30 train from Dover.'* 15: *Moira said, 'I will leave the firm if I am not given a pay rise.'*

C 16: *David said (that) he was tired after his fitness training.* 17: *Marion told us (that) she had bought a new car.* 18: *Gina said (that) she would phone me tomorrow.* 19: *Tom told me (that) he didn't know many people in London.* 20: *Terry said (that) he had a new girlfriend.*

D 21: *Sheila suggested seeing/going to see the new Tom Cruise film. / Sheila suggested that they should see/go to see …* 22: *Jason agreed that it was best to do nothing and wait.* 23: *Daniel advised Tim not to let others influence him.* 24: *Maria admitted that it was her who had downloaded the wrong files, not Sean.* 25: *Ben explained that he wouldn't have time to attend the conference because he was too busy.*

E 26: Correct: reporting verb present, so no tense change necessary 27: *Nazreen wants to know where your brother buys all his fantastic film posters.* 28: Correct: reporting verb past, but 'is' (not only 'was') is possible because the statement is still true when it is reported
29: *Excuse me. Can you tell me where the new job centre is?* 30: Correct: reporting verb past, but 'gives' (not only 'gave') is possible because the statement is still true when it is reported.
31: *Ben told Mary to look for a new job quickly if she felt that she was being bullied.* 32: *Max told his parents that he had been offered a place to study microbiology.* 33: *Beth asked her father if she could borrow the car on Friday evening.* 34: *Sue told Marie/said to Marie that she was having problems with her computer.*

▶ Exercise finder

Sentences	CEG	Exercises
1, 7, 13, 31	▶ 280, 123a	▶ 6, 7
2, 4, 6	▶ 276	▶ 2, 3
3, 9, 11, 15	▶ 277	▶ 3, 4, 7, 8, 9, 10
5, 8, 10, 12, 27	▶ 279	▶ 5, 7, 10
14, 26	▶ 274d	▶ 4, 9
16-20	▶ 274c, 277	▶ 3
21, 22, 24, 25	▶ 274a	▶ 1b, 3, 5, 10
23, 33	▶ 280	▶ 6, 10
28, 30	▶ 278a	▶ 9
29, 32, 34	▶ 274a	▶ 1a, 10

1 *Reporting verbs* **various reporting verbs** ▶ **274a**

a Complete the sentences with a form of *say* or *tell*, adding *to* where necessary.

1 It has often been … that Ireland was the poor man of Europe. That is no longer true.
2 The staff have been … that the proposed changes come into force in April, not July.
3 The law … that no one under 18 is allowed to buy alcohol.
4 The chairman … the committee that he expected their decision by next week.
5 Mike … Peter, 'I think that's a very sensible suggestion.'
6 Layla … that she is going to Pakistan in the holidays to visit her relatives.
7 'Will somebody please … me what's going on here?' … Justin.
8 Lucy … us about her trip to Rome, but she didn't … anything about going to Spain.
9 On the news they … that there has been another crash on the M4.
10 The minister did not … how he proposed to fight unemployment.
11 'Good morning,' Tom … us as he rode past on his bike.
12 You must not … anyone what I have just … My information may be wrong.

b Report what they said using one of the given verbs. Remember to leave out words and phrases which are not important. Read all the sentences through before you start the exercise.

> admit • advise • ~~agree~~ • complain • explain • invite • promise •
> suggest • threaten

Example: John: 'Yes. It would be foolish to spend more money than necessary. I think so too.'
*John **agreed** that it would be foolish to spend more money than necessary.*

1 Anne: 'Sorry. You see, there's only enough room for four people in my car.'
2 Guest: 'The steak is tough. I can't eat it.'
3 Diane: 'I will pay the money back soon. That's a promise, Gina.'
4 Tom: 'Why don't you buy a new computer, Jason?'
5 James: 'All right. It's my fault. Sorry.'
6 Doctor: 'My advice is, stop smoking and go on a diet, Mr Bruce.'
7 Customer: 'If the goods aren't exchanged, I will complain to the store's main branch.'
8 Cathy: 'Oh, by the way, would you like to come to my party on Saturday, Ed?'

2 *Free time* **changes in pronouns; changes in phrases of time/place** ▶ **275, 276**

A group of foreign students on a language course in London talked about what they could do in their free time. Jürgen made some good suggestions.

Two weeks later, another student asked Jürgen about places to go. Jürgen told him about his conversation with Pascale, Juan, Dimitri and Cem. Report it, changing the tenses and the adverb phrases of time and place.

1 the Tate Modern: world-famous museum of modern art, situated on the Thames

Examples: Jürgen: Well, I suggested the Tate Modern.
*Pascale said **she was going** with a friend **that afternoon**.*
*Juan said **he had been there the day before**.*

Jürgen: Then I suggested going to see the musical *Fame*.

1 Pascale: I saw it last week.
2 Juan: I've got a ticket for tomorrow.
3 Dimitri: I'm going next Saturday.
4 Cem: I saw it two weeks ago.

Jürgen: After that I suggested going to Camden Market.

5 Pascale: I was at Camden Market yesterday.
6 Juan: I'm going to Camden Market next weekend.
7 Dimitri: I got a few bargains[1] at Camden Market last Friday.

Jürgen: So then I suggested staying in the café to chat.

8 Cem: But we always sit here to chat.

---

3 *Students in Britain*   **changes in tenses; reporting verb: simple past** ▶ **274a/c, 276, 277**

a A British teenage magazine interviewed some students in Bristol to find out how they lived. Report what the students told the interviewer. Make tense and pronoun changes for indirect speech and vary the reporting verbs by using e.g. *add, mention, think, explain*, etc. where suitable.

I'm a first-year biology student and I live in a hall of residence[2].

Example: *Andrea said (that) **she was** a first-year biology student and **she lived** in a hall of residence.*

1 'I have my own room and I don't have to cook, but hall also has some disadvantages. For example, you have to eat at certain times, or you don't get anything. But you meet a lot of people in hall.'

I spent the first year at home, so it didn't cost me anything.

Example: *Beth explained (that) **she had spent** the first year at home, so it **hadn't cost** her anything.*

2 'But I felt like a schoolgirl, not like a student. My social life was just the same as before because nothing really changed. So I moved into a flat with three other girls.'

I have been studying in Bristol for three years.

Example: *Colin said (that) **he had been studying** in Bristol for three years.*

3 'I have tried hall and flat-sharing, but I still haven't found the ideal place to live. I have just moved out of a private room. I haven't done much studying recently. I have spent too much time looking for somewhere to live.'

---

1 bargain: something bought for less than the usual price   2 hall of residence *Studentenwohnheim*

Next year I will look for a room or I'll share a house with friends.

Example: *David thought that next year **he would look for** a room or **he would share** a house with friends.*

4 'House rents will go up again as usual, but we'll be independent and I'll have more freedom. I will have to choose my friends carefully, but it will be a lot of fun. We probably won't do much studying.'

I'm a second-year maths student and I have just moved out of hall.

Example: *Emma said **she was** a second-year maths student and **had** just **moved** out of hall.*

5 'I liked it in hall, but sharing a small flat is better. But we have to do extra things like shopping and cleaning the flat. Yesterday I didn't have time to do any work at all. We haven't done much cooking yet, in fact we all hate it, but we'll get used to it. And we are managing our own lives at last. A lot of parties! If we get on together and if things work out OK, we will probably spend our third year here too.'

b Translate these sentences into English. Think carefully about time and tense and what the students said in direct speech.

1 Andrea sagte, sie hätte viele neue Freunde gefunden.
2 Colin sagte, er sei gerade umgezogen.
3 Emma sagte, sie würden jedes Wochende Partys feiern *(have)*.
4 Emma sagte, sie würden sich an das Kochen und Putzen gewöhnen *(get used to)*.
5 David sagte, es gäbe im Studentenwohnheim *(hall)* zu viele Regeln.
6 Beth sagte, sie sei mit ihrer Situation ganz zufrieden *(content)*.

c What have you heard about universities and university life in your country? Report to the class or write a short paragraph (4-6 lines). Begin like this: *A friend/Someone/etc. told me that …*

Example: *A friend told me that she **had been studying** physics at the technical university in Munich for two semesters. She said the lectures[1] **were** very impersonal. The lecture halls **were** crowded and …*

---

1 lecture *Vorlesung*

4 *A horoscope*

changes in tenses of modals, reporting verb: simple past; no change in tenses, reporting verb: present

▶ **274d, 277, 278a**

a Everybody reads a horoscope sometimes. This is what last week's horoscope said for Trevor, Kathy and Selima. Unfortunately, none of it came true.

> **LEO (23rd July – 22nd August):**
>
> You have had some money problems, but things will improve. You could receive an interesting offer mid-week. Friday may be a good day for meeting interesting people of the opposite sex.
>
> **VIRGO (23rd August – 22nd September):**
> You have had a boring week, but you will have a very busy weekend. You may have to choose between two unexpected invitations. The week won't end as you planned. A close friend could surprise you.
>
> **LIBRA (23rd September – 23rd October):**
> You have just made the right decision concerning your love life. A change of plans mid-week won't be a disadvantage. Thursday may be a good day for new contacts. Friday could bring a disappointment.

Example: 1 Trevor's birthday is on 1st October. What did his horoscope say?

> *Trevor's horoscope said he **had** just **made** the right decision concerning his love life. It said …*

Continue: 2 Kathy's birthday is on 20th August. What did her horoscope say?
3 Selima's birthday is on 3rd September. What did her horoscope say?

b Cut two horoscopes out of a German teenage magazine, a new one for next week and an old one for last week. Remember that there is no change in tenses when the reporting verb is in the present.

Tell a partner in English: 1 what your new horoscope *says*.
2 what your old horoscope *said*.

5 *At the station*   **indirect questions**

▶ **274a, 279**

Bettina is staying with friends in Oxford. One day on the station platform a woman asks her some questions, quite a lot of questions.

Woman:
1 'Oh, you're a foreigner. Where do you come from?
2 Do you like it here?
3 How long have you been here?
4 Are you on holiday?
5 Is it your first time in Oxford?
6 What have you seen in Oxford?
7 Have you seen all the colleges?
8 When are you going back home?
9 Will you come again?
10 Do you like English food?
11 Have you found an English boyfriend?
12 What do you think of English people?'

Later at home, Bettina told her English friends about the conversation. Add suitable reporting verbs (*ask*, *want to know*, *wonder*) and complete the text with indirect questions.

Example: A woman on the platform asked me **if the 12.30 train to Paddington had already left.**

She heard my accent, so she (1) … Then she (2) … and she (3) … She (4) …, so I told her that I was staying with friends. She (5) … and she (6) … Next she (7) … I didn't have much time to answer before she (8) … Then she (9) … I just said 'yes'. After that she (10) … She recommended beans on toast and apple pie. Then she (11) … After that she (12) … I almost said 'Some of them ask a lot of questions,' but I didn't because my train finally arrived.

6   *Interview tips*   **indirect advice**   ▶ **280**

a   Lara is going to London for a job interview. She wants to make a good impression, so her family and friends have all given her advice. What did they advise/tell her to do or not to do?

Examples:

Her mother …
*Her mother **advised her to get** there early.*

If I were you, I would get there early. (advise)

And don't wear too much make-up. (tell)

Her best friend …
*Her best friend **told her not to wear** too much make-up.*

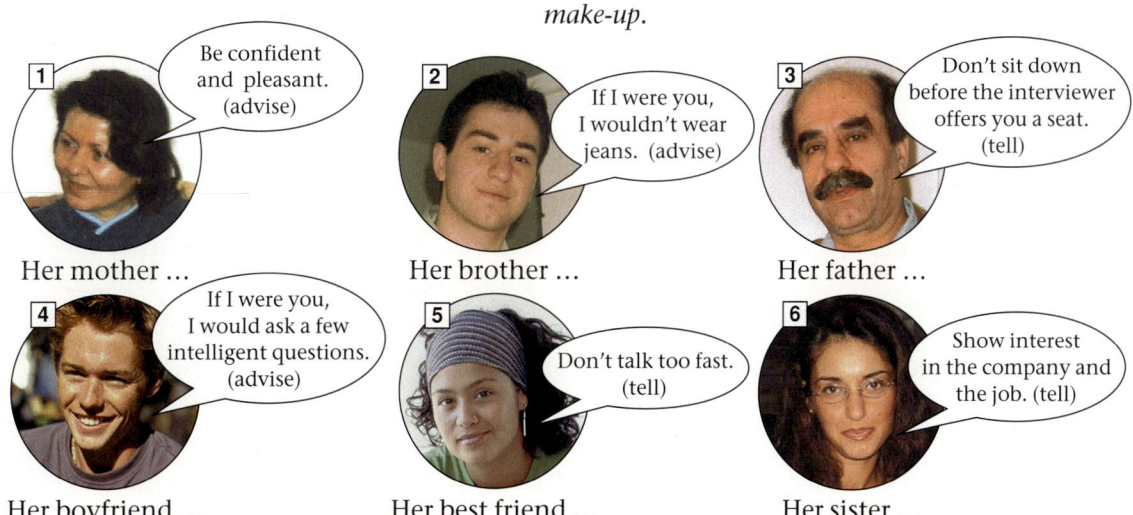

1 *Be confident and pleasant. (advise)*

Her mother …

2 *If I were you, I wouldn't wear jeans. (advise)*

Her brother …

3 *Don't sit down before the interviewer offers you a seat. (tell)*

Her father …

4 *If I were you, I would ask a few intelligent questions. (advise)*

Her boyfriend …

5 *Don't talk too fast. (tell)*

Her best friend …

6 *Show interest in the company and the job. (tell)*

Her sister …

b   Do you think the advice was good? Try to remember who gave Lara which piece of advice. Read the exercise through once more, then close your book and report freely what Lara's family and friends advised her to do and not to do.

Example: *Lara's mother **advised her to get** to/**arrive** at the interview early.*

c   What would you advise an interviewee to do or not to do?

<table><tr><td>**7**</td><td>*A holiday job*   **changes in tenses: indirect to direct speech**</td><td>▶ **277, 279, 280**</td></tr></table>

For the summer vacation, Laura would like a job working with children in a holiday club in Spain. She tells a friend about an interview that she has just had with an agency.

Laura to her friend:

Well, the woman who interviewed me seemed to be quite interested in my application.
She said she had read it through carefully and had a few questions to ask me.

She said (1) she was glad to see that I had already had some experience of working at a holiday camp, and she wanted to know (2) what kind of activities I had been involved with. I told her that (3) I had helped to run a Kids' Club, and that (4) I had mainly been in charge of aqua sports and competitions. I told her a lot of other things as well.

Then she asked me (5) if I was musical. She wanted to know (6) if I could sing or dance. I answered that (7) I preferred sports activities. Then she asked me (8) why I wanted to go to Spain. I said (9) I didn't like the wet English summers and wanted to try something away from home. She asked me (10) how good my Spanish was. I mentioned that (11) I had done a language course in Barcelona, so I was quite good. Then she told me that (12) I might be sent to Ibiza or Gran Canaria and asked (13) if I had a preference.

Then we talked a bit about money and accommodation, that sort of thing. She also wanted to know (14) if I could start as early as May, but I explained that (15) I wouldn't be free until mid-June. She gave me a phone number and told me to (16) talk to the Club management directly if I needed more information. She also asked me to (17) fill in another form with more details. Then she just said (18) she would phone me early next week. All in all, it went quite well, so I think I'll get a job.

What did the interviewer ask or tell Laura? How did Laura answer? Write the numbered sentences in direct speech, remembering to change tenses and pronouns and making any other necessary changes to suit the situation.

Example: Interviewer:
            *I **have read** your application through carefully and **have** a few questions to ask you.*

Space tourist lands back on Earth   direct/indirect speech: mixed ex.   277

Space tourist and multi-millionaire Mark Shuttleworth spent eight days aboard the International Space Station. The Russian Soyuz space shuttle carrying the South African millionaire and two crew members landed in Kazakhstan at 0351GMT on Sunday, 5th May, 2002.

The article shows clearly a typical journalistic mix in the use of direct and indirect speech for variation. How else could the article have been written? Rewrite the numbered sentences, changing direct into indirect speech and indirect speech into direct speech.

Sunday, 5 May, 2002

Examples: Mr Shuttleworth, who is rumoured[1] to have paid $20m for his trip, said
during his stay on the ISS that he was thoroughly enjoying himself.   (indirect)
*Mr Shuttleworth said, '**I am thoroughly enjoying myself**.'*   (direct)
He also said, 'I am enjoying space food – everything from steak to
shrimp cocktail.'   (direct)
He also said **he was enjoying space food**.   (indirect)

He added that (1) he was proud to be the first African in space, or 'Afronaut'. (2) 'I am very proud to carry the flag of an African country to space for the first time,' he said. He is now reported to have bought the Soyuz capsule and his space suit.

Before returning to Earth, the 28-year-old internet tycoon[2] told the BBC, (3) 'It is the holiday of a lifetime, but I may need another holiday to recover from all the excitement.' He said (4) he hoped his trip would inspire people across Africa.

(5) 'One of the things I hope to do by fulfilling my own dream is to reach out to children and learners in Africa and show them that dreams can come true,' he said. (6) 'Africa has a great future – but to reach that future, we have to get every African inspired and dreaming.'

He said (7) part of his mission had been to conduct stem cell and embryology experiments by South African researchers. He was working on Aids, using the weightless environment to grow near-perfect crystals of HIV proteins. (8) 'We hope to get some good quality crystals which will help scientists understand those proteins better and perhaps help develop new drugs,' he said.

Mr Shuttleworth, who made his money from the sale of his internet company, said (9) the 'geek'[3] in him had been fascinated by the mix of low and hi-technology kit installed on the space station. The South African, who actually lives in London, is the world's second holidaymaker in space. He follows in the footsteps of Dennis Tito, a US businessman and former American space agency (NASA) employee, who rode into orbit last year.

Adapted from 'Space tourist lands back on Earth', *BBC News Online*, 5/5/2002

---

1 be rumoured: be reported as a rumour, i.e. perhaps not true   2 tycoon: person who has become very rich in business or industry   3 geek (slang, esp. AE): a boring, conventional person

Josie has met a student at a party. He tells her about his future plans. Here is part of the conversation.

Dave: I want to teach geography. I didn't like school much because most of my teachers weren't very inspiring. Only one was, Mr Parks, the geography teacher, and he has been my role model ever since.

Josie: Mmm. Why do you want to go into teaching, and why geography?

Dave: Well, I think teaching is a very worthwhile job which can give you a great sense of being needed. Teaching is more than passing on your knowledge, it's about awakening interest and enthusiasm for the subject. And geography includes a mixture of subjects – science, economics, sociology, politics, etc. An understanding of the way people live in other countries, in different physical conditions, with different religions, political and economic situations can help young people to access the world more easily, to become global citizens, so to speak.

Josie: That's interesting. Our geography lessons were pretty boring. I hated having to learn things that didn't interest me.

Dave: Well, pupils shouldn't learn because they have to, but because they want to. And the teacher plays an important role here.

Later, Josie tells her sister about her conversation with Dave.

Josie: He said he wants to teach geography. He said he didn't like school much because his teachers weren't very inspiring, but his geography teacher had been his role model ever since school. I asked him why he wanted to teach. He thinks it's a very worthwhile job that can give you a sense of being needed. I have never thought of teaching that way. I wondered why he wanted to teach geography – I used to hate drawing maps at school. He explained that geography covered everything from geology to sociology, and that's why it fascinates him, I expect. He said he thought geography could help pupils to access the world more easily. He believes pupils should learn because they want to, not because they have to. Well, I wished him luck.

a Compare the original conversation with Josie's free report of it. Notice that Josie does not report the conversation word for word. Notice also that Josie has not 'backshifted' the tenses in every case, because sometimes the tenses can stay as they are in direct speech. In Josie's report of the conversation, find as many examples as you can of the following:

1 an indirect question
2 a reporting verb in the past
3 a reporting verb in the present
4 tense forms that are not backshifted *('zurückverschoben')*
5 a modal auxiliary that has changed in indirect speech
6 a modal auxiliary that has not changed in indirect speech.

b Explain simply why the tense forms you found in a) 4 above have not been backshifted. Remember that there is more than one reason why a tense is not backshifted.

Extract from 'Dead Poets Society' mixed ex. ▶ **273, 274a, 277, 279, 280a/b**

Year 11 pupils were shown the film *Dead Poets Society* starring Robin Williams in their English class. They also read the book. Read the following scene, then carry out the pupils' tasks.

Neil attends Welton Academy, a very traditional US boarding school[1] in New England. In the extract Neil speaks with his popular, unconventional English teacher Mr Keating about a family problem. Neil's father insists that he should study medicine, but Neil wants to become an actor.

Neil took a deep breath. 'My father is making me quit the play at Henley Hall. […] I feel like I'm in a prison! Acting is everything to me, Mr Keating. It's what I
5 want to do!
Of course, I can see my father's point. We're not a rich family like Charlie's. But he's planned the rest of my life for me, and he's never even asked me what I want!'
'Have you told your father what you just told me? About your passion for acting?' Mr Keating asked.
10 'Are you kidding? He'd kill me!'
'Then you're playing a part for him, too, aren't you,' Keating observed softly. The teacher watched as Neil paced[2] anxiously. 'Neil, I know this seems impossible, but you have to talk to your father and let him know who you really are,' Keating said.
'But I know what he'll say. He'll say that acting is just a whim[3] and that I should forget
15 about it.' […]
'Well,' Keating said, sitting on his bed. 'If it's more than a whim, prove it to him. Show him with your passion and commitment[4] that it's what you really want to do. If that doesn't work, at least by then you will be eighteen and able to do what you want.'
'Eighteen! What about the play? The performance is tomorrow night!'
20 'Talk to him, Neil,' Keating urged.
'Isn't there an easier way?' Neil begged.
'Not if you're going to stay true to yourself.'
Neil and Keating sat silent for a long time.
'Thanks, Mr Keating,' Neil finally said. 'I have to decide what to do.'

From *Dead Poets Society* by N.H. Kleinbaum

a Rewrite lines 1-15 in indirect speech as freely as you think suitable. Leave out unnecessary details and change words to make the situation clear. In both a) and b), remember to use various reporting verbs in addition to *say, tell* and *ask* for example: *add, advise, answer, continue, exclaim, explain, reply, thank, urge.*

Example: *Neil **explained** that his father **was making** him quit the play. He **said** he **felt** like he **was** in prison and **added** that acting **was** everything to him, it **was** what he **wanted** to do. He **continued** that …*

b Summarize the rest of the scene (ll. 16-24) in a few sentences, i.e. even more freely than in a).

---

1 boarding school *Internat* 2 to pace: to walk up and down 3 whim: a temporary wish or passion that will pass
4 commitment: willingness to work hard, to give time and energy

Extract from 'The Lilac Bus'   'free indirect speech'   ▶ **273 Anm., 277, 279**

Some writers describe the emotions and thoughts of their characters using 'interior monologue' or 'free indirect speech', which is also often mixed with direct and indirect speech. Read the extract and look out for examples of 'free indirect speech'.

Dee suspects that Sam has lied to her about his activities for the weekend. He told her he would be attending a medical conference in London, but she has good reason to believe from Nancy, Sam's receptionist at the hospital, that he is at home with his wife Candy, having a barbecue to celebrate their wedding anniversary. Dee is unhappy, not wanting to believe that Sam has lied to her.

What was she going to do? Was she going to pretend that she knew nothing, let him lie on about London? No, that would be living out a total dishonesty. But then, wasn't he prepared to do that with her? Some of the time. And with Candy some of the time. He didn't have this high regard[1] for total honesty. [...] Should she ring him at home and
5 confront him? What earthly good would that do? None.
She would try to be calm and wait until daylight. [...]

The next day:
Half-way home Dee realised what had happened. That stupid Nancy had got the weekend wrong. That was it. Hadn't Sam said he would be tied up[2] with the family, next
10 weekend? [...]
The relief[3] was immense: it was the joy of getting an exam, [...] it was like passing your driving test.
'Mummy, I was just thinking of the day I passed my driving test,' she began. [...] 'I was just thinking of the lovely feeling when the man said I passed.'
15 [...] Dee thought of Sam in London. He had said there would be papers[4] all of Saturday afternoon, but that he was going to skip[5] the official dinner. Together they had looked at a newspaper and circled plays or shows he might see. She wondered was it a nice warm night in London as it was here. Then it hit her like a tennis ball coming suddenly into her stomach. He had asked Nancy Morris to pray[6] for a fine weekend for the barbecue.
20 *This* weekend.

From *The Lilac Bus* by Maeve Binchy

a Write down an example of a direct statement, an indirect statement and an indirect request/command from the text.

b Compare the free indirect speech used to express Dee's thoughts (mainly ll. 1-6) with the direct and indirect statements in the extract. How is free indirect speech different? Comment on the use of reporting verbs, pronouns, word order in questions and backshift of tenses. Give examples.

c 'She wondered was it a nice warm night in London as it was here.' (ll. 17-18). Write the sentence in direct, then in indirect speech.

---

1 regard: respect   2 tied up: busy with   3 relief *Erleichterung*   4 paper (here): talks, lectures   5 skip: not attend
6 pray *beten*

1 Classroom instructions phrasal verbs: meaning ▶ **165**

Replace the underlined words/phrases with a phrasal verb from the list with the same meaning.

> carry on ▪ find out ▪ hand in ▪ hand out ▪ hold on ▪ look up ▪ make up ▪
> put up ▪ read out ▪ ~~take back~~

Example: Teacher: Can you <u>return</u> your library books by Friday, please?
  Can you **take back** your library books/**take** your library books **back** by Friday, please?

1 <u>Continue</u> writing until I tell you to stop.
2 <u>Wait</u> a moment, Peter, until everybody is quiet.
3 Jason, <u>read</u> the answers <u>aloud</u>, please.
4 For homework I'd like you to <u>invent</u> a story.
5 You could <u>get to know</u> all the facts you need for your projects from the Internet.
6 I'd like you to <u>find the meaning of</u> these words in your dictionaries.
7 Will two of you <u>stick</u> this poster <u>on the wall</u>, please?
8 Katie, can you <u>give</u> the test papers <u>to everyone</u>, please?
9 Can you <u>give me</u> your homework now, please?

2 Get it right phrasal and prepositional verbs: position of the object ▶ **166, 167**

a Add a suitable sentence using the words in brackets and a pronoun object in the correct position.

Examples: Take off your shoes, please. I've just washed the floor. (already – take off)
  *I've already **taken them off**.*
  I can't wait for the holidays to come. (really – look forward to)
  *I'm really **looking forward to them**.*

1 Why don't you visit Brian and see how he is after his accident? (call on – yesterday)
2 Diane arrives back from New Zealand today. (I – pick up – airport)
3 Why don't you phone the head of the complaints department ? (already – ring up)
4 Why did they cancel the football match yesterday? (have to – call off – rain)
5 Some money has been stolen from the school office. (head teacher – look into – carefully)
6 Sheila is very musical, like her mother. (certainly – take after)
7 I really trusted Gemma. (unfortunately – let down – last week)
8 The job interview didn't go very well. I don't think they liked me. (afraid – turn down)
9 The neighbours said our dogs can stay with them while we're in Turkey. (look after)

b Study habits. Use the following or other phrasal and prepositional verbs to answer the questions in full sentences. Use a dictionary to make sure that you understand the meanings.

> catch up (with sth.) ▪ come across sth. ▪ fall behind (with sth.) ▪ finish sth. off ▪
> get on with sth. ▪ give up ▪ keep at sth. ▪ put sth. off ▪ write sth. down

1 What do you do if you fall behind with your work?
2 How do you try to learn and remember new English vocabulary?
3 Do you sometimes leave a piece of homework only half done?
4 Do you ever put off doing your homework or learning for a test?
5 What do you do if you find a piece of work difficult?

Letter to a problem page phrasal and prepositional verbs ▶ **164-167**

Dear Maggie,

I have been a secretary/p.a.[1] to the managing director of a small firm for five years now. I'm twenty-five. I enjoy the work and my boss is satisfied with me. In fact, he counts on me for just about everything.

My problem is that I don't think I earn enough money. My salary in no way measures up to those of friends in similar positions in other firms. My boss has never given me a rise[2], although I have brought up the issue[3] four years in a row. He hasn't turned down my requests, he just ignores them. He says he will deal with the matter, or he will look into it, but he never does.

I think I know the reason for his attitude. Four years ago he asked me out, but I politely refused as I didn't want more than a working relationship. Anyway, he's not my type. Could this be his way of getting back at me? I would like to discuss the problem openly, but I don't know how to go about it. I once threatened to leave, but he talked me into staying. I want to stay. The work is pleasant and varied and I get on well with my colleagues.

I sometimes feel that I can't cope with the situation any longer, but every time I decide to confront him, I put it off. There are so many people out of work. But why should I have to put up with a boss who doesn't take my wishes seriously? I can't do without a rise indefinitely[4]. Please advise me.

Sarah S., Essex

a There are altogether 15 phrasal and prepositional verbs in the letter. Write them down in the order in which they appear.

b With the use of a dictionary, give another verb/verb phrase for the underlined phrasal or prepositional verbs:

1 Sarah has brought up the matter of a salary rise several times.
2 Sarah's boss has not turned down her request.
3 She thinks her boss may want to get back at her.
4 She would like to discuss the problem but she doesn't know how to go about it.
5 Her boss once talked her into staying.
6 She gets on well with her colleagues.
7 She always puts off the confrontation.
8 She can't put up with the situation any longer.

c What do you think Sarah should do? Imagine that this letter is addressed to you. How would you reply? In your answer, use some of the phrasal and prepositional verbs from Sarah's letter.

---

1 p.a.: personal assistant   2 rise: salary increase   3 issue: problem, question   4 indefinitely: without end

Tricky prepositions   prepositions: mixed exercise   ▶ 247, 249

a *In, on, at, to, by, from?* Put in the correct preposition. Sometimes more than one is possible.
I planned to pick up my girlfriend (1) … Heathrow (2) … Friday. She had been (3) … the US
working as an au pair. The plane (4) … Boston lands (5) … nine-thirty (6) … the morning. It's
an hour's drive (7) … Heathrow, so I decided to go (8) … car. There are always so many people
(9) … the train. I went (10) … bed early and the next morning I listened (11) … the traffic
reports (12) … the radio. The phone rang just as I was leaving, but I was (13) … a hurry, so I
didn't answer it. (14) … the airport, I parked the car (15) … the fifth level of the multi-storey
car park and went the rest of the way (16) … Arrivals (17) … foot. I was glad that I was (18) …
time. I was really looking forward (19) … seeing Jessie again. But I waited and waited. All the
passengers had come out. No Jessie. So I went (20) … the United Airlines info desk. (21) …
my surprise I learned that Jessie hadn't been (22) … the flight. Later (23) … home there was a
message (24) … the answering machine. Jessie, still (25) … Boston, had broken her leg and
was not able to travel. She said she had phoned me earlier, (26) … about the time I must
have been ready to leave home …

b *Above* or *over?* Sometimes both are possible.
Ed is a student in Cambridge. He rents a furnished room in an old house, which is well (1) …
a hundred years old. The room's shabby, but it costs (2) … £ 200 a month. There's a bed with
a multi-coloured cover (3) … it. (4) … the bed there was a picture of someone's grandmother
– which Ed replaced with a photo of his girlfriend. There's a big crack in the wall (5) … the
fireplace. He hung the grandmother (6) … the crack. The wardrobe is too small, so he just
throws his clothes (7) … the chairs. There's a crack in the window, but that's all right – as
long as the temperature is (8) … freezing-point. Ed feels at home, and (9) … all, he needn't
worry about breaking anything …

Correct the mistakes   prepositions: mixed exercise   ▶ 247, 248

Correct the mistakes. There is one in each sentence or sentence pair.

1 What's the time, please? – It's exactly three minutes before nine.
2 Who is Barbara talking with?
3 The car before us stopped suddenly. I almost ran into it.
4 Look what I found between some old papers. Some drawings you did when you were six.
5 I couldn't pay for the tickets because I didn't have any money by me.
6 We flew from London to Las Vegas over Chicago.
7 Two people from three think the president should run for a second term of office.
8 Our TV's being repaired. I hope we'll have it back till next Saturday.
9 Scott is going to take Trish in the cinema this evening. It's their first date.
10 Dave often exaggerates things. It's typical for him.
11 Have you read any plays from Arthur Miller?
12 Look at this painting. It's a good example for the kind of work the artist does.
13 Jerry is married with a Spanish girl. He met her in Barcelona when he was on a language course.
14 Jürgen lives in a small town by Munich.
15 Why don't you come to Cologne for a few days? You can stay by us.
16 Which is the longest river of the world?
17 When I'm studying for exams, I work until eight hours a day.

a   Add suitable prepositions to complete the text. In a few cases more than one is possible.

Koalas are Australia's national emblem – and everybody's favourites. They are not bears, but belong (1) … a genus all (2) … their own.
(3) … the wild, a koala lives ten (4) … twelve years (5) … average, but (6) … sanctuaries[1], protected (7) … predators (for example, dingoes or dogs) they can live (8) … fifteen years. They have strong, sharp claws (9) … climbing. (10) … the breeding season the males attract females (11) … grunting loudly. This also frighten off other males.
Koalas inhabit mainly New South Wales (12) … the east, but they have been introduced (13) … western Australia and nearby islands. They feed mainly (14) … eucalyptus leaves. (15) … Australia's 600 species of eucalyptus, koalas only eat about 50 – eucalyptus (16) … breakfast, lunch and supper, about 500g (17) … fresh leaves daily. They are low (18) … nutrients[2], but koalas cope (19) … the lack of energy (20) … sleeping (21) … twenty hours a day. (22) … general, koalas don't drink water – they obtain all the water they need (23) … their leaves. (24) … fact, 'koala' is an Aboriginal word meaning 'no drink'. Koalas spend about 80 per cent (25) … their time sleeping, and the rest just feeding and sitting. They are excellent climbers, but quite slow walkers when (26) … the ground (27) … their lack of energy. Koalas are awake most (28) … night. (29) … the day they sleep. They have no sweat glands[3], so they cool themselves (30) … licking their arms. They have a very small brain – less than 0.2 per cent (31) … their body weight. This is likely to be an adaptation (32) … their low energy diet. The gum leaves contain strong smelling oils that seem to act (33) … a bug repellent[4], keeping the animal free (34) … parasites. They also make the koala smell (35) … very strong cough sweets.
Koalas are listed (36) … the Red List 2000 as 'Lower Risk/near threatened'. The first European settlers hunted koalas (37) … their skins. In 1924 more than 2 million skins were exported. Nowadays the koala population is stable, but loss of habitat, road accidents and attacks (38) … domestic dogs are still a threat. There are estimated to be about 100,000 koalas in Australia.

Adapted from *BBC Nature Wildfacts*

b   Search the text for 1) phrases of place 2) phrases of time. Make two lists. Which preposition do we use to express a way of doing something? Find two examples in the text.

1 sanctuary: safe place/area for threatened or sick animals   2 nutrients *Nährstoffe*   3 glands *Drüsen*
4 bug repellent: a substance used to keep insects away from you

a   The following sentences contain examples of common mistakes. Only two sentences are correct. Which are they? There is one mistake in each of the others. Can you correct them?

1 I have seen our old French teacher yesterday.
2 I explained Tim the situation.
3 Listen. They play my favourite song.
4 There has been an accident, but the police hasn't arrived yet.
5 Dave's new picture phone is smaller than yours.
6 I'm really looking forward to go on holiday.
7 All what I can advise you to do is wait and see what happens.
8 We have been waiting here since an hour.
9 Who gave you these informations?
10 Kate wants that we all go to her party on Saturday.
11 We should respect the nature more.
12 Pat and Dan are leaving for Spain next Friday.
13 I'd like an advice about IT courses. Which would be best for me?
14 I suggest to go to the cinema tonight to see the new Will Smith film.
15 What did you yesterday evening?

b   More common mistakes. Translate into English – be careful!

1 Sollen wir uns um sieben Uhr treffen?
2 Wir müssen die Übungen heute nicht fertig machen.
3 Die meisten Schüler in meiner Klasse arbeiten in den Ferien.
4 Ich kenne Jessica seit fünf Jahren.
5 Serena ist Studentin.
6 Wenn du fünf Minuten wartest, gehe ich mit.
7 In unserer Schule gibt es drei Computer-Räume.
8 Tom arbeitet immer hart.
9 Heute haben wir nicht viele Hausaufgaben.
10 Wenn du das Auto nehmen würdest, würdest du um zehn Uhr da sein.
11 Wir lassen uns oft eine Pizza liefern.
12 Das sind wirklich tolle Nachrichten.
13 Vor zwei Tagen bekam ich ein Job-Angebot.
14 Wir kennen viele Leute, die Englisch sprechen.
15 Dieses Lied wurde von Elton John geschrieben, nicht wahr?

c   Which are your all-time favourite grammar mistakes? Look through a) and b) again and make a list. Compare your list with others and discuss everybody's 'favourites' in class.

Bildquellen

agentur LPM/Henrik Pohl, Berlin (© Henrik Pohl: S. 129 Schokolade); © D. Aitkin, Ottobrunn (S. 43); akg-images, Berlin (S. 88, S. 89, © Tony Vaccaro: S. 95 zweites v. r., S. 95 rechts), S. 99 alle, S. 100 unten, S. 109, S. 110 links); © alltours Flugreisen GmbH (S. 166 unten); © Eray Başkaynak, Berlin (S. 49 linke Reihe oben u. Mitte, S. 165 alle außer links unten u. rechts oben); www.JohnBirdsall.co.uk (S. 87 alle, S. 130 rechts, S. 131, S. 162 Mitte u. unten, S. 163 oben); Anthony Blake Photo Library, London (© Graham Kirk: S. 85 links, © Martin Brigdale: S. 85 rechts unten); www.Britainonview.com (S. 66, S. 85 Mitte); Cinetext, Frankfurt/M. (S. 14 obere Reihe, Mitte, untere Reihe, links, S. 169); Comet Photoshopping GmbH, Zürich / Silvestris (© Bott: S. 67 links); Corbis, Düsseldorf (© Sky One/ Kerry Ghais/Corbis Sygma: S. 22 links, © Bob Krist: S. 38 links u. Mitte, © Alan Schein Photography: S. 38 rechts, © Diego Lezama Orezzoli: S. 42 links, © Stephanie Colasanti: S. 42 rechts, S. 44, © Neil Rabinowitz: S. 50 links, S. 50 Mitte, © Terry W. Eggers: S. 50 rechts, © Ralph A. Clevenger: S. 51 unten, © Adam Woolfitt: S. 51 oben links, © Kit Houghton: S. 51 oben rechts, S. 57, © Bettmann: S. 95 links u. Mitte, © Lewis Alan, Corbis Sygma: S. 104 links, © Jennie Woodcock, Reflections Photolibrary: S. 104 unten, © Chris Andrews, Chris Andrews Publications: S. 107, © Peter Steiner: S. 108 rechts, © Bettmann: S. 156 oben u. Mitte, © Ron Sachs, Corbis Sygma: S. 156 unten, © Olivia Baumgartner, Corbis Sygma: S. 172); Corel-Library (S. 100 oben, S. 104 rechts oben, S. 105 alle, S. 108 links u. Mitte, S. 110 rechts, S. 129 alle außer Brötchen, Ei u. Schokolade, S. 138 rechts, S. 148 rechts u. unten Mitte; Cornelsen Archiv (© Mike Ford Photography, Sheffield: S. 41 Bild 2, © David Dore: S. 129 Brötchen u. Ei, © Lally/York: S. 130 links); dpa-Bildarchiv (S. 95 zweites v. l.); dpa-Fotoreport (© Getty Segretain: S. 14 obere Reihe, zweites v. l., © Consolidated Sachs: S. 14 obere Reihe, zweites v. r., © Forget: S. 14 obere Reihe, rechts, © PA Stephens: S. 14 untere Reihe, zweites v. r., © PA Stillwell: S. 14 untere Reihe, rechts, © epa efe Otin: S. 147 oben, © ZB-Fotoreport/Jan-Peter Kasper: S. 147 links, S. 147 rechts, © epa afp NASA: S. 167 links, © epa Anatoly Maltsev: S. 167 rechts); dpa-Sportreport (© Marcus Beck: S. 14 obere Reihe, links, © Rhona Wise: S. 14 untere Reihe, zweites v. l.); Mary Evans Picture Library, London (S. 90 alle); Das Fotoarchiv, Essen (© Jochen Tack: S. 10, S. 148 links u. Mitte oben, © Tobias Gemme: S. 163 unten links u. rechts, © Manfred Vollmer: S. 163 rechts oben); Getty images, München (© Tama: S. 158); IFA-Bilderteam, München (© Travel Pixs: S. 9 oben, © Edmond Naegele: S. 9 rechts oben); Irish Image Collection (S. 17 unten); Mauritius, Berlin (© Stock Image: S. 165 links unten, © age fotostock: S. 165 rechts oben u. Mitte unten, © Pigneter: S. 166 oben); *Newsweek* (© Laurent Vander Stockt for *Newsweek* special edition, Dez. 02 - Feb. 03: S. 91); © K. Pfeiffer, Unterhaching (S. 60 unten, S. 76 beide rechts); Photofusion, London (© Paul Baldesare: S. 122 links, © Joanne O'Brien: S. 122 Mitte, © Steve Eason: S. 122 rechts); picturealliance (© dpa-Bilderdienste, PA Paul Faith: S. 17 oben links, © dpa-Fotoreport, PA Paul Faith: S. 17 oben rechts); plainpicture, Hamburg (© K. Krebs: S. 73, © M. Lohmann: S. 121, S. 162 oben, S. 163 zweites v. oben); Reuters/E-Lance-Media (© Andrew Wallace: S. 22 rechts); Schapowalow, Hamburg (© Rosenfeld: S. 85); skjoldphotographs.com (S. 35 alle, S. 41 alle außer Bild 2, S. 49 alle außer links oben u. Mitte, S. 127); © J. Seidl, München (S. 12 alle, S. 27 alle, S. 42 Mitte, S. 60 links, S. 61, S. 70 alle, S. 76 links, S. 119 alle, S. 154 alle, S. 174); © A. Sevruk, München (S. 77, S. 118 alle); STOCK4B, München (© Katja Dell: S. 158); TG2 (© Gleize: S. 9 links unten, © Janicek: S. 67 Mitte oben, © Merten: S. 67 Mitte unten, © Ball: S. 67 rechts); © 2002 Universal Studios. All Rights Reserved (S. 149 alle); © J. Wormald, Selby (S. 56 alle, S. 155 Fotos); Zefa Visual Media, Hamburg (S. 161).

Textquellen

Alle angegebenen Internet-Seiten waren gültig bis: August 2003.
The sentence/Word order: 5 www.Sydney.com.au/bridge.htm © 1997-2003 Sydney Online Pty. Ltd: S. 12; **12** Brian Moore, *Lies of Silence*, Longman Group UK Ltd, Harlow, 1995 © Brian Moore 1990: S. 17/18;
Modal auxiliaries and be, have, do: 8 www.tak.schule.de/goldrule.htm: S. 26; **9** Joseph R. Yogerst, *Inside Pocket Guide: Hong Kong* © 2001 APA Publications GmbH & Co. Verlag KG Singapore Branch, Singapore: S. 27;
The tenses of the full verbs: **12** www.berwickacademy.org/lincoln u. home.att/~rjnorton/Loncoln77.Html: S. 43; **15** www.uh.edu/engines/epi969.htm, www.daveslater.telinco.co.uk/sidis.htm u. members.aol.com/popvoid/sidis.html: S. 45; **16** www.GamingMagazine.com/managearticle.asp?c=70&a=228 © Copyright of Telegraph Group Limited 2002: S. 46; **17** © Qaisra Sharaz. In: Liz Rutherford (Ed.): Holding Out. Manchester: Crocus Books, 1988: S. 46/47; **21** www.bbc.co.uk/news: S. 52;
The passive: 1 Nick Middleton, *Atlas of environmental issues*, Oxford University Press, Oxford, 1991 © 1988 Ilex Publishers Limited: S. 55; **7** © 1995 Cornelsen Verlag, Berlin: S. 58/59; **10** www.death.valley.national-park.com/info.htm#esta: S. 61/62;
The infinitive and the gerund: 16 Keith Grimwade, *Physical Geography*, Hodder and Stoughton Educational, Hong Kong, 1992 © Keith Grimwade 1990: S. 76; **17** www.bbc.co.uk/news: S. 77;
The participle: 4 Marchette Chute, *Stories from Shakespeare*, Mentor Books/The New American Library, New York, 1961 © 1956 by Marchette Chute: S. 84; **10** *Oxford Children's Encyclopedia*, Bd. 6 Biography, Oxford University Press, Oxford, 1991 © Oxford University Press 1991 u. Copyright © 1995-2003 Lucid Interactive Article written by Robin Chew - February 1996 www.lucidcafe.com/library/96feb/edison.html : S. 88; **11** www.angliacampus.com/education/fire/london/history/greatfir.htm: S. 89; **12** William Underhill, 'Riding on ... well ... air', in: *Newsweek*, Special Issues Dez. 2002 - Feb. 2003; S. 91;
The noun: 7 www.renaissance.dm.net/compendium: S. 99;
The article: 6 © 1993 Cornelsen Verlag, Berlin: S. 108; **7** www.britainexpress.com/History/bio/shakespeare.htm © 2000 David Ross and Britain Express: S. 109;
The adjective and the adverb: 12 www.thetube.com: S. 122; **13** Copyright © The Economist Newspaper Limited 2003. All rights reserved.: S. 123;
Quantifiers: 4 www.bbc.co.uk/news: S. 130/131;
Pronouns and question words: 7 © 2002 Cornelsen Verlag, Berlin: S. 138/139;
Conditional sentences: 8 © 2002 Cornelsen Verlag, Berlin: S. 149;
Relative clauses: 4 www.whitehouse.gov/history/facts.html: S. 156/157; **5** 'Snuffed out', *The Economist*, 4. Jan. 2003: S. 157;
Indirect speech: 8 www.bbc.co.uk/news: S. 167; **10** N. H. Kleinbaum, *Dead Poets Society*, Petersen Buchimport GmbH, Oststeinbek, 2002 (= PETERSEN Taschenbücher Classics Bd. 170): S. 169; **11** Maeve Binchy, *The Lilac Bus*, Random House, London, 1987 © Maeve Binchy 1984: S. 170;
Mixed Bag: 6 www.bbc.co.uk/nature/wildfacts/factfiles/682.shtml British Broadcasting Corporation © 2002 - 2003: S. 174;

Key to the exercises
Practice Book 2

Cornelsen
English
Grammar

English Edition
Große Ausgabe

Cornelsen

Inhaltsverzeichnis

The sentence/Word order

▶1 An exchange pupil

1 At first the language didn't sound like English to me at all.
2 If my girlfriend doesn't speak carefully,
3 I don't always understand her.
4 I don't think she realizes how difficult …
5 I have to ask her not to talk so quickly,
6 but she doesn't remember most of the time.
7 but of course there are some places that I haven't been able to visit yet, …
8 but there's still a lot of grammar that I cannot/can't use properly.
9 I'm afraid I don't do my homework regularly.
10 In fact, I didn't do any homework at all yesterday.
11 I don't think I take school work here as seriously as I should.
12 The teachers often have to tell me not to waste time in the lessons.
13 They often catch me when I haven't been listening.
14 I would not/wouldn't have been asked to join
15 if I didn't play the guitar pretty well.
16 But what I miss most here is not being able to hang around with my friends …

▶2 The Airport Express

a 1 Where do the buses leave from?
2 What do the buses look like?
3 Does the driver sell tickets in the bus?
4 How much does a one-way ticket cost?
5 Do the buses leave on time?
6 Do you have to queue up?
7 Which places does the bus stop at?
8 Does the bus go past Central Park?
9 How long does the journey take?
10 When does the next bus leave?

▶3 Where do you come from?

a 1 What's your brother's/his name?
2 Where are you from? / Which town/city are you from? / Which town/city do you come from?
3 How long have you been in Germany?
4 Do you like Germany?
5 Why did you come here/to Germany?
6 Do you know many people here?
7 Do you/Can you speak (any) German?
8 Are you taking a course? / Are you learning German?
9 Do you do (any) sports?
10 What are your hobbies?
11 What kind of music do you like/listen to?
12 Would you like to go to a party tonight?

▶4 A film quiz

1 Who directed…? / Which film/When did James Cameron direct …?
2 Who starred in …? / When did Julia Roberts star …? / Which film did Julia Roberts star …?
3 Which film won eleven Oscars in1998? / How many Oscars did *Titanic* win …?
4 Who played the main roles in …? / In which film did P. B. and H. B. play the main roles? / When did P. B. and H. B. play the main roles in …?
5 Who won an Oscar for Best Actor? / In what year did D. W. win …?
6 Which film made $961 million worldwide in …? / How much money did the first *Harry Potter* film make in 2001?

7 Who directed and produced *Braveheart* in 1995? / Which film did M. G. direct and produce …? When did M. G. direct and produce …?

8 How much did … / How many million did *Die Another Day* cost to make?

9 Who directed *The Fellowship of the Rings* in 2001? / Which film did P. J. direct in 2001? / When did P. J. direct *The Fellowship of the Rings*?

10 Which part of the *Rings* trilogy/What was released in December 2002? / When was *The Two Towers* released?

▶ 5 *An interview*

1 How did you get your first (film) role?
2 What did you do before you started making movies?
3 Have you ever wanted to do anything else?
4 Who discovered you?
5 How did you feel when you suddenly became famous?
6 What kind of roles do you like best?
7 What makes you so popular?
8 Would you like to act in comedies?
9 Which film did you enjoy making most?
10 How many films have you made?
11 When will your next film be released? / When is your next film going to be released?
12 What is the film about?
13 Do you play the main role?
14 Who plays the male lead?
15 Do you sometimes wish you weren't famous?

▶ 6 *Sydney Harbour Bridge*

a 1 When did construction begin?
2 Who designed the bridge?
3 How much did it cost to build?
4 How (many metres) high is the bridge?
5 How many tourists visit the bridge every year?
6 How many kilometres away is the Olympic Stadium?
7 When was the bridge opened?
8 How many workers died in building accidents?
9 What can you see from the top?
10 Where is the Opera House?

b 1 How long does it take to reach the top?
2 When can you climb the bridge?
3 How long does the climb take?
4 What do you have to wear?
5 Why do you have to wear a special suit?
6 What can't you take with you?
7 Why is it forbidden to take things with you?
8 How often do climbs leave?

▶ 7 *A blessing in disguise*

1 Never had I faced … 2 Never did I think … 3 Hardly had my father got … 4 Seldom have I seen my father … 5 Never had I seen my father cry … 6 Only later did I understand that … 7 Rarely have I felt so determined … 8 Seldom does one get a second chance … 9 Only later did I realize that …

▶ 8 *TV advertising*

a 1 … that most commercials are totally stupid.
2 … whether/if I am influenced by commercials.
3 When I shop/I'm shopping in a supermarket, …
4 … because I like trying out/to try out new things.
5 He never buys anything unless he has seen it on a TV commercial.
6 Although I often watch commercials, I never really listen to them.

7 … after I had seen the commercial for Flexifone about twenty times on TV.

8 If I see a cool/nice product on TV which interests me, I might buy it.

▶ 9 Famous people

1 Tony Blair was re-elected British Prime Minister in June 2001.

2 Serena Williams is considered the world's best woman tennis player.

3 Do you think Prince Charles will ever be made King of England?

4 George Bush was elected President of the USA in December 2000.

5 Elizabeth II was crowned Queen of England in June 1952.

6 When was Julia Roberts made actress of the year?

7 Prince William is considered the most popular royal.

8 Denzel Washington was voted actor of the year in 2002.

▶ 10 A big win

a 1 me the numbers/the numbers to me   2 my feelings to anyone   3 anything to her   4 us a meal/a meal for us   5 us a table/a table for us   6 the new situation to her   7 them the incredible news   8 invitations to all our friends, neighbours and colleagues   9 a house for our daughter and her family in Scotland   10 a nice flat for our 20-year-old son in London   11 money to various banks   12 generous presents to all our relatives and close friends   13 a nice letter of thanks to the Lottery company   14 large cheques to different national charities   15 interviews to interested radio and TV stations   16 my story to a well-known weekly magazine   17 all the money I got from the media to local charities   18 a sunshine cruise for us and Len and his wife   19 plenty of good ideas to me   20 myself a Harley-Davidson/ a Harley-Davidson for myself

▶ 11 Write the story

a When Sarah got home it was almost midnight. Turning the key in the door, she realized that it wasn't locked. She couldn't understand it because she was always careful with doors and keys. Had the door been unlocked while she had been enjoying herself at the party? She told herself that there was nothing to be afraid of. After she had opened the door very quietly, she went in. Before she closed the door, she listened carefully. What had made that noise upstairs? Might it be a burglar who was looking for money? Never in her life had she felt so scared. On no account would she go upstairs alone. What could she do if there was someone in her bedroom? Should she phone the police and explain the situation to them? Yes. She would report a break-in to them and give them her name and address.

▶ 12 Extract from 'Lies of Silence'

a 1 He took her hand and led her into the lounge. (l. 1)
She did not speak for a moment and then she said, '…' (l. 28)

2 Let's sit over there, where it's quiet. (ll. 1-2)
And now he's going to tell them that you'll testify against his nephew? (ll. 4-5)
I feel I must. (l. 8)
Do you know what you're saying? (l. 14)
Every time I open the door from now on, I'll be waiting … (ll. 14-15)
And if you were, is that so terrible? (l. 23)
Was any country worth the price that Ireland asked …? (ll. 26-27)

3 Why should he risk her life as well as his? (l. 26) /
   And what does that mean? (l. 13) What did it matter? (l. 26) /
   But why did you do it? (l. 7)
4 You're not going to testify, are you? (l. 7) It's for revenge, isn't it? (l. 18)
5 'Wait', ... (l. 1)

b 1 Never do I want to go back there again.
   2 Suggestions:
   A bystander is a person who sees something happening but is not involved.
   Revenge is something you do to pay somebody back because he/she made you suffer.
   A coward is a person who is afraid to do something which others do.

c Suggestions:
   1 Michael Dillon is going to testify because he thinks it is the right thing to do.
   2 Andrea is frightened because she knows that they both will be killed if Dillon testifies.
   3 Dillon tries to comfort Andrea when he tells her that he will have police protection.
   4 Andrea thinks that Dillon's motives are revenge.
   5 At first Andrea is afraid for Dillon ('They're going to kill you.' – l. 10). Later she realizes that she
     will be killed too. ('... I'll be waiting for someone to come in and kill us.' – l. 15). She questions
     Dillon's right to risk her life ('Why should he risk her life as well as his?'– l. 26). She is afraid for
     them both but feels her death would be unjust. She would be killed although she doesn't want
     Dillon to testify.
   6 Andrea is angry about the 'troubles' because the killings are always for revenge. She does not
     feel love or loyalty for the country because she doesn't want to return. She feels that no country
     is worth such a price, a price paid by death again and again. Her feeling of self-preservation is
     greater. (ll. 18-19, 25-28)

Modal auxiliaries, be, have, do

Modal auxiliaries

▶ 1 Mini-dialogues

a 1: 1 could   2 couldn't   3 could   4 was able to
   2: 1 can't   2 could   3 could   4 was able to
   3: 1 have not been able to   2 Can   3 can't   4 won't be able to
   4: 1 can   2 hasn't been able to   3 will be able to/can   4 not being able to
   5: 1 Can   2 could/would be able to   3 could   4 were able to

b 1: 4 I managed to frighten them off.
   2: 4 ... I managed to get things under control.
   5: 4 ... we managed to dry his clothes ...

▶ 2 TV shows

a 1 mustn't   2 needn't   3 mustn't   4 needn't   5 needn't   6 mustn't

b 1 have to   2 mustn't   3 has to   4 needn't   5 have to   6 have to   7 needn't   8 have to
9 have to   10 needn't (or: mustn't)   11 mustn't   12 have to   13 mustn't   14 have to
15 mustn't   16 needn't

▶ 3 Signs

1 a, b, d   2 a, c, d   3 b, d, e   4 a, c   5 a, c, d   6 c

▶ 4 Requests, offers, suggestions

1 May/Could/Can I use your phone, please?
2 Shall/Can I help you with the shopping/bags? / Would you like me to help you with your shopping?
3 Can/Could I check my e-mails on your computer?
4 Shall we go to see a film? / Would you like to go to the cinema?
5 Can/Could you give me my DVDs back? / Can I have my DVDs back soon? / Will you give me my DVDs back tomorrow?
6 Can/Could you phone a garage for me, please? / Would you help me to push? / Can you help me to get it going?
7 Can/Could/Will/Would you lend me twenty pounds? I'll pay you back tomorrow.
8 May I ask you for some advice on subjects and universities? / Could/Would you give me some advice on subjects and universities, please?

▶ 5 German 'sollen'

a 1 Shall   2 had better not   3 ought to/should   4 are we to   5 had better   6 should
7 ought to   8 must   9 is supposed to   10 was supposed to

▶ 6 Probability and possibility

a 1 That must be a very interesting job.
2 John may/could come this evening.
3 It could/may/might rain.
4 That will/must be her.
5 Gemma can't be over 25.
6 He may/might know the answer.
7 The weather in Scotland can sometimes be sunny and warm.
8 Mrs Hadley can't be a foreigner.

b Suggestions:
1 He must/could/may have forgotten about them. / He can't have finished with them yet. / He can't have watched them all yet.
2 You might have lost/lent it to someone. / Someone might have borrowed it. / Someone may have taken it by mistake.
3 She must have gone out. / She may/might have gone to a friend's.
4 He can't have heard it. / He might have had his headphones on.
5 He must have had an accident. / Someone must have crashed into him.
6 He might have won some money. / He may/could have borrowed it from his brother.

▶ 7 Mixed bag

a
1 I had to work last weekend, ...
2 I was able to get up very early this morning, ...
3 You needn't sign the contract now ...
4 Terry was able to/managed to repair his bike yesterday, ...
5 Last Saturday my sister wasn't allowed to go to a party ...
6 ... He may/might like them.
7 ... – When did you have to return them? Last week?
8 ... – I'm not sure, but you may be right.
9 You needn't wait for me ...
10 My little brother was allowed to stay up until ten o'clock last night ...
11 ... I have to go to his room in the second lesson.
12 Mike may/might have a hammer and some nails ...
13 ... I simply must go to bed early tonight.
14 ... They must be rich.

b
1 ... so we were able to play football.
2 Do we really have to copy ...?
3 The story Beth told you might/may be true.
4 You ought to/should go ...
5 That must be the street ...
6 Something must have happened.
7 Could you read/Were you able to read when you were six?
8 You needn't stay/You don't have to stay to supper if ...
9 You mustn't/You are not allowed to take ...
10 You can't have seen Helen ...
11 ... but we just managed to/we were able to stop in time.
12 Max might have met Jane on the management course.

▶ 8 School rules

a 1 had to repaint (l. 10)   2 should have been punished (ll. 10-11)
3 you can get expelled (l. 16), you might get a detention (l. 18), the principal may write (l. 20)
4 you will get expelled (l. 17)

b 1 We are not allowed to have drugs ... / We mustn't have drugs ...
2 ... you can/may smoke when you turn 16 ...
3 But we don't have to stand up when the teacher comes in.

c 1 ... wir dürfen keine Schneebälle werfen ...
2 ... wir können/dürfen anziehen, was wir wollen ...
3 Man darf sich nicht einmal bewegen.
4 Du sollst nicht reden oder andere stören ...
5 ... es wäre besser, wenn du kein Messer bei dir hättest ... /
   ... du solltest lieber kein Messer bei dir haben ...

Be, have, do

▶9 *Hong Kong – past and present*

a 1 There are   2 There is   3 there is   4 there are   5 there was   6 There were   7 there has been
8 there would not have been   9 There has not always been   10 There were/There have been
11 there is   12 There are   13 there may not be   14 there are   15 there was   16 there will
certainly be   17 will there be

▶10 *Write a story*

a 1 never has breakfast   2 does he have lunch   3 had a party, didn't have fun, had a quarrel with
his girlfriend   4 is having a day off   5 is having/is going to have a game of tennis with a friend

b Translation of verbs given:
have breakfast, have a shower, have coffee, have lunch, have a sleep, have a drink
have a break/a rest, have fun, have a party, have a good time
have a day off, have a swim, have a walk, have a meal, have a quarrel

▶11 *Doing things*

1 do   2 Did you do, do   3 made   4 didn't do   5 do   6 Have you done   7 was doing   8 make
9 does   10 is doing   11 make   12 didn't do   13 Are you doing   14 don't do/aren't doing
15 did

The tenses of the full verbs

Full verbs

▶1 *Quick and easy*

a A4   B1   C5   D2   E6   F3

b 1 s   2 p   3 p   4 s   5 p   6 s

▶2 *Get it right*

a State verbs: consist of, understand, cost, know, contain, own, sound, mind, believe, prefer, seem,
doubt

b 1 doesn't consist of   2 contains   3 are working   4 don't believe   5 don't know   6 is doing
7 Do you mind …?   8 prefer   9 seems   10 doesn't own   11 understand   12 is collecting

Present and past

▶3 Our website

a Lines: 1-2 … we all go skiing every winter.   3-4 … we sometimes go home at weekends …
4 … we often give …   4-5 … Basti still goes to school …   5 He doesn't like school much usually.
/ He doesn't usually like school much.   5-6 Just now he is doing his Abitur …   7 Basti plays …
7-8 He usually writes …   10 … this week we aren't meeting at all …   11 Just now we are
working on …   13 … if you live close by …

▶4 Mini-dialogues

a 1: 1 is still looking for   2 needs   3 is always needing   4 is spending   5 lives   6 goes   7 takes
8 is going up   9 cost   10 is working   11 need   12 pay   13 is babysitting

2: 1 Are you doing   2 am helping out   3 like   4 rains   5 work   6 is delivering   7 is emptying
8 are working

▶5 What's it about?

a *Maid in Manhattan* stars Jennifer Lopez and Ralph Fiennes … Jennifer Lopez plays Marisa. She is
a room maid in a hotel in Manhattan. She makes beds and tidies rooms for rich people … One
day in one of the hotel rooms she tries on some clothes of one of the rich guests – just for fun …
He thinks she is a rich guest too, and he falls in love with her. Of course, Marisa tries to hide the
truth at first …

▶6 A problem

a Typical signal words for the present perfect are: always, often, already, never, recently, so far,
up to now, just, ever, not … yet
Typical signal words for the simple past are: in 2002, last year, two months ago, last week,
yesterday

b Suggestion:
Jonathan is having problems with his parents about his future. He has always wanted to go into
acting, but his parents have never taken his wishes or his activities seriously, because they want
him to study law.
He stayed on at school to do A-levels to please his parents, but he has told them clearly what he
wants. A few years ago he even won an award for acting. He has applied to RADA and has been
invited to an audition. The problem is, he didn't tell his parents about the application. He doesn't
know what do do. Should he risk an uncertain future, or should he do what his parents want?

c 1 Jonathan has quarrelled a lot with his parents recently.
2 He has always wanted to be an actor.
3 In 2002 he even won a prize.
4 Two months ago he applied for a place at RADA.
5 He hasn't told his parents (anything) about it yet.
6 Yesterday he received a reply.
7 He has just spoken to his girlfriend.

8 He has already told her about his problem.
9 Up to now/So far, his parents haven't realized the seriousness of the situation.
10 Jonathan doesn't know what to do. He hasn't decided yet.

▶7 *Have you ever …?*

a 1: 1 have never been   2 went   3 did   4 made   5 Have you ever thought   6 have applied
7 Have you heard   8 sent off

2: 1 went   2 Have you ever been   3 has already been   4 has only been   5 loved
6 has never eaten   7 did you order   8 had   9 ordered

3: 1 Have you seen   2 hasn't called   3 haven't seen   4 have just spoken   5 has been
6 started   7 has never worked   8 has had to

▶8 *Sentence pairs*

1a have fallen   1b fell   2a have worn   2b wore   3a saw   3b didn't see   4a lost   4b have lost
5a haven't heard   5b didn't hear   6a has been   6b was   7a found   7b hasn't found
8a has written   8b wrote   9a didn't fail   9b has failed   10a haven't had   10b have had

▶9 *Describe the pictures*

1a has been reading   1b has read   2a has trained   2b has been training
3a has been driving   3b has driven   4a has rained   4b has been raining

▶10 For *or* since?

a for: … ages, about three months, a long time, weeks, a year or so
since: … last week, Christmas, my birthday, I was on holiday last summer, we moved here 2001,
someone gave me two free tickets

b 1 Polly has been studying economics since October last year.
2 Doug has been working for a firm of architects in the accounts department for a year.
3 Chris and Scott have been doing a training course with British Airways for eighteen months.
4 Val has been taking a gap year since last summer.
5 Emma and Lucy have been learning fashion design since September last year.
6 Owen has been training as a helicopter pilot for two years.

▶11 *A trip down under*

a 1 Did you have   2 phoned   3 answered   4 didn't go   5 were you doing   6 weren't doing
7 heard   8 was cleaning   9 rang   10 didn't answer   11 was listening   12 forgot
13 drove   14 were all looking   15 was just taking   16 looked   17 saw   18 was moving
19 was beating   20 did you do?   21 were all wearing   22 slid   23 went   24 happened
25 thought   26 got   27 drove

▶12 *Abraham Lincoln*

a 1 spent   2 went   3 liked   4 was always borrowing   5 moved   6 were looking
7 determined   8 was walking   9 saw   10 were being sold   11 were treating   12 swore
13 tried   14 was working   15 impressed   16 worked   17 was not earning   18 was studying
19 qualified   20 believed   21 stood   22 was dividing   23 made   24 was becoming
25 became   26 did not agree   27 left   28 began   29 wrote   30 did not free
31 was assassinated   32 were attending   33 shot   34 grieved   35 was erected

▶13 *Bad luck*

1 had forgotten   2 had been looking forward   3 hadn't taken   4 had gone   5 had just spent
6 had lent   7 hadn't come   8 had been running   9 had been watching   10 had been waiting
11 had been taking   12 had explained   13 had wasted   14 had already played

▶14 *Join the sentences*

1 Ben was sick after the party because he had eaten too much at the buffet.
2 I didn't know that my pen pal had moved to another town.
3 My brother finally passed his exams after he had studied for seven years.
4 As soon as I had read the questions through, I started to write the answers.
5 I felt really hungry in the fourth lesson because I hadn't eaten any breakfast.
6 I paid John the money I owed him as soon as I had been to the bank.
7 When I had read the novel, I passed it on to a friend.
8 After the maths teacher had marked our tests, he gave them back to us straightaway.

▶15 *The greatest mind ever*

a 1 had also learnt   2 taught himself   3 had learnt   4 taught himself   5 had completed   6 took
7 had already written   8 passed   9 had also learnt   10 took   11 stayed   12 had learnt
13 read   14 had mastered   15 enrolled   16 had studied   17 gave   18 followed   19 avoided
20 had already graduated   21 went   22 became   23 had ridiculed   24 gave up   25 went
26 had already studied   27 had been driven   28 led   29 disappeared   30 won
31 had already predicted   32 had been ignored   33 died   34 had spent

▶16 *A plane crash*

1 has crashed   2 was carrying   3 came   4 was making   5 crashed   6 was circling
7 had failed   8 died   9 died   10 remain   11 have not yet been accounted for
12 has sent   13 has been closed   14 said   15 had been   16 is believed   17 was said
18 have also been reported

a Suggestions:
1 Miriam had been on a hill-walking trip with some friends from college.
2 When she was getting close to her home, she began to feel uncomfortable because of her western clothes.
3 The 'other world' was the western world with its western values, the world of English girls.
4 Her future in-laws had never seen her in western clothes because she had always worn the traditional dress of her Asian culture on their visits.
5 In her traditional dress she felt a new person with a new set of values and a new personality. Her outward clothing represented her inner thoughts, feelings and actions.
6 She wanted to play that role that her future in-laws preferred, the role of a demure, elegant daughter-in-law.

b 1 came, was wearing   2 had already arrived   3 went, changed   4 have seen
5 had changed, felt   6 felt, was acting

c 1 in the simple past
2 'saw' is simple past. It refers to a particular point of time in the past (i.e. 'first, at a party'). 'was seeing' is past progressive. It refers to an action that was still in progress in the past, i.e. the action was not complete.
3 The present perfect form have seen refers to an action that has happened. The exact time is not important and is not mentioned.
4 The past perfect is used to express the idea that one past action ('had earlier traipsed') came before another past action ('was now dressed').

d 1 'As she was crossing the road near her own street, she suddenly became very conscious of her appearance.' (ll. 3-4)
2 'Once in her room, she closed the door behind her and breathed out deeply.' (l. 5)

Ways of expressing future time

a Suggestions:
1 I'll get it. / I'll answer it. / I'll go.
2 Manchester are going to win. / Leeds are going to lose.
3 He's going to fall off the ladder. / The ladder's going to fall.
4 Don't worry. I'll call an ambulance. / I'll get help.
5 They're going to miss the bus. / They're not going to catch the bus.
6 Thanks. I'll pay you back tomorrow/as soon as I can. / You're a friend. I won't forget this.

b 1 will take   2 will you be   3 won't forget   4 is going to have   5 is going to study   6 will drive
7 are going to start   8 will crash   9 am going to stay   10 will enjoy

a Ali: 1 will go   2 won't be/is not going to be   3 am leaving/am going to leave   4 will be
Kim: 1 am going to do/am doing   2 will probably go   3 finishes
4 am signing up/am going to sign up   5 will miss   6 will help

Don: 1 am doing/am going to do   2 will travel   3 am definitely going/will definitely go
        4 am going to do
Owen: 1 will be able to   2 will be   3 will send   4 will be able to
Kate: 1 am going   2 is taking/is going to take   3 starts   4 will be   5 will probably share
Mel: 1 am not going to get/am not getting   2 will study   3 will go   4 am going to relax

▶20 An unusual holiday

a be about to: … are about to start out on a holiday … (l. 1)
   going to-future: They are going to travel … (ll. 1-2)
   present progressive: Where are they going? (l. 2)
   will-future: And we'll send lots of photos. (ll. 5-6)
   be to: … we are to give a TV special … (ll. 7-8)
   simple present: Our plane leaves from Heathrow … (l. 12)
   future progressive: … we will be driving … (l. 13)
   be certain to: We are certain to have a few breakdowns … (l. 19)
   be likely to: … the roads are likely to be bad … (l. 19)
   future perfect: … we will have seen … (l. 23)

b Suggestions:
   1 The Wilsons are about to set off on a long and unusual holiday. They are going to travel from
      Alaska to Tierra del Fuego by motorbike.
   2 They are going to send detailed reports of their journey every two weeks by e-mail. They are
      also going to take a lot of photos. After their trip they are to make a TV special for a local
      channel. They will also be giving an exclusive interview to a magazine.
   3 They will be taking the coastal routes down through Alaska, Canada, the USA, Central and
      South America.
   4 They will most likely have problems such as bad weather, extreme heat, bad roads and
      breakdowns.
   5 They are probably taking only necessary things such as spare parts for the motorbikes, a tent,
      sleeping bags, cooking utensils, water bottles, a few clothes for cold and hot weather, first aid
      kit, medicine, cameras, etc.
   6 They will most probably be sightseeing, cooking, doing the washing, studying maps and
      taking photos. Pat will also be writing her diary.
   7 They will probably have been away for almost six months.
   8 They will have driven through Alaska, Canada, the west coast US states, Mexico, Guatemala,
      Honduras, Nicaragua, Costa Rica, Panama, Columbia, Ecuador, Peru and Chile.
   9 They will have driven about 26 thousand kilometres by the time they get back.
   10 After their return Pat thinks she is likely to be planning their next exciting holiday.

▶21 A question of identity

1 moved   2 has lived   3 has ordered   4 has lived   5 is   6 said   7 going to do
8 Are they going to arrest/Will they arrest   9 Am I going to be deported? / Will I be deported?
10 have been/were   11 haven't slept   12 haven't eaten   13 lives   14 discovered   15 died
16 found out   17 had never been registered/had never registered   18 applied   19 was rejected
20 had lived   21 had sent/sent   22 does not possess/did not possess   23 arrived
24 are supporting   25 is trying   26 will be sitting   27 was   28 have lived /have been living
29 will die   30 Does that not make

The passive

▶1 *Quiet, please!*

simple present: is exposed, are increased, is hoped
present progressive: are being introduced
simple past: were exposed, were reported
present perfect: has been done, have been found
past perfect: had not been noticed, had been damaged
will-future: will be enforced
modal aux. + present infinitive: cannot be measured, can be disrupted, may be disturbed,
have to be paid
modal aux. + perfect infinitive: should have been introduced

▶2 *Famous 'firsts'*

a 1 The first balloon flight was made by the Montgolfier brothers in 1783.
2 The first sharp photograph was taken by Louis Daguerre in 1837.
3 The first man was put into space by the Russians in 1961.
4 An electric current was first produced by Galvani in 1780.
5 The first school was set up by Plato in 387 BC.
6 The first petrol-powered car was developed by Benz in 1885.
7 The first heart transplants were performed by Christiaan Barnard in 1967.
8 The first Oscar for Best Actor was won by Emil Jannings in 1927.

▶3 *School rules*

a 1 School property should not be removed from the premises.
2 The computer room must be locked after use.
3 Electronic equipment may be used during the breaks only.
4 Wet clothing should not be hung on radiators.
5 Mobile phones must be switched off during lessons.
6 Food and drinks should not be left in classrooms overnight.
7 Sports equipment must be returned to the gymnasium after use.
8 Equipment may not be removed from the music room without permission.

▶4 *A trip to Ireland*

1 Sixth form pupils were allowed …   2 We were recommended …   3 We were helped …
4 We were told …   5 All pupils were advised …   6 It will be remembered …

▶5 *First jobs*

a 1 … I was taught how to deal with complaints.
2 I have already been given a 20% discount card.
3 I was sent a really nice get-well letter and a big cake.
4 … she has been promised a job in one of their London branches.
5 I haven't even been shown how to work the machines yet.

6 We have both been offered the chance to stay on after our training.
7 We are paid £50 a week.
8 I will be told their decision …

b 1 I was sent some application forms by the firm.
2 At the interview I was given a questionnaire to fill in.
3 I also had to do an aptitude test. Unfortunately, we were not taught these things at/in school.
4 We were given further information about the firm.
5 A week later I was sent a letter.
6 I was offered a job as a trainee in the personnel department.

▶ 6 Street chat

1 was broken into   2 will be/is going to be looked after   3 was paid for   4 haven't been asked out
5 be taken notice of   6 haven't been shouted at   7 was laughed at   8 would be dealt with

▶ 7 The threat to the environment

a 1 In the past ozone was destroyed by CFC's, for example in aerosols and fridges.
2 If the ozone layer is damaged, skin cancer can be caused by the sun's ultra-violet rays.
3 The use of CFC's has been eliminated or reduced by new technologies.
4 The lungs are attacked by too much ozone caused by traffic smog.
5 Domestic and industrial waste is still dumped in landfills.
6 The soil is still polluted by fertilizers and pesticides.
7 Rivers, lakes and seas are still used as dumping grounds for toxic waste.
8 Global warming is caused by the greenhouse effect.
9 Every year an area of rainforest as big as Denmark is destroyed.
10 Rainforest plants which might give us a cure for diseases are destroyed.

b 1 It is known that some nations hunt whales and dolphins in spite of international agreements.
2 It has often been claimed that the 'ozone hole' is the earth's greatest problem.
3 It is thought that half the world's species of birds, insects, flowers and trees live in tropical rainforests.
4 It is believed that the Amazon rainforest alone produces 25% of the world's oxygen.
5 It is expected that the world population will have doubled by 2050.
6 It is estimated that an average American uses twice as much energy as an average European.
7 It has often been said that unlimited population growth is the most important issue facing the world.

c 1 Some nations are known to hunt whales and dolphins in spite of international agreements.
2 The 'ozone hole' has often been claimed to be the earth's greatest problem.
3 Half the world's species of birds, insects, flowers and trees are thought to live in tropical rainforests.
4 The Amazon rainforest alone is believed to produce 25% of the world's oxygen.
5 The world population is expected to have doubled by 2050.
6 An average American is estimated to use twice as much energy as an average European.
7 Unlimited population growth has often been said to be the most important issue facing the world.

▶8 An accident report

a One crash victim, a 25-year-old man, was taken to hospital by an air ambulance. He is said to be in critical condition. An injured woman was pulled from a burning car by passing motorists. Unfortunately, the driver could not be rescued. It is thought that the car was a silver Toyota. / The car is thought to have been a silver Toyota.
The woman was air-lifted to hospital. The passenger in the Ford was unhurt but in shock. He was also taken to hospital in Swindon, where he is being kept under observation. It is believed that the driver of the Ford had lost control … / The driver of the Ford is believed to have lost control … Motorists who witnessed the accident are being interviewed by the police.

▶9 Green Cards

1 are invited   2 are changed   3 must be sent   4 have to be filled in   5 is made   6 to be disqualified   7 were rejected   8 had even been opened/were even opened   9 had been posted/ were posted   10 had been filled in/were filled in   11 is received/has been received   12 will be automatically disqualified/is automatically disqualified   13 being selected/having been selected   14 are notified   15 have not been selected   16 Will I be informed   17 am rejected/have been rejected   18 are informed   19 will soon be invited   20 are applicants interviewed   21 are usually issued   22 will be announced/is going to be announced   23 to be selected

▶10 Death Valley

a is recognized, is believed, is called: simple present passive
wasn't established, were saved, were discovered/rescued: simple past passive
could have been prevented: modal aux. + perfect passive infinitive

b 1 The landscape has been shaped over millions of years by climatic changes, wind and water.
2 Evidence of the presence of man through hundreds of years can be found in almost every part of the valley …
3 In the 1930's a new industry was discovered – tourism.
4 Death Valley was proclaimed a national monument by President Hoover in 1933 …
5 The roads through the valley have certainly been improved since then.
6 Is the valley closed in winter?
7 Many of the side roads are closed in summer …
8 Campgrounds and facilities are being improved continually.

c 1 A national park is a huge area of land which is protected by the government. It is visited by tourists because of its natural beauty or historic importance.
2 A myth is an old story which is generally believed even though it may be false.

d Suggestion:
It is often forgotten that the Forty-Niners crossed other deserts, not only Death Valley.
It is wrongly believed that all the pioneers died here. Only one old man died. Secondly, it is thought that it was very hot when the pioneers crossed the valley. It was winter and therefore not hot. Thirdly, it is said that there was no water in Death Valley. But the pioneers found springs and snow.

e *Man glaubt, dass mehrere Pioniere in Death Valley gestorben seien.*
Several pioneers are believed to have died in Death Valley.
Man glaubt/Es heißt, dass mehrere Pioniere in Death Valley gestorben seien.
Angeblich sollen mehrere Pioniere in Death Valley gestorben sein.

f Park rules that must be obeyed by visitors for their own safety at all times:
Vehicles must be parked on roads and parking lots, not off-road. Contact with animals must be avoided. Flowers may not be picked and rocks may not be collected. Mineshafts or tunnels must not be entered. Strong shoes and hats should be worn.

The infinitive and the gerund

The infinitive

▶ 1 At an activity camp

1 He advises them to get enough sleep.
2 He warns non-swimmers not to go canoeing alone.
3 He tells them to stay in their groups during the outdoor activities.
4 He asks them to do what their instructors say.
5 He reminds them to register for activities the evening before.
6 He expects everybody to keep the washrooms clean.
7 He asks them not to be late for meals.
8 He would like them to look after camp equipment.
9 He tells them not to play loud music in their tents after ten p.m.
10 He warns campers under 18 not to leave the camp without permission.
11 He reminds everybody to read the information on the noticeboard regularly.
12 He advises campers under 14 not to make camp fires without supervision.

▶ 2 Jeff's future

a Jeff's father is a doctor and he would like Jeff to study medicine too. Jeff's mother also wants him to go to university to study something useful. They often tell him to do more in school to get better marks, because they expect him to pass his A-levels without difficulty. Of course they would like him to have a good start in life, and they expect him to apply for a university place soon.
Jeff's girlfriend wants him to stay at home. She doesn't want him to study in another town far away. But Jeff expected her to be more understanding.
They all expect him to do what they want. But Jeff has other ideas. He doesn't want others to plan his life for him. He tells them not to worry about him, and he has decided to travel round the world for a year – alone. Nothing could cause him to change his mind.

▶ 3 Get it right

a 1 … for us to come here.   2 … for Sheila/her to be so careless.   3 … for John to take us to the station.   4 … for me to finish this essay in such a short time.   5 … for my brother/him to finish his homework.   6 … for everyone to know the procedure in case of fire.

b 1 It isn't necessary for you to go shopping today.   2 I had to wait for my sister to come home.
3 I have arranged for a taxi to collect us/pick us up at 8.30.
4 It is essential for young people to have good qualfications these days.
5 I have made a few sandwiches for you to eat on the journey.

▶ 4 We don't know where to stay

a Suggestions:
You can find out what to see, what to do; where to go, where to stay, where to eat, where to shop, where to buy tickets, which places to visit, which sights to see, which hotels to stay at, which restaurants to eat at, how to get to different places, how to use city transport.

▶ 5 Spot the mistakes

Correct: 4, 7, 9
Corrected:
1 I would rather not take the early flight … 2 Does your maths teacher make you learn formulas by heart? 3 Tim hopes to go to university after school to study law. 5 Susan would like to be chosen for a part in the school play … 6 Let's stay at home and cook pasta rather than go out for a meal. 8 If Leo thinks his moped has been stolen, he had better report it to the police. 10 Do they let you take photos in the museum? 11 … It appears that there is nothing to be done. 12 … I thought I heard someone come in.

The gerund

▶ 6 What I like

a 1 + -*ing* form/*to*-inf. 2 + -*ing* form/*to*-inf. 3 + *to*-inf. 4 + *to*-inf. 5 + -*ing* form/*to*-inf. 6 + *to*-inf. 7 + -*ing* form 8 + -*ing* form

c 1 *to*-inf. 2 -*ing* form/*to*-inf. 3 -*ing* form 4 *to*-inf. 5 -*ing* form/*to*-inf. 6 -*ing* form

▶ 7 Which form is correct?

a 1 to call, calling 2 buying, to buy 3 giving, to give 4 answering, to answer 5 to say, not saying 6 discussing, to discuss

b 1 Max went on talking about his new car for hours, although nobody/no one was interested. 2 My father has stopped learning Japanese. 3 I mustn't forget to send David a birthday card. 4 Please remember to collect the things from the cleaner's. 5 I have tried to phone the bank three times, but the number is engaged.

▶ 8 A job advert

1 good at organizing 2 interested in making 3 keen on travelling 4 tired of being 5 clever at solving 6 used to taking up 7 sick of doing 8 bad at waiting 9 afraid of missing 10 fond of doing 11 used to taking 12 interested in working

▶ 9 Working au pair

a opportunity of spending, reasons for going, idea of travelling, hope of learning, experience of doing, difficulty in getting, chance of living

b 1 of communicating   2 in making   3 of getting   4 of not being   5 of being
6 for not getting on   7 of doing   8 of not having   9 about going   10 of spending
11 of living   12 between going

▶10 *A boat trip*

1 After jumping on the boat, Steve started the engine.
2 Before getting on the boat, she looked up at the dark clouds again. /
   After looking up at the dark clouds again, she got on the boat.
3 On/After hearing thunder in the distance, she started to panic.
4 In spite of seeing that a storm was coming, Steve still wanted to take the boat out.
5 Instead of turning off the engine, he just laughed.
6 Suddenly Cheryl climbed off the boat without saying a word.
7 After turning off the engine, Steve ran after Cheryl.
8 Cheryl thought for a few seconds before answering.
9 She tried to hide the fact that she was afraid by saying it was too cold.
10 Without saying another word, Cheryl ran to the main road and took the next bus home.

▶11 *Class gossip*

a 1 a Brian doesn't mind his friends borrowing all his CDs.
        b But he doesn't like them borrowing his mobile.
     2 a Nick is not very pleased about his new girlfriend always arriving late.
        b He hates her wearing too much make up.
     3 a Jenna objects to her parents telling her when to come home.
        b But she doesn't mind them giving her lots of pocket money.
     4 a Sharon's parents are proud of her getting a place at university.
        b But they aren't keen on her going to study in London.
     5 a Sarah is not fond of her little brother sometimes using her computer.
        b And she's tired of him leaving all his stuff in her room.

▶12 *Jeff's old car*

a 1 … said it was difficult (for him) to start.
     2 … thought it was stupid to buy a car that wouldn't start.
     3 They suggested that he should buy a new one.
     4 … decided not to buy a new one. / … decided that he wouldn't buy a new one.
     5 The reason why Jeff bought an old car …

b 6 Before buying the car, Jeff …
     7 Jeff loved repairing things.
     8 He was glad about/at having something to do …
     9 After putting in some new parts, he …
    10 And his friends didn't mind him driving them about in it …

▶13 *Interview with a band*

1 … at writing lyrics.   2 … by playing support …   3 … signing our first recording contract.
4 … travelling a lot.   5 … to working late hours.   6 Giving interviews …
7 … to going to New York.   8 … of not being …   9 … about playing …   10 … buying.

▶14 Write a dialogue

1 + inf.   2 + -*ing* form   3 + inf.   4 + *to*-inf.   5 + inf.   6 + -*ing* form   7 + -*ing* form   8 + inf.
9 + *to*-inf.   10 + inf.   11 + -*ing* form   12 + inf.   13 + -*ing* form   14 + -*ing* form   15 + -*ing* form

▶15 Your star sign

a Pisces: 1 being/to be   2 helping   3 painting   4 organizing
Aries: 1 doing   2 competing/to compete   3 to win   4 losing/to lose
Taurus: 1 doing   2 doing/to do   3 listening   4 drawing   5 accepting
Gemini: 1 working   2 discussing   3 doing   4 to get on with
Cancer: 1 swimming   2 collecting   3 to help   4 taking
Leo: 1 being   2 telling/to tell   3 to do   4 doing   5 getting
Virgo: 1 to know   2 spending   3 to rely on   4 to say
Libra: 1 wasting/to waste   2 arguing   3 being   4 Travelling
Scorpio: 1 to do   2 solving/to solve   3 to make   4 to be
Sagittarius: 1 playing   2 being/to be   3 to follow
Capricorn: 1 working   2 to concentrate   3 being   4 doing

▶16 Rainforests

1 to be cleared   2 to set up   3 to disappear   4 Clearing   5 storing   6 farming   7 making
8 to provide   9 eating   10 to ranch   11 to note   12 to go on   13 destroying   14 to be
15 to persuade   16 to change   17 making   18 realize   19 to carry out   20 to prove
21 to fight   22 to miss   23 finding   24 take away   25 allowing/to allow   26 to make
27 sacrificing   28 making   29 realize   30 to bring in   31 doing   32 to destroy/
to be destroyed   33 to ignore/to be ignored   34 to destroy   35 to replace   36 fighting

▶17 Dolphins in danger

a 1 escape suffering (l. 7), consider including (l. 10)
2 before … running out (l. 8)
3 too late to save (l. 14)

b 1 being wiped out (l.17), [getting caught] (l. 19)
2 danger of dying out (title), danger of being wiped out (l. 17)
3 to monitor (l. 27), to prevent (l. 33)
4 urge the government to adopt (ll. 32-33)

c 1 *Wir erwarten, dass die Regierung und die EU harte, neue Maßnahmen ergreifen werden,
die das Töten beenden.*
2 … but we cannot allow this situation to drag on.

d 1 by pair trawling   2 without considering the fate of the dolphins   3 instead of decreasing
4 In spite of fighting hard, conservationists have not …   5 before dying from lack of oxygen
6 for killing or harming dolphins

e Suggestions:
1 … of dying out/of being wiped out / of disappearing from the South West coast.
2 … to take immediate action to prevent dolphin deaths / to pass strict laws to stop the killing.

3 ... the situation continue for years / foreign industrial vessels harm dolphins unnecessarily.

4 ... to have the situation monitored by independent observers / to stop pair trawling.

5 ... dolphins from dying (from being killed) in fishing nets.

6 ... to free themselves / to escape.

7 ... to persuade the government to take necessary measures to save the dolphins / to urge the government to present plans to stop the dolphin deaths.

8 ... to act quickly because soon there will not be any dolphins left / to save the dolphins before they are all killed.

9 ... feeling angry and sad / feeling that the EU is indifferent to the dolphin deaths.

10 ... to help the dolphins would be to put more pressure on the government/EU through public protest. / ... to improve the situation would be to get more media interest/coverage.

f Suggestions:

1 A conservationist is a person who takes an active part in protecting nature and the environment. / ...who works to conserve the environment, especially nature and wildlife.

2 A trawler is a fishing boat that pulls a large net to catch fish in. / ... that catches fish by pulling a huge net behind it.

3 The RSPCA is a society which works to protect animals or to improve their situation. / ... which works to prevent animals from being treated cruelly.

The participle

▶1 Making adjectives

a 1 a well-dressed man   2 a French-speaking secretary   3 tight-fitting jeans
4 a hard-working schoolgirl   5 a well-paid job   6 fun-loving teenagers   7 a good-looking girl
8 a badly-written application

▶2 An eye-witness account

a 1 ... smelt something burning ...   2 ... saw flames coming ...   3 ... heard people shouting.
4 ... saw a big crowd standing ...   5 ... heard the fire brigade coming.   6 ... watched the firefighters setting up ...   7 ... noticed two people climbing ...   8 ... saw a cat running ...
9 ... noticed a woman waving ...   10 ... smelt wood burning ...

b Correct: 3, 7   Corrected: 1 I saw the robber suddenly pull ...   2 I noticed a dark-haired man with a beard waiting in the get-away van.   4 Through my rear mirror I noticed the car behind me crash into a tree.   5 We smelt rubber burning ...   6 I overheard two men in a pub talking about a break-in ...   8 I felt something hit my car ...   9 I noticed a man lying on the pavement ...   10 ... A minute later we heard the bomb explode.

▶3 Having things done

a 1 He is going to have a pizza delivered.   2 She has had her hair cut.
3 She is having her nails manicured.   4 He is having his motorbike repaired.
5 They are going to have their car washed.   6 He is having his eyes tested.
7 She has had the windows cleaned.   8 They are having some (wedding) photos taken.

b 1 Where can I have these trousers shortened?
2 Why don't you have your hair dyed?
3 Dr Sutton has had a new computer system installed.
4 Where's Jack? – At the garage. He is having his tyres changed.
5 The parcels are very heavy. We can have them sent.

▶4 Romeo and Juliet

Participle constructions (ll. 1-12):
<u>Having become</u> the symbol of love and youth, the story …
… the city of Verona, <u>troubled</u> by fighting …
… Romeo <u>wearing</u> a mask …
<u>Being</u> fascinated by Juliet's beauty, Romeo …
<u>Not knowing</u> who Juliet is, he asks …
<u>Discovering</u> that Juliet is a Capulet, …, Romeo …
…, <u>not being</u> able to sleep, Juliet goes onto the balcony <u>overlooking</u> the orchard.
<u>Passing</u> Juliet's window on the way home, Romeo decides to climb over the wall into the orchard
<u>hoping</u> to see Juliet again.

Possible participle constructions (ll. 13-33):
<u>Having decided</u> to marry Juliet without delay, … (l. 13)
The old priest, <u>thinking</u> that the two families … (l. 14)
Later in the day, Romeo, <u>having killed</u> Juliet's cousin … (l. 17)
… Paris, the husband <u>chosen</u> for her by her father. (ll. 20-21)
<u>Having</u> no one to talk to, she turns to Friar Laurence, <u>asking</u> him to help her. (ll. 21-22)
<u>Having told</u> her his plan, he gives her a potion of herbs putting her … (ll. 22-23)
… a letter to Romeo <u>telling</u> him … (l. 24)
<u>Trusting</u> Friar Laurence's words, Juliet … (l. 26)
<u>Believing</u> her to be dead, Juliet's grief-stricken family … (ll. 26-27)
<u>Hearing</u> the news that Juliet is dead, Romeo … (l. 28)
<u>Taking</u> her in his arms, in his grief he drinks poison, <u>dying</u> beside her. (ll. 29-30)
<u>Awaking</u> from the long sleep, Juliet … (l. 31)
<u>Not wanting</u> to live without Romeo, Juliet … (ll. 32-33)

▶5 Christmas in England

1 Although costing   2 being   3 if caught   4 Although celebrated   5 After going/having gone
6 Before going   7 After hanging up/having hung up   8 although sleeping/having slept
9 While opening   10 When pulled   11 when eating   12 If given

▶6 Get it right

1 *correct*   2 when queuing up   3 [when]   4 when running   5 [when]   6 when putting up
7 when waiting   8 *correct*   9 [when]   10 when walking

▶7 Written English

a 1 …, several trains being delayed.   2 Interest rates having fallen, …   3 Demonstrators blocking the streets, …   4 Camera phones costing more than expected, …   5 …, sales having dropped by more than 10%.   6 More and more teachers falling ill with influenza, …

b 1 The captive having been kept in a dark room for five days, the kidnappers finally released him.
2 The new motorway exit being difficult to see in the fog, several drivers missed it.
3 The property costing over a hundred thousand pounds, the tenants are not willing to buy it.
4 The dog having bitten three people, the owner was forced to have it destroyed.

▶8 *Street talk*

1 With Christmas getting closer, I've started looking for presents.
2 And with exams finished, we'll be able to enjoy Christmas.
3 But with all the shops closed over Christmas, there will be nowhere to go.
4 With my mum losing her job, we haven't got much money for presents anyway.
5 With my boyfriend's family living in Scotland, I might not see him over Christmas.
6 With train fares going up, I can't afford to go to Scotland with him.
7 And with petrol costing so much, it's too expensive by car, I expect.
8 Well, with my computer repaired at last, I will have enough to do over Christmas.

▶9 *Spot the mistakes*

Correct: 1, 2, 4, 8, 10, 15
Corrected: 3 The weather being warm and sunny, Angela ...   5 The book being long and boring, the class didn't want to read it.   6 ... a herd of bulls, when cycling ...   7 With the new computers costing over a thousand pounds, people ...   9 The train leaving very early in the morning, Ben and Anna missed it. / Though leaving very early in the morning, Ben and Anna missed their train.   11 His favourite jeans having a big hole in the knee, Pete threw them away.
12 ... with a very long beard, when eating her lunch at the *Hard Rock Café*.
13 Strictly speaking, ...   14 Having already seen *Scream 6* at the cinema, we ...

▶10 *Thomas Alva Edison*

a 1 ... Edison from school thinking that the seven-year-old was too slow to learn.
2 Though having only three months of formal education, he became ...
3 His mother knowing full well that her son was intelligent, she began to teach him at home.
4 Noticing that he enjoyed doing experiments, she encouraged him ...
5 But not being able to afford books for her son, she realized that she could not help him further.
6 Needing money for books, at the age of twelve Edison began selling newspapers ...
7 Having nothing to do while the train stood in the station, he set up ...
8 Having great faith in scientific progress, Edison valued ...
9 He stretched himself to his limits, sometimes working twenty hours a day.
10 After having invented the light bulb in 1879, Edison went on ...
11 He made great improvements to the telegraph, telephone and in film-making technology, also founding the first modern research laboratory.
12 Edison was a clever businessman, setting up companies worldwide to manufacture and sell his inventions.
13 Edison was also a hard businessman, fighting fiercely to defeat his competitors.
14 Edison having encouraged Henry Ford to use the gasoline-powered engine for the automobile, ...
15 Edison obtained 1,093 United States patents, the biggest number ever issued to any individual.

▶11 The Great Fire of London

a 1 Active: destroying eighty per cent, smelt something burning, Finding the house, sleeping family, Climbing through a window, Being too frightened, burning building, setting it on fire, destroying not only houses
Passive: started perhaps by the carelessness, Awakened, Accelerated by the strong winds, Being built of wood, packed with flammable materials
2 the sleeping family (l. 11), the burning building (l. 15), the demolished houses (l. 29)

b 1 present participle after a verb of perception ('smell') + object
Further examples: He saw houses on both sides of the bridge burning. (l. 23)
… and noticed people trying to remove … (l. 24); He watched sick people being carried away in their beds. (l. 25);
Translation: *Er sah auf beiden Seiten der Brücke Häuser brennen.*
… und bemerkte, wie die Menschen versuchten, ihre Sachen … zu entfernen.
Er beobachtete, wie Kranke in ihren Betten weggetragen wurden.
2 present participles after the verbs *keep* and *leave* + object (as after verbs of rest and movement)
Translation: *Die starken Ostwinde ließen die Flammen immer weiter fortschreiten.*
Bald hinterließen sie die ganze Stadt in Flammen.
3 a participle construction instead of an adverbial clause of reason, with its own subject ('water')

c 1 When he found the house full of smoke …
2 … and set it on fire too.
3 … warehouses which were packed with flammable materials …
4 After/When he had been sent for by the King, Pepys …
5 Since/As/Because he was greatly troubled, the King …
6 Since/As/Because they had started the demolition too close to the fires, …
7 … and all were reduced to ashes.
8 For three more days the fire raged through the city and destroyed 13,200 houses and 87 churches.
9 Since/As/Because they had lost everything, many people were reduced …
10 … wooden houses which dated back to the medieval period were replaced …

▶12 Riding on … well … air

a 1 smog-belching (l. 4), air-powered (l. 8), hydrogen-powered (l. 11)
2 compressed … (l. 14)
3 After having worked for almost ten years on the project, … (ll. 7-8)
4 … including … (l. 22)

b 1 traffic which/that pollutes the air with smog
2 air which/that is compressed
3 a car which/that is powered by hydrogen

c 1 running on compressed air
2 producing zero emission
3 pressure used for the standard car tire …
4 Big carmakers not being interested …
5 It also needs refueling every 120 miles, which makes it essentially a short-distance city car.
6 Though having won the backing of the big auto companies, hydrogen-powered cars won't be ready for the road for five years at the very least.

d 1 a participle construction expressing accompanying circumstances
   2 a present participle used after the verb *leave* + object (as with verbs of rest and movement)

e Suggestions:
   1 ... using/running on compressed air. / ... producing zero emission. / ... designed to prevent air pollution/designed for city-use/designed by the Frenchman Guy Nègre.
   2 ... the hydrogen-powered car. / ... a car powered by hydrogen.
   3 ... the company set up/founded by Guy Nègre to build and market his invention.

The noun

▶ 1 Words, words, words

a Plural: bacteria, media, passers-by, phenomena, teeth, women
   Singular: analysis, city, crisis, criterion, life, roof, studio, tomato
   Singular and plural: crossroads, means, series, sheep, spacecraft, species

b 1 Plural forms: analyses, crises, criteria, cities, lives, roofs, studios, tomatoes
   2 Singular forms: bacterium, medium, passer-by, phenomenon, tooth, woman

c 1 means   2 criteria   3 series   4 analysis   5 spacecraft   6 species   7 sheep
   8 phenomenon   9 women   10 tomatoes   11 teeth   12 roofs

▶ 2 What nationality were they?

a 1 a Spaniard   2 a Frenchwoman   3 an Indian   4 a Russian   5 an Austrian   6 an Italian
   7 a Chinese   8 a Hungarian   9 a Norwegian   10 a Scot   11 a Pole   12 a Greek   13 a Swede
   14 a Japanese   15 a Dutchman   16 an Irishman

b 1 The English ...   2 The French ...   3 The Germans ...   4 The Greeks ...   5 The Dutch ...
   6 The Italians ...   7 The Japanese ...   8 The Russians ...   9 The Scots ...   10 The Spaniards ...
   11 The Swiss ...   12 The Turks ...

▶ 3 More words

a 1 Verb always singular: maths, news, politics, the USA
   2 Verb always plural: belongings, cattle, glasses, goods, jeans, police, scissors, shorts, surroundings
   3 Verb singular and plural: band, crowd, family, government, team

b a pair of glasses/jeans/scissors/shorts

c 1 is   2 do the jeans in the window cost   3 speaks/speak   4 is having
   5 politics doesn't interest   6 is leaving/are leaving   7 are not   8 have already arrested
   9 is   10 don't cut   11 were stolen   12 don't fit   13 are   14 thinks/think   15 is/are

▶ 4 Food and drinks

a 1 some/six *(or any number)*   2 some/six pieces of   3 some/two bottles of   4 some/a/a bowl of
5 – /some/some cans of/some bottles of   6 – /some/some bottles of/some cartons of   7 – /some
8 – /some/some cartons of/three big cartons of/etc.

b We'd like two colas, an/one orange juice, two coffees, a/one mineral water, two strawberry ice
creams and a/one tea.

▶ 5 Mini-dialogues

a Uncountable nouns: accommodation, damage, furniture, information, music, pollution,
progress, sun, traffic, travel, weather, work

1 some very good, was, awful, any/much   2 – , a, –   3 a, – , some   4 any, some/a lot of, A lot of
5 a lot of, some good/good

b 1 A friend gave me some good advice. / A friend gave me a bit/piece of good advice.
2 This homework is difficult. / This piece of homework is difficult.
3 I have some good news for you. / I have a bit/piece of good news for you.
4 I got a lot of useful information. / I got a lot of bits/pieces of useful information.
5 The police have found some new evidence. / The police have found some new bits/pieces
of evidence.

▶ 6 What's the name of the store?

a 1 my brother's birthday   2 the name of the store   3 friend's   4 the name of the street
5 hairdresser's   6 the name of the Italian restaurant   7 the end of the street   8 Luigi's
9 men's department   10 ladies' department   11 the price of the blouse
12 this season's colours   13 chemist's   14 aunt's

b 1 James's best friend   2 Ireland's economy/the economy of Ireland   3 the children of friends
who live in Leeds   4 the students' applications   5 the government's decision/the decision
of the government   6 today's paper   7 women's magazines   8 the son of the people who have
moved in next door   9 Lisa and Patrick's/Lisa's and Patrick's address   10 the meaning of this
word   11 children's books   12 my last month's pocket money

▶ 7 Elizabethan life

a 1 children, cities, coaches, deer, dresses, elves, fairies, furniture, potatoes, witches
2 'tights'; other pair nouns: e.g. trousers, pants, shorts, jeans, pyjamas, glasses, goggles, scissors,
binoculars, headphones, pliers
3 'hair' + singular verb, e.g.: Your hair looks nice today.
'hairs' + plural verb, e.g.: There are two dog hairs on your jacket.

b 1 Uncountable nouns ll. 1-14: progress, travel, furniture
2 a loaf/slice of bread, a cup/pot/packet/jar of coffee, a jar of honey, a slice/piece/kilo of meat,
a bag/kilo/spoon of sugar

c 1 England's population – the population of England; girls' education – the education of girls; rich people's houses – the houses of rich people; London's theatres – the theatres of London; Elizabeth's England – the England of Elizabeth; Shakespeare's England – the England of Shakespeare

2 'the children of rich people' (l. 15), or: 'rich people's children'
'the daughter of King Henry VIII and his second wife Anne Boleyn' (ll. 1-2): too long for the use of the possessive form
'the rooms of their houses' (ll. 13-14): we use the *of*-phrase for things
'the taste of chocolate' (l. 29): we use the *of*-phrase for things
'the growth of the merchant class' (l. 30): too long for the use of the possessive form

d 1 At court looks were very important.
2 Clothes were complicated and elaborate.
3 In court circles hair was very important for men and women.
4 Elizabeth was slim with pale skin and red hair.
5 Manners did not always correspond to our idea of good manners.
6 During Elizabeth's rule/reign, a lot of/much social and economic progress was made.

The article

▶1 Mini-dialogues

1 Crime, The crime, city life, Pollution, traffic, noise   2 people, the people, Life   3 The pizza, pizza, cooking, The food   4 industry, The tourist industry   5 the music, the noise, Music
6 Coffee, the coffee, cake, the cakes   7 Paper, the paper, The waste, developed countries
8 nuclear power, electricity, the electricity, wind power, wave power, solar power

▶2 Get it right

a 1 to hospital   2 at work   3 on television   4 on the radio   5 at university/college   6 by train
7 to the cinema   8 at home   9 to prison   10 to court   11 to the theatre   12 in town

b 1 School, the school, the church   2 the hospital, the hospital   3 university   4 the prison
5 the college

▶3 A trip to London

a 1 –   2 –   3 –   4 the   5 the   6 –   7 –   8 –   9 the   10 –   11 the   12 –   13 –   14 –   15 the
16 The   17 –   18 the   19 –   20 –   21 –   22 –   23 –   24 the   25 –   26 the   27 –   28 the
29 –   30 the   31 the   32 the   33 –

c Suggestions:
the Hudson River, the East River, the Guggenheim Museum, the Metropolitan Museum, Times Square, Union Square, Central Park, Battery Park, Wall Street, Fifth Avenue, Park Avenue, Broadway, Madison Avenue, Madison Square Garden, Rockefeller Center, Lincoln Center, Brooklyn Bridge, the Statue of Liberty, the New York Stock Exchange, the Waldorf-Astoria, the Ritz-Carlton, Ellis Island, the Empire State Building, the Trump Tower, the Chrysler Building, Harlem Market, the Apollo Theater

▶4 Correct the mistakes

Correct: 5, 11
Corrected:
1 ... how life began?
2 ... double the salary ...
3 ... three nights a week ...
4 ... as a systems analyst ...
6 As a result ...
7 ... quite a nice town ...
8 ... with the exception of Peter ...

9 She plays the guitar ...
10 ... on Saturday.
12 Most of the pupils ...
13 ... for breakfast.
14 ... on condition that ...
15 ... on Pennsylvania Avenue ...
16 Half the time ...

▶5 Going to university

a 1 –   2 –   3 a   4 a   5 –   6 –   7 –   8 an   9 such a   10 the   11 the   12 –   13 –   14 a   15 a
16 Most of the   17 quite a   18 half the   19 Both (the)   20 –   21 –   22 –   23 –   24 a

▶6 The 'American Dream'

a 1 a   2 a   3 –   4 the   5 –   6 –   7 –   8 –   9 the   10 –   11 –   12 –   13 a   14 a   15 the/ –
16 the   17 the   18 the   19 the   20 –   21 the   22 –   23 –   24 –   25 –   26 –   27 –   28 –

▶7 Shakespeare's life

a 1 '... was a glove maker and a wool dealer'.' (= war Handschuhmacher und Wollhändler);
'... success as a merchant ...' (= Erfolg als Kaufmann);
'... worked as a school teacher.' (= arbeitete als Schullehrer)
2 The word 'wool' is a material noun, usually uncountable. There is no definite article before
'wool' because it is used in a general sense.
3 The word 'life' is an abstract noun. In 'Life in Shakespeare's day ...' it is used in a general sense,
so there is no definite article. In '... the life of an actor ...' it is more concrete and specific (with
an of-phrase), so it has a definite article.
4 In '... went to school ...' the word 'school' is used without the definite article because the
purpose or function of 'school' is meant.
In 'The school he attended ...' the building itself (not the purpose or function) is meant, so
it has a definite article. Also, 'school' is more specific because of the relative/contact clause
'he attended'.

b 1 was a glove maker, a wool dealer (l. 3); a merchant (l. 5)
2 two plays a year (l. 27)
3 as a merchant (l. 5); as a child (l. 17); as a school teacher (l. 19); as a writer (l. 22); without a
roof, without a curtain (l. 40)
4 Without 'the': in Henley Street (l. 2), He bought New Place (l. 34),
in Holy Trinity Church (l. 36);
With 'the': the south bank of the River Thames (l. 28), the Globe (Theatre) (ll. 29, 33-34, 37)

c 1 an, the   2 the   3 The, the   4 –   5 –, –   6 a, a   7 –, –   8 –

The adjective and the adverb

The adjective

▶ 1 Find the mistakes

a Correct: 1, 4, 6, 8
Corrected: 2 The sick child … 3 The sleeping man … 5 The happy girl …
7 The frightened children … 9 … my brother is older. 10 … a living language …

b 1 alike, similar 2 sleeping, asleep 3 frightened, afraid 4 alive 5 sick

▶ 2 School subjects

a 1 more enjoyable than 2 harder than 3 more useful than 4 more interesting than
5 more boring than 6 easier than 7 more difficult than

c 1 My best friend is better than me at … 2 But she/he is not as/so good at … as I am/as me.
3 My marks in … are getting better and better/worse and worse. 4 My friend is less interested in
… than me/than I am. 5 Fewer pupils learn/are learning … than …, because … is more useful.
6 The Abitur is/A-levels are getting closer and closer. 7 The more I think of the exams, the more
nervous I get. 8 But school will soon be over. The sooner the better!

▶ 3 Mini-dialogue

1 older/elder 2 latest 3 last 4 older 5 next 6 nearest 7 further/farther 8 further

▶ 4 Add a word

1 people 2 one 3 thing 4 – 5 woman 6 people/men/women 7 man 8 thing 9 –
10 ones 11 – 12 people/men/women 13 one 14 thing 15 ones

The adverb

▶ 5 My ideal teacher

c 1 boring 2 patiently 3 stupid 4 angry 5 idiotically 6 angrily 7 noisy 8 unfair
9 seriously 10 popular 11 well 12 clearly 13 fast 14 interesting

▶ 6 Get it right

a 1 cheaply, cheap 2 daily, daily 3 long, long 4 high, highly 5 early, early 6 prettily, pretty
7 hard, hardly 8 right, rightly

▶ 7 How to be a winner

a 1 more intensively 2 physically 3 mentally 4 firmly 5 most seriously
6 most confidently 7 most successfully 8 fully 9 more aggressively 10 faster 11 harder
12 more skillfully 13 earlier 14 better 15 worse 16 competitively 17 longer
18 more sensibly 19 less 20 more slowly 21 nervously 22 best

▶ 8 A disappointing weekend

1 The exams would soon be starting.
2 Paul had been working very hard at home every evening.
3 He really felt that he needed a break. / He felt that he really needed a break.
4 So he asked his girlfriend if she'd like to go to his brother's cottage in Cornwall for the weekend.
5 They had had a great time there the year before.
6 The cottage was empty because Paul's brother had gone to work in the States for six months.
7 Cathy welcomed the idea, so Paul arranged to collect her from the office at about five the next day.
8 The journey to Tintagel usually took about three hours,
9 so they expected to arrive at the cottage at about eight on Friday evening.
10 Paul was looking forward to having a swim in the sea before breakfast
11 and to taking a walk on the beach in the afternoons.
12 And perhaps a barbecue in the garden on Saturday evening.
13 Unfortunately, Paul had trouble with his car on the way.
14 Luckily, they easily managed to find a garage,
15 but the mechanic politely told them that he was just closing.
16 He said they could collect the car at about lunchtime the next day.
17 In fact, Paul didn't have enough money to pay the bill.
18 They arrived at the cottage at four in the afternoon, only to discover that Paul had forgotten to take the keys with him.

▶ 9 Living in London

1 ... I used to live in Tottenham, ...   2 ... are known to be very high.   3 ... flat rents are unlikely to/not likely to fall.   4 I happen to have a friend ...   5 I'm afraid I don't earn ...
6 You are sure/certain to know ...   7 I suppose she earns a lot of money.   8 ... prefer to live ...
9 They seem to get used to it.   10 I hope ...

▶ 10 Anke's English

a 1 easily 2 fast 3 properly 4 fluently 5 stupid 6 strange 7 funny 8 badly 9 unusual
10 in a friendly way/manner 11 wrong 12 highly 13 amusing 14 extremely 15 nervous
16 fairly 17 late 18 tired 19 hardly 20 hard 21 really 22 particularly

c 1 Anke speaks English quite well.
2 At first she found the grammar terribly complicated.
3 She found 'th' extremely difficult to pronounce.
4 She practised in front of the mirror. Her little brother thought she was totally crazy.
5 She bought an English grammar, but she found it terribly boring.
6 After six months in London her English was considerably better.

▶11 A camping trip

'I remember quite <u>clearly</u> the first time I went camping. I was just thirteen. My friends Sebastian and Andreas were twelve.
We weren't very <u>well</u> prepared for the trip. The tent was my Dad's – not the <u>latest</u> model and <u>extremely</u> awkward to put up. <u>Admittedly</u>, we could have put it up more <u>easily</u> if we had practised at home, but we felt <u>excited</u> about our first time in a tent, and tried not to get <u>angry</u> just because a few tent pegs were missing.

At seven o'clock it started to get dark. We all felt <u>hungry</u>, so we decided to make a fire and cook something to eat. Unfortunately, most of the wood we collected was damp, so the fire started smoking <u>terribly</u>, making us all cough. As soon as it was burning properly, we warmed up our cans of chilli con carne. Actually, it smelt <u>awful</u> and it tasted even worse. But we ate it <u>hungrily</u>.

Just as we were getting into our sleeping bags, Basti heard a strange noise. It sounded fairly <u>close</u>, in the bushes right behind our tent. We felt pretty frightened, because it seemed to be getting <u>closer</u>. We lay in our tent staring into the darkness, not daring to speak <u>loudly</u>. One of us switched on a torch. I looked at the two <u>frightened</u> faces – but I probably looked just as <u>nervous</u> myself. I told the others that we were <u>perfectly</u> safe, and to prove it I got up, took my torch and went outside to look. Everything seemed calm. I felt my way <u>carefully</u> through the bushes and I felt <u>proud</u> of myself for having overcome my fear. But then, it was <u>highly</u> unlikely that I would meet a <u>dangerous</u> animal in our local woods.
Anyway, we felt <u>greatly</u> relieved, and at some time in the early hours we must have fallen asleep.'
(23 mistakes)

▶12 The London 'Tube'

a 1 oldest 2 publicly 3 privately 4 continually 5 slowly 6 fastest 7 most popular
8 surprisingly 9 less/more crowded 10 earlier 11 later 12 comfortably 13 less stressful
14 quieter 15 better 16 temporarily 17 busiest 18 least crowded 19 more convenient
20 less congested 21 farther/further 22 cheaper 23 fairly 24 smoothly 25 safer

▶13 The triumph of English

a 1 messier (l. 13), stronger (l. 13), better (l. 26), lazier (l. 28)
2 worst (l. 9), cleverest (l. 31)
3 highly flexible (l. 16), infinitely tolerant (l. 16), particularly true (l. 19),
   thoroughly dubious (l. 35)
4 competently (l. 5), fluently (l. 33)
5 truly (l. 7), indeed (l. 26), unfortunately (l. 28)
6 even (ll. 11, 22), only (l. 31)

b 1 more highly motivated 2 less lazy 3 least clever 4 best

c 1 the most powerful 2 simpler/more simple than 3 worse 4 the laziest/the least motivated

d 1 rightly 2 mostly 3 highly 4 pretty 5 hard 6 wrongly

e 1 English is usually understood in most countries in the world.
2 English doesn't seem particularly difficult for people from EU countries.
3 Foreigners often speak better English than the British.
4 Unfortunately, 66% of British people do not speak a foreign language at all.

f Suggestion:

First, in the author's opinion English is the world language because it is the language of the USA, the world's most powerful country. So the English that influences, even damages other languages and cultures is American, not British English. The spread of American culture is also very obvious in Britain – and is often lamented.

Secondly, as English is so widely spoken, the British are less motivated than other peoples to learn foreign languages. They seem to be the laziest and worst language learners in the EU. This lack of knowledge cuts them off from the literature and ideas of other peoples.

Quantifiers

▶1 Mini-dialogues

1: 1 some   2 some   3 anything   4 any   5 any   6 any   7 some   8 anything
2: 1 some   2 some/any   3 Any   4 some   5 somewhere   6 some/any
3: 1 anybody   2 some   3 Somebody   4 their   5 they
4: 1 anybody   2 somebody   3 Anything   4 somebody   5 their   6 them   7 some
   8 somebody/anybody   9 them   10 they

▶2 There isn't much left

a There's a lot of … bread, chocolate mousse. There are a lot of tomatoes.
There's a little … noodle salad, orange juice, ice cream.
There are a few … pizza slices, crisps, cans of cola.

b Possible answers:
I ate/drank a lot of … (all words are possible)
I didn't drink much … mineral water, cola, orange juice.
I didn't eat much … chocolate cake, bread, chocolate mousse, noodle salad, ice cream, cheese.
I didn't eat many … sandwiches, pizza slices, crisps, grapes, tomatoes.
I didn't drink many … cans of cola, glasses of orange juice, glasses of mineral water.

c Possible answers:
I eat/drink (quite) a lot of … (all words are possible).
I drink … (very) little milk, fruit juice, diet cola.
I eat … few vegetables, sweets, low-calorie products, eggs, fries, burgers.
I eat … (very) little fruit, fish, red meat, chicken, chocolate, yoghurt, convenience food.

▶3 Get it right

1 all   2 either   3 Both the   4 Either   5 All the   6 None   7 every   8 neither   9 any
10 each of them   11 each   12 Every   13 none   14 any   15 neither   16 Both of the
17 Every   18 Any   19 no   20 Either

▶4 Young people vote against politics

a Lines:
1 <u>All</u> young people …   4 <u>Each</u> young person …   6 <u>Many</u> politicians …   7 … <u>no</u> politicians …
8 … <u>any</u> of them, … <u>all</u> the same …   9 … <u>little</u> has been done. <u>A lot of</u> young people …
11 … had not done <u>much</u> …   12 <u>All</u> the sixth formers …   14 … <u>little</u> connection …
17 … <u>little</u> knowledge …   18 … not have any idea. <u>A few</u> pupils …   19 … <u>few</u> distinctions …
20 … hardly <u>any</u> differences …

b 1 'all' means 'all in general'; 'all the' means 'all of a definite group or number'
2 'any' means here *'jeden beliebigen, irgendeinen egal welchen'*
3 Few young people …
4 'little' means 'sehr wenig'; the meaning is negative; 'a little's means *'ein bisschen, etwas'*; the meaning is positive
5 In positive statements 'any' is used after words with a negative or restricted *(einschränkend)* meaning (i.e. 'never', 'hardly').

c 1 British sixth formers do not show much interest in politics.
2 Not many can name the leader of the Opposition.
3 The government has done little to improve …
4 Most pupils had no idea who …
5 Pupils didn't show much knowledge of politics.
6 Some/Not many pupils knew the answer.
7 All the young people interviewed were asked to …
8 The youngsters could not see much connection between …
9 They could not draw many distinctions between …
10 The school makes all possible efforts to get the pupils …
11 Not any of the pupils interviewed expects to vote.
12 The two major parties have similar political aims. /
The major parties both have similar …

Pronouns and question words

Pronouns

▶1 The German 'man'

a 1 you/one   2 they   3 You/One   4 They   5 They   6 you   7 you   8 They   9 One/You
10 You   11 One/You   12 You/One

▶2 A flat of her own

a 1 mine   2 her   3 of her   4 hers   5 her   6 my   7 our   8 hers   9 yours   10 his   11 her
12 mine   13 her   14 her

c 1 … a friend of mine.   2 … a classmate of his.   3 … some friends of theirs …
4 … an idea of yours …   5 … some neighbours of ours.   6 … a colleague of hers.
7 … some CDs of mine.   8 … a teacher of theirs.

▶3 Don't hurt yourself!

a 1 herself   2 myself   3 ourselves   4 –   5 themselves   6 –   7 –   8 –   9 Yourself   10 yourself
11 himself   12 himself   13 –   14 themselves

▶4 Interview tips

a 1 –   2 himself/herself   3 –   4 themselves   5 –   6 –   7 –   8 yourself   9 yourself
10 yourself   11 themselves   12 –   13 –   14 myself   15 –

▶5 Situations

1 They are writing to each other.
2 They are looking at themselves in the mirror.
3 They are thinking about each other.
4 They are helping each other.
5 They are enjoying themselves.
6 They are speaking French to each other.
7 They don't understand each other.
8 They are helping themselves.

▶6 Mixed bag

1 each other   2 his   3 ourselves   4 each other   5 –   6 himself   7 of hers   8 –
9 his own car   10 her   11 ideas of his own   12 of mine

▶7 Being Australian

a 1 be proud of oneself (l. 3)   2 express oneself (l. 14)   3 imagine (l. 16)   4 differ (l. 17)
5 consider oneself (l. 12)   6 agree (l. 9)   7 think of oneself (l. 4)
8 identify oneself with sth. (l. 9)

b remember: *sich erinnern*   wonder: *sich fragen*
mix with: *sich mischen unter*   fall in love: *sich verlieben*
adapt: *sich anpassen*   recover: *sich erholen*
change: *sich ändern*   settle down: *sich häuslich niederlassen*
meet: *sich treffen*   worry about sth.: *sich Sorgen machen*

c 1 –   2 herself   3 themselves   4 –   5 each other, each other   6 themselves
7 yourself, –   8 each other

d Suggestions:
1 The teachers at McQuarrie High School try to encourage their students to be proud of
themselves and their cultural heritage. They do not try to influence them on the question of
national identity. They want them to see themselves as Arabic-speaking Australians, etc.
2 The three girls agree that their parents mix mainly with their own ethnic communities. Their
parents still find it hard to adapt to Australian customs and the 'new' way of life. They
remember the 'old' way of life in their home countries and identify themselves strongly with it.

3 Maria sees herself as an Australian with a Chinese background. She tries to identify herself with the Chinese culture.
4 Amanda worries about her future because her parents expect her to settle down with someone from the Lebanese community. She thinks they may never recover from the shock if she falls in love with an English-speaking Australian.
5 The main problem of people from a different ethnic background is basically one of 'acceptance' of the new culture.
First-generation immigrants have been used to a their own culture with its traditions, customs, beliefs and lifestyle. For years they have known nothing else. They share all this only with people from the same ethnic community and they naturally share a strong feeling of belonging together. The question of learning to accept the 'new' culture is perhaps one of attitude. The new language is perhaps one of the main reasons for not mixing. Immigrants simply feel more comfortable using their native language. One can understand the strong parental desire for children to value their heritage and continue the parents' customs and traditions. These, however, are only part of their children's lives, the smaller part, a fact which the parents must also learn to accept.

Question words

▶ 8 *At the scene of the crime*

a 1 Who knows the injured man?
2 What did you see on the way to the changing rooms?
3 Who did you see running away?
4 Which of you can describe the men?
5 What did they look like?
6 What were they wearing?
7 Who has a key to the changing rooms?
8 Who could/might have had a key?
9 Which player came into the changing rooms first?
10 Who found the injured man?
11 Which of you phoned the police?
12 Who have you spoken to about this? / With whom have you spoken about this? (formal)

▶ 9 *Find the mistakes*

Correct: 3, 11
Corrected:
1 Which of you would like to go to a concert in Bath with me?
2 Whose CDs are these? They're not mine.
4 What did Alexander Fleming discover in 1928?
5 What kind of book are you looking for?
6 That was a stupid thing to do. What did you do it for?
7 Which of the pupils hasn't made any mistakes?
8 To whom did you give the information?
9 Which of these paintings do you like best?
10 What is this metal ring for?
12 What is the weather like in Berlin today?

Conditional sentences

▶1 Mini-dialogues

a 1 When, if, if, if, When   2 When, If, If

b 1 in case, unless, Supposing, as long as   2 unless, as long as, in case, Supposing

▶2 What will happen if …?

a 1 manages   2 will sell   3 doesn't clean   4 won't sell   5 phone   6 will tell   7 will let   8 ask

b Suggestions:
1 …, he will have a better chance of selling it. / …, it will look a lot better.
2 …, she may/might buy it.   3 … if it costs too much. / … if she doesn't like it.
4 … if the car needs repairs.   5 …, she probably won't buy it.   6 … if it isn't too expensive.

▶3 Problems

a 1 wouldn't have to   2 didn't want   3 got   4 wouldn't be   5 would help   6 had   7 wanted
8 would ask

b Suggestions:
1 If I were you, I would get more sleep/see a doctor.   2 If I were you, I would start tidying up/
try to be a bit tidier.   3 If I were you, I would explain to her why it's important to you.
4 I would stop going out so much if I were you. / I would stop buying unnecessary things if
I were you.   5 I would do what's best for your mark in French if I were you.

▶4 Situations

a Suggestions:
1 If I lost my passport in a non-EU country, I would report it to the German consulate. /
… I might go to the police and report it.
2 If a stranger asked me for 20 euros on the street, I would ask for his/her name and telephone
number. / … I might give him/her only ten.
3 If I was alone at home and the doorbell rang in the night, I would look out of the window and
ask who it was. / … I wouldn't open the door. /… I might stay in bed and do nothing.
4 If I missed the last bus home, I would phone my parents. / … I wouldn't walk home alone.
5 If my bicycle had a puncture on a lonely road late at night, I would push the bike and look for
help.
6 If a pickpocket stole my purse, I would report it at a police station. / … I might ask someone for
help or for money to phone home.

b Suggestions:
1 If my parents were rich and famous, I could stop worrying about my future. / … I might not be
able to go out without a bodyguard.
2 If my family lived in the US, I could probably drive to school in my own car/I could be a
cheerleader/I could play baseball. / … I might not have much free time because of the long
schooldays.

3 If I won a car, I could sell it and save the money. / … I couldn't drive it because I'm not 18. /
   … I might keep it until I'm old enough to drive.
4 If I went to university in the UK, I could have a degree after three years. /… I might have
   problems with the language.

▶ 5 *It wouldn't have happened if …*

a 1 If Steve hadn't left his rucksack in a café, it wouldn't have disappeared.
2 The maths teacher wouldn't have confiscated Sita's mobile if it hadn't rung in his lesson.
3 Rachel wouldn't have lost her walkman if she hadn't left it lying about.
4 If Tom had paid his bill, his mobile phone wouldn't have been de-activated.
5 If Emma hadn't been driving too fast on her moped, she wouldn't have had the accident.
6 Lucy's university application would have been accepted if she hadn't sent it off too late.

b 1 If Laura had locked her bicycle, it wouldn't have been stolen.
2 Julia wouldn't have lost her camera if she had taken more care.
3 If Alan hadn't driven too fast, he would have passed his driving test.
4 David wouldn't have fallen if he hadn't wanted to show off with his snowboard.

▶ 6 *A bus accident*

a Suggestions:
1 If there hadn't been a lot of traffic in France, the coach would/might not have been delayed.
2 If the coach had not been behind schedule, the driver would/might not have been driving too
   fast.
3 The accident might not have happened if the driver had not been overtired.
4 The coach might not have skidded if it hadn't rained heavily.
5 The driver wouldn't have lost control if the roads hadn't been wet.
6 The bus wouldn't have hit the crash barrier if it hadn't skidded and swerved.
7 If the passengers hadn't been asleep, more of them might have been wearing seatbelts.
8 If the injured passengers had been wearing seatbelts, they might not have been hurt.
9 If there had been more traffic on the mortorway, the accident could/might have been worse.
10 If the driver hadn't been in shock, he could have told the police how the accident happened.

▶ 7 *Holiday plans*

1 will have   2 hadn't spent   3 unless   4 spent   5 wouldn't have   6 didn't earn   7 book
8 will get   9 go/went   10 doesn't start   11 Supposing   12 won't have to
13 in case   14 didn't get   15 had to   16 booked   17 could walk   18 had bought
19 would/could/might have saved   20 are

▶ 8 *Extract from 'About a Boy'*

a 1 If there was a disadvantage … , then he had finally found it … (ll. 13-14)
      (simple past – past perfect: mixed type)
2 If you were falling in love …, then feeling like a blank twit put you at something of a
   disadvantage. (ll. 16-17) (past progressive – simple past: mixed type)
3 … he got a glimpse of what life could be like if he were in any way interesting. (l. 20)
   (modal aux. + infinitive – simple past: type II)

4 … he would be far happier if she turned round to look at him … (ll. 21-22)
  (modal aux. + infinitive – simple past: type II)

  If the *if*-clause comes before the main clause, a comma is used.
  If the *if*-clause comes after the main clause, a comma is not usually used.

b 1 had lived   2 had not earned/made, would/could not have (or: would/could not lead)
  3 would have to (or: would)   4 would/could not have   5 would/could not have, had lived
  6 would have gone   7 would/might have been (or: would be), had had (or: had/did)
  8 would/might be, turned

c 1 If only Rachel was interested in me.   2 If only I had a job.
  3 If only I could think of something interesting to say.   4 If only I did something with my life.
  5 If only I had learnt something.   6 If only she didn't ask awkward questions.
  7 I only I didn't have to lie about myself all the time.   8 If only I hadn't wasted my life.

Relative clauses

▶1 Definitions

a 1 It's someone/a person who/that acts in a film or play.
  2 It's a sign that/which shows you the way.
  3 It's someone/a person who/that works with wood and makes things, for example, furniture.
  4 It's a small book/brochure that/which tells you when trains or buses leave and arrive.
  5 It's someone/a person who/that doesn't smoke.
  6 It's someone/a person who/that comes to another country to live there permanently.
  7 It's a machine that/which records telephone messages (when nobody is at home).
  8 It's someone/a person who/that is part of /belongs to your family.
  9 It's someone/a person who/that can see the future/tell your fortune.
  10 It's a book that/which gives you (travel) information about a country, city, etc. /
    It's someone/a person who/that shows groups of tourists around interesting places.

▶2 The hotel we stayed at

a 1 What was the name of the theatre we went to?   2 What was the name of the big tower we
  climbed up?   3 Where was the castle we drove to?   4 What was the name of the big museum
  we looked round?   5 What was the name of the Italian restaurant we sometimes used to go to?
  6 Where was the sushi restaurant we ate at?   7 What was the name of the musical we went to?
  8 Where was the park we sometimes had lunch in?   9 What was the name of the store we often
  shopped at?   10 What was the name of the lake we rowed the boat on?

▶3 Places to visit

a 1 Hawaii, which is not one island but several, became …
  2 … James Cook, who also discovered Australia.
  3 Cook, whom the natives killed in 1779, had been …
  4 … Honolulu, which is situated on …

5 Oahu is the island that most tourists visit.
6 Pearl Harbor, which was attacked by the Japanese in 1941, is on Oahu …
7 The beaches where the world surfing championships take place are on Oahu and Maui.
8 … Waikiki Beach near Honolulu is the one that is most famous.
9 … on Kauai, which is the greenest of the islands.
10 The island of Hawaii, which is also called Big Island, is …
11 Hawaii is also the home of Kilauea, the volcano which is known to be the world's most active.
12 *Aloha*, which means *Hello* and *Goodbye*, is the first Hawaiian word which you learn.

b 1 The Channel Islands, which belong to Britain, are closer to France than to England.
2 The largest of the four islands, which is called Jersey, is only about 20 kilometres from the French coast.
3 The nearest island to England is Alderney, which is 80 kilometres from the English coast.
4 The Channel Islanders, who speak both English and French, are very friendly.
5 The island of Sark, which is the smallest island, is only 5.5 square kilometres.
6 The islands, which are known for their mild climate and beautiful beaches, are visited by …
7 The tourists, who come mainly from England, are fond of the street cafés …
8 The English, whom the Channel Islanders warmly welcome, particularly enjoy …

▶4 *The White House*

a 1 that/which   2 whose   3 that/which   4 which   5 which   6 where   7 who
8 which   9 – /that/which   10 where   11 – /that/which   12 which   13 where
14 – /that/which   15 – /that/which   16 whom   17 whom   18 whose

b 1 The architect James Hoban, by whom the 'President's House' was built, was born in Ireland.
2 The British, against whom the Americans fought in the War of 1812, set the White House on fire in 1814.
3 Theodore Roosevelt, by whom the White House was officially given its name in 1901, was the 26th president of the USA.
4 Theodore Roosevelt, for whom the West Wing was built as extra working space, had six children.
5 The Oval Office, from which important presidential speeches are often broadcast, is situated in the West Wing.
6 The White House, in which there are 132 rooms and 35 bathrooms, is 200 years old.
7 The State Dining Room, in which 140 guests can be seated, was enlarged in 1902.

▶5 *Snuffed out*

a the city that never sleeps (also: which) (l. 1); … the city that never smokes (also: which) (l. 1); New Yorkers whose New Year Resolution (l. 2); … a bill … that bans smoking … (also: which) (ll. 2-3); … legislation that banned smoking … (also: which) (l. 5); …, which adds to the risks … (ll. 7-8); … tobacco company, which happens … (ll. 11-12); … those who work in restaurants and bars (also: that) (l. 13); … any bar that has … (also: which) (l. 18); … a special room smokers can use (contact clause) (l. 18); … any bar … which builds … (l. 18); … a special smoking room that employees do not have to enter … (also: which) (ll. 18-19)

b 1 the city <u>that</u> never sleeps (l. 1); ... the city <u>that</u> never smokes (l. 1); ... a bill ... <u>that</u> bans smoking
... (ll. 2-3); ... legislation <u>that</u> banned (l. 5); ... a company, <u>which</u> happens to have (ll. 11-12);
... those <u>who</u> work (l. 13); ... any bar <u>that</u> has; ... any bar <u>which</u> builds ... (l. 18)
2 a special smoking room <u>that</u> employees do not have to enter (ll. 18-19)
3 ..., which happens to have its headquarters in New York. (ll. 11-12)
4 ... a special room (which/that) smokers can use ... (l. 18)
5 ..., which adds to the risks of their habit. (ll. 7-8)

c 1 ... in restaurants which/that seat more than 35 customers.
2 ... second-hand smoke which/that is breathed in involuntarily.

d 1 A non-smoker is a person who does not smoke.
2 A New Year resolution is something that you determine to do, to stop doing or to change in the
coming year.
3 A mayor is a person who is elected by a city or town council to represent and govern the city.
4 A habit is something that you often do, whether it is good or bad.
5 A cigarette-lover is a person who loves to smoke cigarettes.
6 A smoking room is a special room where/in which smokers are allowed to smoke. /
A smoking room is a special room smokers are allowed to smoke in.

e 1 whose   2 which/that   3 who   4 which   5 where   6 which   7 whose   8 why

Indirect speech

▶1 Reporting verbs

a 1 said   2 told   3 says   4 told   5 said to   6 says/said   7 tell, said   8 told, say   9 said
10 say   11 said to   12 tell, said

b 1 Anne explained that there was ...
2 The guest complained that the steak was tough.
3 Diane promised Gina that she would pay the money back soon.
4 Tom suggested to Jason that he should buy ...
5 James admitted that it was his fault.
6 The doctor advised Mr Bruce to stop smoking and go on a diet.
7 The customer threatened to complain to the store's main branch if the goods were not exchanged.
8 Cathy invited Ed to her party on Saturday.

▶2 Free time

1 Pascale said she had seen Fame the week before/the previous week.
2 Juan said he had got a ticket for the next/following day.
3 Dimitri said he was going the following Saturday.
4 Cem said he had seen it two weeks before/earlier.
5 Pascale said she had been there the day before.
6 Juan said he was going there the following weekend.
7 Dimitri said he had got a few bargains there the Friday before/the previous Friday.
8 Cem said we always sat there to chat.

▶3 Students in Britain

a 1 Andrea: She said she had her own room and she didn't have to cook, but hall also had some disadvantages. She mentioned that you had to eat at certain times, or you didn't get anything. She also said you met a lot of people in hall.
2 Beth: But she had felt like a schoolgirl, not like a student. She explained that her social life had been just the same as before because nothing had really changed. So she had moved into a flat with three other girls.
3 Colin: He said he had tried hall and flat-sharing but he still hadn't found the ideal place to live. He said he had just moved out of a private room and he hadn't done much studying recently. He explained he had spent too much time looking for somewhere to live.
4 David: He thought house rents would go up again as usual, but they would be independent and he would have more freedom. He said he would have to choose his friends carefully, but it would be a lot of fun. He admitted that they probably wouldn't do much studying.
5 Emma: She said she had liked hall, but sharing a small flat was better. She said that they had to do extra things like shopping and cleaning the flat. The day before she hadn't had time to do any work at all. She admitted that they hadn't done much cooking, in fact they all hated it, but added that they would get used to it. And they were managing their own lives at last. She mentioned that if they got on together and if things worked out OK, they would probably spend their third year there too.

b 1 Andrea said she had found a lot of new friends.
2 Colin said he had just moved.
3 Emma said they had parties every weekend.
4 Emma said they would get used to cooking and cleaning.
5 David said there were too many rules in hall.
6 Beth said she was quite content with her situation.

▶4 A horoscope

a 1 It said that a change of plans mid-week would not be a disadvantage. It said Thursday might be a good day for new contacts, but Friday could bring a disappointment.
2 It said she had had some money problems, but that things would improve. It said she could receive an interesting offer mid-week, and Friday might be a good day …
3 It said she had had a boring week, but she would have a very busy weekend. It said she might have to choose between … It said the week wouldn't end as she had planned, and that a close friend could surprise her.

▶5 At the station

1 … asked me where I came from.   2 … asked me if I liked it here.   3 … wanted to know how long I had been here.   4 … wanted to know if I was on holiday …   5 … asked if it was my first time in Oxford …   6 … wanted to know what I had seen in Oxford.   7 … asked me if I had seen all the colleges.   8 … asked me when I was going back home.   9 … wanted to know if I would come again.   10 … wondered if I liked English food.   11 … wanted to know if I had found an English boyfriend.   12 … wondered what I thought of English people.

6 Interview tips

a 1 Her mother advised her to be confident and pleasant.
2 Her brother advised her not to wear jeans.
3 Her father told her not to sit down before the interviewer offered her a seat.
4 Her boyfriend advised her to ask a few intelligent questions.
5 Her best friend told her not to talk too fast.
6 Her sister told her to show interest in the company and the job.

7 A holiday job

1 Int.: I'm glad to see that you have already had some experience …   2 What kind of activities were you involved with?
3 Laura: I helped to run a Kids' Club, and   4 I was mainly in charge of aqua sports …
5 Int.: Are you musical?   6 Can you sing or dance?
7 Laura: I prefer sports activities.
8 Int.: Why do you want to go to Spain?
9 Laura: I don't like the wet English summers and I want to try something away from home.
10 Int.: How good is your Spanish?
11 Laura: I have done a language course in Barcelona, so I'm quite good.
12 Int.: You may be sent to Ibiza or Gran Canaria.   13 Do you have a preference?   14 Can you start as early as May?
15 Laura: I won't be free until mid-June.
16 Int.: Talk to the Club management directly if you need more information.   17 Could you/Would you please fill in this form?   18 I will phone you early next week.

8 Space tourist lands back on Earth

1 'I am proud to be the first African in space …,' he added.
2 He said he was very proud to carry the flag …
3 … told the BBC that it was the holiday of a lifetime, but he might need another holiday …
4 'I hope my trip will inspire people across Africa,' he said.
5 He said that one of the things he hoped to do by fulfilling his own dream was to reach out to children and learners in Africa and show them that dreams could come true.
6 He added that Africa had a great future – but to reach that future, they had to get every African inspired and dreaming.
7 'Part of my mission was to conduct … '
8 He said they hoped to get some good quality chrystals which would help scientists …
9 … said, 'The 'geek' in me was fascinated by the mix of …'

9 Future plans

a 1 I asked him why he wanted to teach. I wondered why he wanted to teach geography …
2 said (2 x, l. 1), asked (l. 3), wondered (l. 5), explained (l. 6), said (l. 7)
3 thinks (l. 3), believes (l. 8)
4 wants, didn't like, weren't (ll. 1-2), it's, can (ll. 3-4), should, want to, have to (l. 9)
5 could (l. 8)
6 can (l. 4), should (l. 9)

b 'wants' (l. 1): not backshifted because the statement is still true when it is reported
'didn't like', 'weren't' (ll. 1-2): not backshifted because in informal English past tense forms in indirect speech often stay the same
'it's', 'can' (ll. 3-4): not backshifted after a reporting verb in the present ('thinks')
'should' (also 'would', 'could', 'might', 'ought to') stays the same in indirect speech
'want to', 'have to' (l. 9): not backshifted after a reporting verb in the present ('believes')

▶10 *Extract from 'Dead Poets Society'*

a Suggestion:
… he could see his father's point, they were not a rich family, but his father had planned the rest of his life for him, and had never even asked him what he wanted. Keating asked Neil if he had told his father what he had just told him, about his passion for acting. Neil exclaimed that his father would kill him. Keating observed that Neil was playing a part for his father, too, and although it seemed impossible, Neil advised him to talk to his father and let him know who he really was. Neil replied that he knew what his father would say, that acting was just a whim and that he should forget about it.

b Suggestion:
Keating said that if acting was more than a whim, Neil should prove it to his father. He added that if that didn't work, at eighteen he would be able to do what he wanted. But Neil explained that the play was the following night. So Keating urged Neil to talk to his father. He told him there was no easier way, not if he was going to stay true to himself. Neil thanked Mr. Keating and said that he had to decide what to do.

▶11 *Extract from 'The Lilac Bus'*

a Direct statements in ll. 13-14: 'Mummy … test,' and 'I was just … passed.'
Indirect statement in ll. 15-16: He had said there would be papers …
   but that he was going to skip …
Indirect request/command in l. 19: He had asked Nancy Morris to pray …

b Free indirect speech: Dee's thoughts, mainly in ll. 1-12
(excluding: Half-way home … happened.)
In free indirect speech reporting verbs are not usually used. Example: What was she going to do? (Indirect speech: She <u>wondered</u> what she was going to do.) Pronouns are as in indirect speech. Example: What was <u>she</u> going to do? The word order in questions is as in direct speech. Example: <u>Should</u> she ring him at home …? The backshift of tenses is as in indirect speech. Example: She <u>would</u> try to be calm …

c Direct: 'Is it a nice warm night in London as it is here?' Dee wondered.
Indirect: Dee wondered if/whether it was a nice warm night in London as it was there.

Mixed bag

▶1 Classroom instructions

1 Carry on writing ...   2 Hold on a moment ...   3 ... read the answers out/read out the answers ...   4 ... make up a story/make a story up.   5 ... find out all the facts ...
6 ... look up ...   7 ... put up this poster/put this poster up ...   8 ... hand out the test papers/hand the test papers out ...   9 ... hand in your homework/hand your homework in ...

▶2 Get it right

a 1 I called on him yesterday.
2 I'm going to pick her up/I'm picking her up from the airport.
3 I've already rung him/her up.
4 They had to call it off because of rain/because it rained.
5 The head teacher is going to look into/is looking into it very carefully.
6 She certainly takes after her.
7 Unfortunately, she let me down last week.
8 I'm afraid they turned me down/will turn me down.
9 They are going to look after them.

b Suggestions:
1 If I fall behind I usually try to catch up as soon as possible.
2 I write the new words down and go over them a few times.
3 Sometimes, but I usually try to finish it off.
4 Yes, I do. But it's best just to get on with it. Otherwise I fall behind.
5 I sometimes give up. / I just try to get on with it.

▶3 Letter to a problem page

a count on sb., measure up to sth., bring sth. up, turn sth. down, deal with sth., look into sth., ask sb. out, get back at sb., go about sth., talk sb. into sth., get on with sb., cope with sth., put sth. off, put up with sb., do without sth.

b 1 ... has mentioned the matter/has started talking about the matter ...
2 ... has not rejected/not refused her request.   3 ... take revenge on her.   4 ... approach it.
5 ... persuaded her to stay.   6 ... has a good relationship with her colleagues.
7 ... postpones the confrontation.   8 ... tolerate ...

▶4 Tricky prepositions

a 1 from/at 2 on 3 to/in 4 from 5 at 6 in 7 to 8 by 9 on 10 to 11 to 12 on
13 in 14 At 15 on 16 to 17 on 18 on 19 to 20 to 21 To 22 on 23 at 24 on
25 in 26 at

b 1 over 2 over 3 over 4 Above/Over 5 above/over 6 over 7 over 8 above 9 above

▶5 Correct the mistakes

1 to nine   2 talking to   3 in front of us   4 among some old papers   5 on/with me
6 via Chicago   7 Two people out of three   8 by next Saturday   9 to the cinema
10 typical of him   11 plays by Arthur Miller   12 example of   13 married to
14 near Munich   15 stay with us   16 in the world   17 up to eight hours

▶6 Koalas

a 1 to   2 of   3 In   4 to   5 on   6 in   7 from   8 up to/for   9 for   10 During/Throughout/In
11 by   12 in   13 into   14 on   15 Out of/From   16 for   17 of   18 in   19 with   20 by
21 up to/for   22 In   23 from   24 In   25 of   26 on   27 because of/owing to   28 at
29 During   30 by   31 of   32 to   33 as   34 of/from   35 like/of   36 on   37 for   38 by

b Phrases of place: in the wild, in sanctuaries, in the east, into western Australia, on the ground
Phrases of time: at night, during the day
'by' is often used to express a way of doing something: 'by grunting, by licking their arms'

▶7 Quick and easy

a Correct: 5, 12
Corrected: 1 I saw …   2 I explained the situation to Tim.   3 They are playing …
4 … the police haven't arrived yet.   6 I'm really looking forward to going …
7 All that I can advise you to do …   8 … for an hour.   9 … this information?
10 Kate wants us all to go …   11 We should respect nature more …   13 I'd like some advice …
14 I sugggest going …   15 What did you do yesterday evening?

b   1 Shall we meet at seven?
    2 We needn't/don't have to/ haven't got to finish the exercises today.
    3 Most (of the) pupils in my class work in the holidays.
    4 I have known Jessica for five years.
    5 Serena is a student.
    6 If you wait five minutes, I'll go with you.
    7 In our school there are three computer rooms.
    8 Tom always works hard.
    9 We haven't got much homework today.
    10 If you took the car, you would be there at ten o'clock.
    11 We often have a pizza delivered.
    12 That's really great news.
    13 Two days ago I got a job offer.
    14 We know a lot of people who speak English.
    15 This song was written by Elton John, wasn't it?

Notes